2 8 NU

To be returned on

Struggles for Equity in Education

In the **World Library of Educationalists** series, international experts compile career-long collections of what they judge to be their finest pieces – extracts from books, key articles, salient research findings, major theoretical and practical contributions – so the world can read them in a single manageable volume. Readers will be able to follow the themes and strands and see how their work contributes to the development of the field.

Spanning Mel Ainscow's accomplished 30-year international career in education, the texts in this book trace his efforts to find ways of fostering more equitable forms of education. This has involved a series of struggles as he has experimented with different approaches – in a variety of contexts – to find new possibilities for responding to learner diversity. Over the years this has related to a variety of headline themes, starting from special education, through to integration, on to inclusive education, and then, more recently, educational equity.

The readings have been chosen to illustrate the changes that have occurred in Ainscow's thinking and practices and a short introduction is provided for each chapter that is intended to help readers to understand the significance of what is presented and how this relates to other chapters in the book. The writings in this text reinforce the idea that the promotion of equity in schools is essentially a social process that has to occur within particular contexts.

Mel Ainscow is Professor of Education and Co-director of the Centre for Equity in Education at the University of Manchester, and Adjunct Professor at Queensland University of Technology, Australia. In the Queen's 2012 New Year honours list he was made a CBE for his services to education. Currently he is leading Schools Challenge Cymru, the Welsh Government's multi-million pound flagship programme to accelerate the rate of improvement across the country's schools.

World Library of Educationalists Series

Constructing Worlds through Science Education
The selected works of John K. Gilbert
John K. Gilbert

Making Sense of Learners Making Sense of Written Language
The selected works of Kenneth S. Goodman and Yetta M. Goodman
Kenneth S. Goodman and Yetta M. Goodman

Learning, Curriculum and Life Politics
The selected works of Ivor F. Goodson
Ivor F. Goodson

Education and the Nation State
The selected works of S. Gopinathan
S. Gopinathan

Educational Assessment, Evaluation and Research
The selected works of Mary E. James
Mary E. James

Teaching, Learning and Education in Late Modernity
The selected works of Peter Jarvis
Peter Jarvis

Education, Markets, and the Public Good
The selected works of David F. Labaree
David F. Labaree

Politics, Policies and Pedagogies in Education
The selected works of Bob Lingard
Bob Lingard

A Life in Education
The selected works of John Macbeath
John Macbeath

Overcoming Exclusion
Social Justice through Education
Peter Mittler

Learner-Centered English Language Education
The selected works of David Nunan
David Nunan

Educational Philosophy and Politics
The selected works of Michael A. Peters
Michael A. Peters

Encountering Education in the Global
The selected works of Fazal Rizvi
Fazal Rizvi

The Politics of Race, Class and Special Education
The selected works of Sally Tomlinson
Sally Tomlinson

Corporatism, Social Control, and Cultural Domination
in Education: From the Radical Right to Globalization
The selected works of Joel Spring
Joel Spring

The Curriculum and the Child
The selected works of John White
John White

The Art and Science of Teaching and Learning
The selected works of Ted Wragg
E.C. Wragg

Landmarks in Literacy
The selected works of Frank Smith
Frank Smith

Multiculturalism in Education and Teaching
The selected works of Carl A. Grant
Carl A. Grant

Thinking and Rethinking the University
The selected works of Ronald Barnett
Ronald Barnett

China through the Lens of Comparative Education
The selected works of Ruth Hayhoe
Ruth Hayhoe

Educational Experience as Lived: Knowledge, History, Alterity
The selected works of William F. Pinar
William F. Pinar

Faith, Mission and Challenge in Catholic Education
The selected works of Gerald Grace
Gerald Grace

Dysconscious Racism, Afrocentric Praxis, and Education for
Human Freedom: Through the Years I Keep on Toiling
The selected works of Joyce E. King
Joyce E. King

A Developing Discourse in Music Education
The selected works of Keith Swanwick
Keith Swanwick

Struggles for Equity in Education
The selected works of Mel Ainscow
Mel Ainscow

Struggles for Equity in Education
The selected works of Mel Ainscow

Mel Ainscow

 Routledge
Taylor & Francis Group

LONDON AND NEW YORK

First published 2016
by Routledge
2 Park Square, Milton Park, Abingdon, Oxon OX14 4RN

and by Routledge
711 Third Avenue, New York, NY 10017

Routledge is an imprint of the Taylor & Francis Group, an informa business

© 2016 M. Ainscow

British Library Cataloguing in Publication Data
A catalogue record for this book is available from the British Library

Library of Congress Cataloging in Publication Data
Ainscow, Mel.
  Struggles for equity in education : the selected works of Mel Ainscow / Mel Ainscow.
   pages cm
  Includes index.
  1. Educational equalization.   2. Inclusive education.
  3. School improvement programs.   I. Title.
  LC213.A56 2016
  379.2'6—dc23   2015004941

ISBN: 978-1-138-91886-3 (hbk)
ISBN: 978-1-138-10007-7 (pbk)
ISBN: 978-1-315-68821-3 (ebk)

Typeset in Sabon
by RefineCatch Limited, Bungay, Suffolk

MIX
Paper from
responsible sources
FSC   FSC° C013056
www.fsc.org

Printed and bound in Great Britain by
TJ International Ltd, Padstow, Cornwall

CONTENTS

ACKNOWLEDGEMENTS

The following articles have been reproduced with the kind permission of the respective journals.

Ainscow, M. (2000) Reaching out to all learners: some lessons from international experience. *School Effectiveness and School Improvement* 11(1), 1–9.

Ainscow, M. (2005) Developing inclusive education systems: what are the levers for change? *Journal of Educational Change* 6(2), 109–124.

Ainscow, M. (2010) Achieving excellence and equity: reflections on the development of practices in one local district over 10 years. *School Effectiveness and School Improvement* 21(1), 75–91.

Ainscow, M. and Miles, S. (2008) Making education for all inclusive: where next? *Prospects* 37(1), 15–34.

Ainscow, M., Booth, T. and Dyson, A. (2006) Inclusion and the standards agenda: negotiating policy pressures in England. *International Journal of Inclusive Education* 10(4–5), 295–308.

Ainscow, M., Dyson, A., Goldrick, S. and West, M. (2012) Making schools effective for all: rethinking the task. *School Leadership and Management* 32(3), 1–17.

The following chapters have been reproduced with the kind permission of the respective publishers.

Ainscow, M. (1999) Chapter 2: Learning from experience. In *Understanding the development of inclusive schools*. London: Routledge.

Ainscow, M. (2002) Using research to encourage the development of inclusive practices. In P. Farrell and M. Ainscow (eds.), *Making special education inclusive*. London: Fulton.

Ainscow, M. (2006) Towards a more inclusive education system: where next for special schools? In R. Cigman (ed.), *Included or excluded? The challenge of the mainstream for some SEN children*. London: Routledge.

Ainscow, M. (2013) Developing more equitable education systems: reflections on a three-year improvement initiative. In V. Farnsworth and Y. Solomon (eds.), *What works in education? Bridging theory and practice in research*. London: Routledge.

Ainscow, M. and Hopkins, D. (1994) Understanding the moving school. In G. Southworth (ed.), *Readings in primary school development*. London: Falmer.

Ainscow, M. and Tweddle, D.A. (1979) Chapter 1: Peter, and Chapter 2: Teaching slow learners. In *Preventing classroom failure: an objectives approach*. London: Wiley/Fulton.

Ainscow, M. and Tweddle, D.A. (1988) Chapter 1: Success in the classroom. In *Encouraging classroom success*. London: Fulton.

Ainscow, M. and West, M. (eds.) (2006) Chapter 12: Drawing the lessons. In *Improving urban schools: leadership and collaboration*. Maidenhead: Open University Press.

CONTRIBUTORS

Tony Booth, formerly Professor of Education, Canterbury Christ Church University, Canterbury, UK

Alan Dyson, Professor of Education and Co-director, Centre for Equity in Education, School of Education, University of Manchester, Manchester, UK

Sue Goldrick, Research Associate, Centre for Equity in Education, School of Education, University of Manchester, Manchester, UK

David Hopkins, Professor Emeritus, Institute of Education, University of London, UK

Susie Miles, Senior Lecturer, School of Education, University of Manchester, Manchester, UK

Dave Tweddle, formerly Research Fellow, University of Manchester, Manchester, UK

Mel West, Professor of Educational Leadership, School of Education, University of Manchester, Manchester, UK

CHAPTER 1

INTRODUCTION: THE COLLECTIVE WILL TO MAKE IT HAPPEN

Over the years my work has been related to a variety of headline themes, starting from special education, through to integration, on to inclusive education, and then, more recently, educational equity. Drawing on the formulation used by OECD, I take this latter theme to have two interconnected dimensions (OECD, 2007). First, it is a matter of *fairness*, which implies ensuring that personal and social circumstances – for example, gender, socio-economic status or ethnic origin – should not be an obstacle to achieving success in learning. Second, it is to do with *inclusion*, which is about ensuring a basic minimum standard of education for all.

Bearing this formulation in mind, this introductory chapter provides an overview of the evolution of my ideas regarding how to foster fairness and inclusion within education systems. In particular, it explains how my thinking has moved in the following directions:

- From a narrow focus on special education to a much wider concern with processes I have called *school improvement with attitude*.
- From efforts to achieve integration for particular groups of learners towards the development of inclusive forms of education that focus on the *presence, participation and achievement* of all children and young people.
- From an analysis of the characteristics of individual learners to the analysis of *barriers and resources* that exist within particular learning contexts.
- From an emphasis on the development of individual schools towards efforts to achieve system-level reform through a focus on *levers for change*.

The chapter also provides an overall timeline of my career development that pinpoints key events, projects and publications that have informed these changes in thinking. A pattern emerges from these accounts. This involves periods of uncertainly as my thinking is challenged by new experiences and different contexts, through a process I have described as 'making the familiar unfamiliar'. What also becomes evident is the way that working with colleagues has helped me to cope with these disturbances, such that they often became critical incidents that led to developments in my ideas.

Pathways to learning

In selecting the readings I have tried to provide an illustrative map of the development of my thinking and practice as a teacher, researcher and activist.

The varied styles of the readings reflect efforts to reach different audiences: practitioners, administrators, policy makers and researchers, in the UK and overseas. Inevitably there are some overlaps between the various texts, as earlier ideas are revisited, refined and, sometimes, replaced with new thinking. Together, they illustrate my on-going struggles to find forms of education that can make sure that all children and young people get a fair deal. These struggles have also involved attempts to convince others that this is in everybody's best interest.

Over many years I have argued that the most important factor that will enable us to achieve this goal is the collective will to make it happen. Occasionally, those who have heard this have suggested that it is an unrealistic aspiration. As I understand it, their point is that in unequal societies – such as Australia, Chile, the UK and the USA – it will never be possible to get everybody pulling in the same direction. While recognising the power of this argument, I remain convinced that it should be possible to mobilise everybody who has an interest in education to work together for the common good. Perhaps somewhat idealistically, I also take the view that a system of schools that treats every child fairly is, ultimately, in the interests of everybody – an argument that is made so convincingly by Wilkinson and Pickett (2009) in their influential book *The Spirit Level*.

Inevitably, my commitment to this way of thinking is related to my own life experience. I was born into a working-class Manchester family that had an instinctive view that more education was a good thing. However, they had little or no understanding of what was involved in ensuring children found an appropriate pathway through a highly selective education system. Consequently, while I enjoyed my time at school, I lacked any real sense of direction or understanding of how to move forward.

At the age of eleven, like other children in the city, I took the examination that would decide which type of secondary school I would attend: grammar (for those seen to be academically able), technical (for those whose future would involve forms of practical knowledge), or secondary modern (for the rest). The decision was made that it was appropriate for me to go along the technical route. Those who know me will recognise how laughable this is, in that I still struggle to change a plug. To further reinforce how farcical it was, attending the same school was John Thaw, who was eventually to become an internationally known actor, not least because of his role in the TV series *Morse*. I am not sure if he could change a plug either.

In later years I found myself reflecting on these experiences in relation to what happens to other young people who come from families with limited knowledge of how systems of education work. In particular, how do they acquire information that allows them to ensure that their daughters and sons get a 'fair deal'? And, of course, how do processes of selection within education systems privilege young people who have certain backgrounds?

Having survived and, indeed, enjoyed my years in the secondary school, I chose to train as an art teacher. The main influence regarding this decision was a pupil in the year group above me who had decided to follow a similar direction. Such an option had never crossed my mind and the school provided little guidance on career pathways. Of course, my family was delighted, seeing the idea of being a teacher as something to boast about.

Becoming a teacher

My first teaching post, in the mid-1960s, was in a secondary modern school for boys. It was located in a poor, working-class district on the east side of Manchester, not far from my family home. This was a tough environment in which to work, dealing with boys who in many cases saw little purpose in going to school. And, of course, at that time there were plenty of jobs available that required no formal qualifications. The overall atmosphere was brutal, with frequent use of a leather strap as a form of punishment. Nevertheless, there were colleagues on the staff who were deeply committed to providing a rich educational diet for the boys.

I recall that during this period I started to think that I wanted to find ways of intervening in the education system in order to bring about some significant change, although I had no specific idea of what form this might take. Retaining my family's instinctive commitment to the idea that more education was a good thing, I certainly had it in my mind that I would need to do further study.

After three years, during which my confidence as a teacher gradually developed, I took up a post in a newly opened special school in the then notorious Manchester district of Moss Side. There the students I worked with were all rejects of a mainstream school system that had limited tolerance of differences and, indeed, little capacity to support learners who experienced difficulties. I recall that going to this school was like starting my career all over again. Strategies that I had found to be effective in the tightly organised secondary modern school did not seem to work in this new, less rigid context. In addition, the bringing together of young people who had all been excluded from their former schools understandably had an impact on their attitudes to schooling. All of this made an impression on me that was to be influential to the work I was to do later.

At the same time, the informality of the special school opened up spaces for experimentation that were not much available in mainstream schools during that era. This idea of special education contexts providing opportunities for innovation was one that was picked up years later by the American scholar, Tom Skrtic, who argued that this was the gift that should be given to mainstream education in order to foster processes of integration (Skrtic, 1991).

After a period at this school, in 1970 I was fortunate to be seconded for a year to Liverpool University, where I gained an additional qualification as a special educator. This opened up a whole new world of ideas, including literature from a sociological perspective that certainly made me stop and think. In particular, it created a feeling of turbulence regarding the ways in which some children become categorised as deviant and are excluded from mainstream education opportunities. Having a chance to visit schools I also became increasingly troubled by what was offered to many of these learners in various forms of special provision. For example, a visit to what was called an 'opportunity class' attached to a primary school led me to comment rather sarcastically that the last thing the pupils were getting was opportunity. Similarly, I was staggered at what I saw in the classroom of an inner-city special school. On each desk there was a label with two numbers. The teacher explained that one was the child's school number and the other was their IQ score. This was, she explained, so that she was able to pitch tasks at the right level.

At the end of the course I was left feeling better qualified and, at the same time, more confused as to where I stood in relation to the field of special education. Nevertheless, at the age of twenty-seven, I took up the post of deputy headteacher at a newly opened special school in Bedfordshire, in the south of England. The students at that school were far less challenging, and it was a pleasant environment in which to work and explore what is involved in managing an organisation. A feature of the school that was to stay with me was the emphasis we placed on team work. Each day began with a short staff meeting, some of which took the form of an informal case study discussion of a particular pupil. We also introduced a programme of staff development workshops that seemed to encourage a collaborative problem-solving atmosphere among the team of colleagues.

A centre of innovation

In 1974 I was successful in my application to be headteacher of Castle Special School in the West Midlands. Following my period in the relatively peaceful environment in the South, this took me back into an economically poor and socially troubled community of the sort that I had previously experienced. In addition, the school itself was troubled, having had years of poor management that had left the staff low in confidence and many of the pupils out of control. As one of the youngest members of staff, I faced what was to be the biggest challenge in my professional career. This included the requirement to bring order to a pupil population that was running wild – in classrooms and in the playground – and the need to lift the morale of staff in order to convince them that, together, we could turn the school round.

It is a complex story, the details of which are irrelevant to the argument I wish to make. Simply to say that I was able to pinpoint some key staff members who were able to help me in providing effective leadership. I also had some luck in that a few colleagues decided it was time for them to move on, which allowed me to bring in some new blood. Finding new teachers was difficult in those days, particularly for a school that had such a bad reputation. Indeed, I recall going round to the house of a newly qualified teacher to persuade him to join us.

Having gradually established stability in the school, we began the process of creating what came to be seen as a centre of innovation. Building on strategies that I had experienced elsewhere, particularly the idea of staff collaboration, Castle School became known nationally for its work on curriculum development. A key factor in all of this was the contribution of the educational psychologist attached to the school, Dave Tweddle. Seeing the opportunity to be involved in something that was potentially ground breaking, he gave the school an enormous amount of his time, collaborating with me and working with the staff in supporting the development of their skills in designing and implementing the new curriculum. Chapter 2, which is an extract from my book *Understanding the development of inclusive schools* published in 1999, provides an account of what this involved.

It is worth noting that all of this was going on during a period when the world of special education was subject to considerable criticism, particularly with respect to curriculum thinking and assessment practices. This was part of a wider concern about the purposes and quality of schooling, leading to demands for greater accountability. In addition, there were other, more specific pressures that seemed to draw attention to the need for an examination of what happened in special schools. The influential Warnock Report had suggested that the quality of education offered to pupils in special provision was unsatisfactory, particularly with respect to the curriculum opportunities provided, and that many special schools underestimated their pupils' capabilities (Department for Education and Science, 1978). A number of other publications were also critical of existing practice (e.g. Brennan, 1979; Tomlinson, 1982).

As the work of the school developed, I found myself returning to my concerns about the way the education system categorised and marginalised some groups of learners. With this theme in mind, Tweddle and I set out to develop Castle School as a support hub for teachers working in local mainstream schools. We did this by offering intensive workshops on how to design what we referred to as individualised programmes for children experiencing learning difficulties. All of this signalled a move away from what some have called a medical model – where the main focus of special education practices was on analysing learner characteristics – towards an emphasis on analysing tasks so that learning objectives could be designed to suit the level of achievement of each pupil.

During this period, Tweddle and I were fortunate to have the advice and encouragement of two eminent academics at the University of Birmingham, Ron Gulliford and Klaus Wedell. Their involvement and encouragement added to our feeling that we were involved in something significant, and, at the same time, contributed to the promotion of the approach we had developed.

Our work at Castle led Tweddle and I to write the book *Preventing Classroom Failure: An Objectives Approach*, which was published in 1979 (Chapter 3 reproduces two short chapters from the book). At that time getting a book published was extremely difficult, not least because of the cost implications. Consequently, there was limited literature available regarding the education of children in special provision. As I have noted, there was also considerable pressure on the field to address the challenges provided by various national reports. Perhaps as a result, the book became a big seller and had an enormous influence on thinking and practice in the field.

From special education to integration

After five years as headteacher of Castle School, I was fortunate to be offered another opportunity to study. This time it involved a year at Birmingham University, studying for a master's degree. This interlude provided me with a timely opportunity to reflect on what I had experienced and to consider where I might go next with my struggle to make education fairer for all children and young people. This led me in 1979 to take up the post of Adviser for Special Needs in the Coventry local authority.

This move opened up wonderful new opportunities for me to reposition myself and to take my thinking forward. Alongside my specialism, the role included providing general advice on school development matters to a group of primary and secondary schools. For somebody who had spent so much time in special provision, this presented a set of new challenges. At the same time, it opened up splendid opportunities to explore how mainstream schools could develop ways of working that could promote the integration of children who might otherwise be placed in special provision.

At that time, the Coventry authority had an enormous commitment to encouraging innovation in its schools and to providing professional development for teachers in order to encourage improvements in practice. As I got involved with some of these developments, I formulated a proposal for a large-scale initiative to promote integration across the authority's schools. Working with another committed and innovative educational psychologist, Jim Muncey, we designed what came to be known as the Special Needs Action Programme (SNAP) – a detailed account of this is provided in Chapter 2. In order to take SNAP forward, we asked each school to designate a member of staff as the special needs coordinator, somebody who could act as the lead for developments across the staff. Later this approach was to become part of national policy. Linked to this, our mantra was 'every teacher a special needs teacher'.

The initial phase of SNAP concentrated on the primary sector (Ainscow and Muncey, 1989). The core activity was a staff development pack called 'Small Steps', which involved helping teachers to design the sorts of individualised learning programmes, based on task analysis and objectives, that we had used at Castle School. In addition, other staff development packages were developed, including one that focused on ways of addressing difficulties in behaviour and others that addressed issues to do with various impairments.

Eventually the decision was made to extend SNAP into the secondary sector. With this in mind, Muncey and I formed a working group of teachers to help us formulate a way forward. Discussions in this group led to yet another period of personal turbulence, as it became clear that the sorts of individualised approach that we had used in primary schools would not be feasible in secondary schools. However, the debate went beyond a consideration of practicalities, leading to a major rethinking of my orientation.

In many ways this was for me the most important turning point in my career. It involved me in moving away from a narrow concern with individual learners deemed to be vulnerable, to a focus on the wider contexts in which learning takes place. As a result, the SNAP staff development package for secondary sector shifted the agenda to a consideration of all aspects of a school's work: the curriculum, teaching practices, management and leadership, monitoring of pupil progress and support for learning. This was, I now realise, pushing me to reposition my work as being about overall school improvement, a theme I will return to later.

While this was going on, our publisher, David Fulton, suggested to Tweddle and me that we should write a new edition of *Preventing Classroom Failure*. Fulton's argument was that, since the book had been so successful, an updated version would be timely. Over many months we discussed how best to deal with this request. After a lot of rather painful debate, we came to the conclusion that, since our thinking had changed so radically, a new version was simply not possible. Consequently, we agreed to write a new book, *Encouraging Classroom Success* (Ainscow and Tweddle, 1988), which presented our new thinking in a way that, in essence, contradicted the argument we had given in 1979. Chapter 4 in this book reproduces the introductory chapter.

Effective schools for all

In 1986 I moved to Cambridge, where I spent almost ten years working at the Institute of Education. This small unit within the Faculty of Education concentrated on research, in-service training and higher degrees. It had a staff of committed academics, most of whom have subsequently become well known for their research nationally and, in some cases, internationally.

This move gave me the opportunity to clarify the changes in thinking that had occurred during my time in Coventry. It also led me to make links with new bodies of knowledge, particularly the fields of school effectiveness and school improvement. This, in turn, led to new partnerships with colleagues whose work was associated with these traditions.

At this stage I became increasingly confused about where to position myself: was I still part of the special education tradition, with its own debates and disputes about directions of travel? Or was I now part of the then emerging school improvement world? As I will show later, I was eventually able to resolve this apparent contradiction through my positioning around the theme of inclusive education and then, much later, in relation to notions of equity.

The nature of this particular struggle was reflected in an edited book, *Effective Schools for All* (Ainscow, 1991), which consisted of papers that had been presented at a symposium I organised at the International Conference of Special Education in 1990. In arranging that event I had chosen to invite key figures from the school effectiveness tradition, such as Dave Reynolds and Louise Stoll, and others concerned with teacher effectiveness, including Neville Bennett and Margaret Wang. Contributions were also made by scholars who, like me, were grappling with the need to rethink the special education field, such as Judy Sebba, Roger Slee and Tom Skrtic.

During this period of uncertainty I spent many hours talking things through with various of my Cambridge colleagues, one of whom, Susan Hart, was particularly helpful in guiding me through a process of clarification. This led us to map out possible perspectives on educational difficulties in order to assist ourselves (and possibly others) in gaining a better understanding of our own current positions (Ainscow and Hart, 1992).

We defined three overall perspectives. The first of these, we suggested, seeks to explain educational difficulties in terms of the characteristics of individual pupils. This remains the dominant perspective in the special needs field, where the nature of educational difficulties is explained in terms of particular disabilities, social background and/or psychological attributes. The frame of reference created by this perspective is the individual child, and responses are chosen that seek to change or support the child in order to facilitate participation in the process of schooling. Traditionally, responses informed by this perspective take the form of removal of the child from the mainstream curriculum for specialist help. We noted, however, that responses had begun to develop that allowed help to be provided in the context of the regular classroom.

The second perspective explains educational difficulties in terms of a mismatch between the characteristics of particular children and the organisation and/or curriculum arrangements made for them. Here support may be directed towards helping the child to meet the demands and expectations of the system, if this is assumed to be fixed or – for the time being at least – unchangeable. Or it may be directed towards making modifications to the system in order to extend the range of pupils who can be accommodated. The frame of reference in this interactive perspective once again focuses attention on individual pupils, but this time is concerned with the ways they interact with particular contexts and experiences. So much so that those adopting this perspective had, during that period, tended to argue for the use of the term 'individual needs' rather than 'special needs' (Ainscow and Muncey, 1989). Responses chosen in the light of this perspective included curriculum adaptations, alternative materials for pupils, or extra support in the classroom. Sometimes, these responses are also seen as being of benefit to pupils other than those designated as having special needs.

The third perspective explains educational difficulties in terms of curriculum limitations, using the term curriculum in a broad sense to include all the planned and, indeed, unplanned experiences offered to pupils. Thus in this perspective there is a concern with what can be learnt from the difficulties experienced by some children about the limitations of provision currently made. The assumption is that changes introduced for the benefit of those experiencing difficulties can improve learning for all children. Those adopting this perspective are critical of the limitations of an individual frame of reference, even where this is used to raise questions about the adequacy of curriculum organisation and practice as currently provided for individual pupils. They argue that a wider frame is needed, focusing on curriculum organisation and practice as currently provided for all pupils. The task involves continually seeking ways of improving overall conditions for learning, with difficulties acting as indicators of how improvements might be achieved. Those who adopt this perspective are likely to favour approaches that encourage inquiry as a means of achieving improvement, e.g. various forms of partnership teaching, action research. Of course, this third perspective defined what had become the basis of my work.

As I emerged from this period of rethinking and repositioning, I began a programme of research that involved a way of working – collaborative inquiry – that has continued to the present day. It started with a conversation with another of my Cambridge colleagues, David Hopkins, in 1988, during which we decided we would like to bring together our different expertise to address issues of school improvement. This led to the initiative that we called Improving the Quality of Education for All (IQEA). Initially, it involved Hopkins and me working with nine schools in and around London (Chapter 5 describes this early phase of the project). Subsequently, IQEA grew as other Cambridge colleagues became involved – Michael Fielding, Geoff Southworth, Judy Sebba and Mel West – and then later led to developments in other parts of the world that were influential to the development of policies in a range of countries (for more detailed accounts of some of these projects, see Ainscow, 1999; Clarke et al, 2005; Hopkins, 2007; Hopkins et al, 1994; West and Ainscow, 2010). All of these activities involved teams of researchers working in partnership with colleagues from schools to identify ways in which the learning of all members of the school community – students, parents and staff – could be enhanced.

Work with schools in the IQEA projects was based on a contract that attempted to define the parameters for our involvement, and the obligations those involved owed to one another. In particular, the contract emphasised that all staff be consulted; that an in-school team of coordinators be appointed to carry the work forward; that a critical mass of staff were to be actively involved; and that sufficient time would be made available for necessary classroom and staff development activities. Meanwhile we committed ourselves to supporting the school's developments, usually in the first place for one year. Often the arrangement continued, however, and in some instances we were involved for periods as long as seven years. We provided training for the school coordinators, made regular school visits and contributed to school-based staff development activities. In addition, we attempted to work with the schools in recording and analysing their experiences in a way that also provided data relevant to our own on-going research agendas.

As a result of such engagements with schools involved in the IQEA project, we evolved a style of collaboration that we referred to as 'working with, rather than working on' (Ainscow and Southworth, 1996). This phrase attempted to sum up an approach that deliberately allowed each project school considerable autonomy to determine its own priorities for development and, indeed, its methods for achieving these priorities. In attempting to work in this way, we found ourselves confronted with staggering complexity, and by a bewildering array of policy and strategy options. It was our belief, however, that only through a regular engagement with these complexities could a greater understanding of school improvement be achieved.

Taking an inclusive turn

In parallel with the development of IQEA, during my time at Cambridge I became involved in another project that was to grow in size and influence far beyond what I had anticipated. This was a UNESCO teacher education initiative to do with the development of more inclusive forms of schooling. Called 'Special Needs in the Classroom', it originally involved research in eight countries (i.e. Canada, Chile, India, Jordan, Kenya, Malta, Spain and Zimbabwe), but subsequently led to dissemination activities of various kinds in over eighty countries (Ainscow, 1994). As with all my work, the project again involved me in collaborating with a team of colleagues from each of the eight countries. It also formed the basis of my doctoral thesis, completed in 1995.

The approach taken in the UNESCO project reflected the rethinking that had occurred during and following my time in Coventry. This revised thinking was characterised by Dyson and Millward (2000) as the 'organisational paradigm'. In general terms it involves moves away from explanations of educational failure that concentrate on the characteristics of individual children and their families towards an analysis of the barriers to participation and learning experienced by students within school systems (Booth and Ainscow, 2002). In this way, those students who do not respond to existing arrangements come to be regarded as 'hidden voices', who, under certain conditions, can encourage the improvement of schools (Ainscow, 1999).

I have argued that this approach, which I defined as involving an 'inclusive turn', is more likely to be successful in schools where there is a culture of collaboration that encourages and supports problem-solving. It involves those within a particular context in working together to address barriers to education experienced by some learners.

During the early phases of the UNESCO project it was assumed that materials and methods would be developed that could be distributed in a straightforward way for use in different parts of the world. Gradually those of us leading the project came to realise – as others involved in international development activities in education have done (e.g. Fuller and Clark, 1994) – that schooling is so closely tied into local conditions and cultures that the importation of practices from elsewhere is fraught with difficulties. In other words, learning from other people, particularly those who live their lives in far-away places, is by no means straightforward (Booth and Ainscow, 1998).

The UNESCO project took as its starting point existing practice within mainstream classrooms. It also adopted a particular view of how teachers develop their practice. Specifically, it assumed that the development of practice occurs in the main through a largely 'trial and error' process within which teachers extend their repertoires as a result of finding out what works for them. Their previous experience as pupils themselves may be very influential in shaping this developmental process, in addition to their observations of other practitioners – including those who lecture to them in teacher education contexts. In this way, teachers create their own individual theories of teaching that guide their day-to-day practice. Such theories are largely unarticulated. They represent the 'tacit knowledge' that has been created through what seems to be a mainly intuitive process of learning from experience using processes of improvisation.

Within the UNESCO project we attempted to work in ways that were consistent with this view of how teachers learn. Specifically we tried to encourage teachers to become more confident and skilful in learning from experience through processes of reflection, in ways that we hoped would stimulate further experimentation. Rather than simply leaving this to chance, we believed it was possible to create workshop contexts that would enable teachers to recognise the value of this form of learning and to gain greater control of the processes involved.

As we worked on this initiative, the idea of inclusive education was gaining ground in many parts of the world. This was given further impetus by the ground-breaking UNESCO World Conference on Special Needs Education, held in Salamanca, Spain, in 1994. The conference considered the future direction of the special needs field in the light of international efforts to ensure the rights of all children to receive basic education. Specifically it examined how far the field of special needs is part of this 'Education for All' movement. In other words, is the aim to move towards a unified system of schooling that is capable of responding to all children as individuals? Or, is it to continue with the tradition of parallel systems whereby some children receive separate forms of education? The implications of this theme are examined in Chapter 12.

Subsequently, I have worked with many colleagues in taking the thinking and materials generated by the UNESCO project forward in countries as diverse as Australia, Brazil, Iceland, Laos, Romania, Portugal, Spain and Zambia (see Chapter 6). More recently, this has led me to experience new challenges, as those guiding national policies in many countries have become preoccupied with measuring school outcomes in terms of test scores and comparing progress with that of other countries through systems such as PISA (Programme for International Student Assessment). At the same time, a growing number of countries are using the idea of an educational 'market place' that emphasises increased school autonomy, competition between schools, parental choice and accountability as central strategies for improving schools. Many in the field argue that these policy trends represent obstacles to the creation of more inclusive education systems. While sharing their concerns, I also think that it is possible to occupy the spaces that are created by the new policy contexts in order to move thinking and practice forward (Ainscow, 2014).

Networking and collaboration

In 1995 I returned to Manchester, taking up the Chair at the University that had previously been held by Peter Mittler, an academic who had made an enormous impact – nationally and internationally – on the development of what had come to be known as the field of inclusive education. The move was particularly painful in that it meant leaving behind the outstanding team of scholars that

I had worked with at Cambridge. In addition, I left the extensive network of school and local authority contacts that I had developed, moving to a region where I had no links.

Gradually, over the following years, I was able to build a new set of partners and contacts. This led to a plethora of projects and research studies, many of which became focused on the challenges facing urban schools, particularly in respect to the low levels of achievement of learners from economically disadvantaged backgrounds.

Eventually I was joined in Manchester by my colleague from Cambridge, Mel West, and, together, we coordinated a national project on behalf of the government to strengthen school leadership within the Excellence in Cities initiative. This occurred during a period when funding was made available to encourage urban secondary schools to collaborate. This experience alongside a series of other related studies, some of which were carried out by doctoral students, was reported in an edited book, *Improving Urban Schools* (Ainscow and West, 2006). The concluding chapter of that book is reprinted here as Chapter 11.

Much of our research during this period was focused on the idea of networking and collaboration between schools. For example, between 2004 and 2006, my colleague Andy Howes and I carried out a study on behalf of the government of an improvement process known as Transforming Secondary Education, in a city in the Midlands where the performance of the school system was a cause for considerable concern. The initiative made collaboration within four networks of secondary schools the main route to sustainable higher achievement (Ainscow and Howes, 2007). During the same period, Andy and I carried out an evaluation of developments in another local authority that encouraged school partnerships, where we were privileged to be able to observe closely the work of its team of school improvement officers as they worked together in order to improve the work of schools. An account of this study is provided in Chapter 13.

Alongside these two studies, with various colleagues, I carried out a programme of research that generated considerable evidence that school-to-school collaboration can strengthen improvement processes by adding to the range of expertise made available (see Chapters 12 and 13 for details). Together, these studies indicate that collaboration between schools has an enormous potential for fostering the capacity of education systems to respond to learner diversity. More specifically, they show how collaboration between schools can help to reduce the polarisation of schools, to the particular benefit of those students who seem marginalised at the edges of the system, and whose performance and attitudes cause increasing concern.

It is worth adding that networking can be extended much more widely to encourage the sharing of experiences and ideas regarding ways of developing inclusive practices across national borders. It was with this possibility in mind that I worked with Sue Stubbs from Save the Children and my Manchester colleague Susie Miles in setting up the Enabling Education Network (EENET), with the technical and financial support of a group of concerned international organisations, including UNESCO. The purpose of EENET is to contribute to the development of effective, relevant, appropriate sustainable education policy and practice internationally, and to support and promote the inclusion of marginalised groups in education worldwide. EENET's annual publication, *Enabling Education*, is disseminated to almost 2000 individuals and organisations in over 150 countries, and its website has been accessed by people in over 190 countries (see Chapter 12 for further details).

School improvement with attitude

My thinking regarding ways of helping schools to become more inclusive was much influenced as a result of the development of the 'Index for Inclusion' (Booth and Ainscow, 2002). Designed originally for use within the policy context of England at the turn of the century by a team of activists, the Index is a set of school review materials that has been refined as a result of over ten years of collaborative action research in many countries (see *The International Journal of Inclusive Education*, volume 8 number 2, for articles about some of these developments). As a result, it is now available in more than 30 languages and is widely used internationally.

The Index enables schools to draw on the resources of staff, students, parents/ carers and community representatives in order to address barriers to the participation and learning of pupils that exist within their existing 'cultures, policies and practices'. In connecting inclusion with the detail of policy and practice, the Index encourages those who use it to build up their own view of inclusion, related to their experience and values, as they work out what policies and practices they wish to promote or discourage. Such an approach is based on the idea that inclusion is essentially about attempts to embody particular values within specific contexts. In other words, it is 'school improvement with attitude' (Ainscow et al, 2006).

The Index approach also involves an emphasis on collaborative inquiry, involving coordinated and sustained efforts around the idea that changing outcomes for all students is unlikely to be achieved unless there are changes in the behaviours of adults. Consequently, the starting point for inclusive school development is with teachers: in effect, enlarging their capacity to imagine what might be achieved, and increasing their sense of accountability for bringing this about. This may also involve tackling taken-for-granted assumptions, most often relating to expectations about certain groups of students, their capabilities, behaviour and patterns of attendance. At the same time, such efforts have to be linked to what is happening in other schools and in the wider community. Chapter 7 provides accounts of my use of the Index in various countries.

The work on the Index for Inclusion, alongside the findings from our earlier efforts to explore the potential of inquiry-based approaches, influenced the design of another project, 'Understanding and Developing Inclusive Practices in Schools'. This initiative, which took the form of a collaborative action research project, took place between 2000 and 2004, and involved 25 urban schools, their associated local education authorities and three universities (i.e. Canterbury Christ Church, Manchester and Newcastle). It was funded by the ESRC as part of its Teaching and Learning research programme.

I led the study in partnership with Tony Booth and Alan Dyson. Together we explored ways of developing more inclusive practices in the schools. In designing the study, we saw inclusion as a value and set of practices about which something was already known. Moreover, as established authors and researchers in the field, we had played our part in generating this prior knowledge. We also knew – from our own work and from others in this field – that acceptance of the values and practices of inclusion were frequently resisted by practitioners who saw themselves as having other priorities and as working within constraints that made inclusive practice impossible. This was particularly the case in the then English policy context, where a relentless focus on 'raising standards' was being imposed on schools by the Labour government.

We therefore needed a means of releasing practitioners from the constraints of national policy and enabling them to change their value positions and assumptions. We saw the use of research evidence as offering this means. Furthermore, we made the assumption that when practitioners were confronted by evidence about their practices, they would – with appropriate encouragement from their critical friends – begin to recognise the non-inclusive elements of those practices and would find ways of making them more inclusive. Fortunately, this is what did most often happen. Chapter 8 provides an account of what this involved.

Using collaborative inquiry

Our attempts to learn how collaborative inquiry can be used to foster equity continue to this day, not least through the work of the University of Manchester Coalition of Research Schools (Ainscow et al, in press). Schools joining the Coalition commit themselves to engage in systematic inquiry processes, informed by evidence from national and international research studies. As with our earlier projects, this requires them to establish a staff research group, selected on the basis of their capacity to lead developments in school. This group works with the team from the Centre for Equity in Education in order to collect and analyse contextual evidence, develop improvement plans and evaluate the impact of actions taken. While the short-term aim is improved learning outcomes for specific pupil groups, in the longer term it is anticipated that this will develop the school's capacity to use collaborative inquiry more generally as a vehicle for improvement.

A similar approach has been a feature of a recently completed study, 'Responding to diversity by engaging with students' voices'. This involved two cycles of collaborative action research carried out by teams of teachers and researchers in three countries (i.e. England, Portugal and Spain) that led to the creation of what we see as an innovative strategy for teacher development (Messiou et al, in press). This aims to support teachers in developing inclusive classroom practices by engaging with the views of students.

Central to the strategy is the idea of engaging with the views of students, a process that, we argue, should permeate all the processes involved and can take many forms. Our research suggests that it is this factor, more than anything else, that makes the difference as far as responding to learner diversity is concerned. In particular, it is this that brings a critical edge to the process that has the potential to challenge teachers to go beyond the sharing of existing practices in order to invent new possibilities for engaging students in their lessons. Where such changes take place, it is useful to think of them as the result of an interruption to continuing thinking and practice which brings about a transformation from 'single-loop' to 'double-loop' learning (Argyris and Schon, 1996) – that is, from learning that enables practice to be improved incrementally, to learning that shifts the assumptions on which practice is based.

Our experiences of working with schools in such projects have, for me, confirmed Kurt Lewin's suggestion that the best way to understand an organisation is by trying to change it (Schein, 2001). Specifically, it has put my colleagues and me in privileged positions to learn from the successes of the schools, as well as their frustrations, as they have attempted to work collaboratively in order to find more effective ways of educating all of their students within national policy contexts that, at times, seem perverse. This leads me to argue that, despite good intentions, efforts to encourage collaboration between schools will remain something of a disappointment in respect to their capacity to foster equity within education policies that places some emphasis on competition.

All of this has significant implications for national policy makers. In order to make use of the power of collaboration as a means of achieving equity in schools, I argue that they need to foster greater flexibility at the local level so that practitioners have the space to analyse their particular circumstances and determine priorities accordingly. This means that policy makers must recognise that the details of policy implementation are not amenable to central regulation. Rather, these have to be dealt with by those who are close to and, therefore, in a better position to understand local contexts. They should be trusted to act in the best interests of the children and young people they serve, and encouraged to work together, pooling their knowledge and experience, for the benefit of students and teachers alike.

Changing systems

In 2004 I was joined in Manchester by Alan Dyson, with whom I had previously collaborated on a series of projects. With the support of Sue Goldrick and Kirstin Kerr, we launched the Centre for Equity in Education. Our stated aim was to do research that makes a difference (Ainscow et al, 2009). In particular, by adopting a social justice stance, we wanted to have a direct impact on policy and practice. Moreover, we sought to have an impact on as large a scale as possible, which meant moving from work with individual practitioners and institutions, to work with groups and systems, and, in this sense, to move from work at the level of specific practices to work at the level of policy. An example of such a project that involved work with schools in one local authority over a five-year period is described in Chapter 14.

We see the role of the Centre as being a form of disturbance, where we use evidence from our research to provoke debate in the field. Following the advice of Andy Hargreaves, who was a visiting professor at Manchester at the time, our aim is to be there 'at the table' when policies are being formulated at different levels of the education system, even though sometimes people may not like what we have to say. This is a difficult stance to take: being at the table can often involve collusion with the status quo, while challenging what is being said risks the possibility of being asked to withdraw, as often happens with researchers. Fortunately, Alan Dyson and I have had considerable experience of walking this line and the existence of our Centre provides a vehicle for us to carry out such interventions, not least through the publication of our occasional reports and manifestos (these can be accessed on the Centre for Equity in Education website).

The rationale of our Centre has led me to focus increasingly on finding what I have referred to as high-leverage strategies for system-level change, as explained in the paper reproduced in Chapter 10. However, what was to be the greatest opportunity to be 'at the table' and 'say things that would sometimes not be liked' came about as a result of my involvement in a three-year initiative known as the Greater Manchester Challenge. The purpose of this government-instigated project was to improve outcomes for children and young people across the city region, focusing in particular on those from low-income families. The budget for the project was £50 million and I had the role of Chief Adviser.

Chapter 15 provides an account of what this involved. This adds to the growing literature that attempts to make sense of the successes of the much-publicised City Challenge initiative in England, first of all in London, and then later in the Black Country (in the West Midlands) and Greater Manchester (i.e. Barrs et al, 2014; Claeys et al, 2014; Greaves et al, 2014; Hutchings et al, 2012; Hutchings and Mansaray, 2013; Kidson and Norris, 2014; Ofsted, 2010). What is distinctive about my contribution is that as a participant observer I am able to explain what happened from the inside. This has enabled me to draw lessons that will, I believe, be useful to those in other parts of the world who are interested in system-level change, as I explain in the book *Towards Self-Improving School Systems: Lessons from a City Challenge* (Ainscow, 2015).

This does not result in the sorts of simplistic and prescriptive recommendations that too often permeate the literature on school improvement. Rather, my insider stance enabled me to engage with matters of detail that draw attention to local complications that can act as barriers to change processes. This led me to formulate a strategic framework that can be used to analyse existing arrangements in order to develop powerful improvement approaches. More specifically, this framework helps to pinpoint resources that can be mobilised in order to overcome the barriers that exist through collective efforts that involve many stakeholders. I argue that this is a *different way of thinking* about how to develop school systems that are more equitable, one that requires an engagement with the social and political factors that are fundamental to the way these systems work.

Central to the way of thinking that I present are attempts to develop new, more fruitful working relationships: within and between schools; between schools and their wider communities; and between local and national government. This brings together lessons from all of my earlier experiences and research. It is worth adding that the flexible and responsive nature of this approach means that it can be adapted for use in different national contexts. Interestingly, it also took me back to reconsider the role of special schools within attempts to reform an education system (see Chapter 9).

Subsequently I have been able to work on a series of new projects based on this thinking. These include: an improvement initiative in the small island of Anglesey, off the north west of Wales; a collaborative action research network in Queensland, Australia; and a project with schools facing challenging circumstances in the Yorkshire Humber region of England. In these varied contexts, I have seen how a way of thinking about system change – developed as a result of experiences in the dense urban context of Greater Manchester – can make a difference. In particular, it has stimulated new thinking and the formulation of strategies to put this into action. At times, however, the pace of change has remained frustratingly slow. This reminds us that what we are promoting is a process of cultural change that challenges deeply held beliefs and well-established patterns of working across different levels of an education system.

The progress achieved in Anglesey subsequently led me to become involved in other developments in Wales, particularly the design of the Central South Wales Challenge, which involves over 400 schools in five local authorities, and Schools Challenge Cymru, the Welsh Government's multi-million pound flagship programme to accelerate the rate of improvement across the country. These developments allow me to continue my search for ways of developing more equitable education systems.

Some final reflections

I was privileged to be closely involved in the process of the Salamanca conference in 1994, working alongside many colleagues from around the world. Over the following twenty years, the theme of inclusive education has influenced thinking internationally to a level that I suspect none of us had anticipated. More recently, the formulations explained in this chapter influenced the conceptual framework for the 48th session of the International Conference on Education, held in 2008, and attended by Ministers of Education and officials from 153 countries (see Chapter 12).

No doubt in another ten years we will once again stop to reflect on the continuing influence of Salamanca. My hope is that the progress that has been made in fostering more inclusive and fairer education systems over the last twenty years will have continued. For this to happen, however, those involved have to be effective in analysing the barriers that are preventing progress in their own contexts and in mobilising available resources in order to overcome these barriers. In this way, efforts to promote equity within education systems can, I believe, refocus national policies to 'raise standards' in a way that reflects the spirit of Salamanca.

Bearing this in mind, the argument I have developed in this introductory chapter points to a series of propositions that could be useful to those seeking to foster more equitable developments in their own contexts. These are as follows:

* In order to move policy and practice forward, there needs to be clarity regarding what is meant by equity.
* The development of inclusive practices must involve mobilising available human resources in order to overcome barriers to participation and learning.
* An engagement with various kinds of evidence can be a powerful stimulus for encouraging teachers to develop more inclusive practices.
* Inclusive schools take many forms but what is common is the existence of an organisational culture that views student diversity positively.
* Schools need to work together and with the wider community in promoting equity.
* National policies have to create a framework for making all of this happen.

These ideas reinforce the idea that the promotion of equity in schools is essentially a social process that has to occur within particular contexts. In this sense, it is about learning how to live with difference and, indeed, learning how to learn from difference. And, as I have argued many times, the most important factor is the collective will to make it happen.

References

Ainscow, M. (1991) (Ed.), *Effective schools for all*. London: Fulton.
Ainscow, M. (1994) *Special needs in the classroom: a teacher education guide*. London: Jessical Kingsley/UNESCO.

Ainscow, M. (1999) *Understanding the development of inclusive schools*. London: Falmer Press.

Ainscow, M. (2015) *Towards self-improving school systems: lessons from a city challenge*. London: Routledge.

Ainscow, M. and Hart, S. (1992) Moving practice forward. *Support for Learning* 7(3), 115–120.

Ainscow, M. and Howes, A. (2007) Working together to improve urban secondary schools: a study of practice in one city. *School Leadership and Management* 27, 285–300.

Ainscow, M. and Muncey, J. (1989) *Meeting individual needs in the primary school*. London: Fulton.

Ainscow, M. and Southworth, G. (1996) School improvement: a study of the roles of leaders and external consultants. *School Effectiveness and School Improvement* 7(3), 229–251.

Ainscow, M. and Tweddle, D.A. (1979) *Preventing classroom failure*. London: Fulton.

Ainscow, M. and Tweddle, D.A. (1988) *Encouraging classroom success*. London: Fulton.

Ainscow, M. and West, M. (Eds.) (2006) *Improving urban schools: leadership and collaboration*. Maidenhead: Open University Press.

Ainscow, M., Booth, T. and Dyson, A. (2004) Understanding and developing inclusive practices in schools: a collaborative action research network. *International Journal of Inclusive Education* 8(2), 125–139.

Ainscow, M., Booth, T., Dyson, A., with Farrell, P., Frankham, J., Gallannaugh, F., Howes, A. and Smith, R. (2006) *Improving schools, developing inclusion*. London: Routledge.

Ainscow, M., Dyson, A., Goldrick, S. and Kerr, K. (2009) Using research to foster equity and inclusion within the context of New Labour educational reforms. In C. Chapman and H. Gunter (Eds.) *Radical reforms: perspectives on an era of educational change*. London: Routledge.

Ainscow, M., Dyson, A., Goldrick, S. and West, M. (in press) Using collaborative inquiry to foster equity within school systems: opportunities and barriers. *School Effectiveness and School Improvement*.

Argyris, C. and Schon, D.A. (1996) *Organisational learning II: Theory, method and practice*. Reading, MA: Addison-Wesley.

Barrs, S., Bernardes, E., Elwick, A., Malortie, A., McAleavy, T., McInerney, L., Menzies, L. and Rigall, A. (2014) *Lessons from London schools: investigating the success*. Reading: CfBT Trust.

Booth, T. and Ainscow, M. (1998) (Eds.) *From them to us: an international study of inclusion in education*. London: Routledge.

Booth, T. and Ainscow, M. (2002) *Index for inclusion: developing learning and participation in schools*. Bristol: Centre for Studies on Inclusive Education.

Brennan, W. (1979) *Curricular needs of slow learners*. Milton Keynes: Open University.

Claeys, A., Kempton, J. and Paterson, C. (2014) *Regional challenges: a collaborative approach to improving education*. London: CentreForum.

Clarke, P., Ainscow, M. and West, M. (2005) Learning from difference: Some reflections on school improvements projects in three countries. In A. Harris (Ed.) *International developments in school improvement*. London: Continuum.

Department for Education and Science (1978) *Report of the Committee of Enquiry into Special Educational Needs (The Warnock Report)*. London: HMSO.

Dyson, A. and Millward, A. (2000) *Schools and special needs: issues of innovation and inclusion*. London: Paul Chapman.

Fuller, B. and Clark, P. (1994) Raising school effects while ignoring culture? Local conditions and the influence of classroom tools, rules and pedagogy. *Review of Educational Research* 64(1), 119–157.

Greaves, E., Macmillan, L. and Sibieta, L. (2014) *Lessons from London schools for attainment gaps and social mobility*. London: the Social Mobility and Child Poverty Commission.

Hopkins, D. (2007) *Every school a great school: realizing the potential of system leadership*. Maidenhead: Open University Press.

Hopkins, D., Ainscow, M. and West, M. (1994) *School improvement in an era of change*. London: Cassell.

Hutchings, M. and Mansaray, A. (2013) *A review of the impact of the London Challenge (2003–08) and the City Challenge (2008–11)*. London: Ofsted

Hutchings, M., Hollingworth, S., Mansaray, A., Rose, R. and Greenwood, C. (2012) *Research report DFE-RR215: Evaluation of the City Challenge programme*. London: Department for Education. Kidson, M. and Norris, E. (2014) *Implementing the London Challenge*. London: Joseph Rowntree Foundation/Institute of Government.

Messiou, K., Ainscow, M. and others (in press) Learning from differences: a strategy for teacher development in respect to student diversity. *School Effectiveness and School Improvement*.

OECD (2007) *No more failures: ten steps to equity in education*. Paris: OECD Publishing.

Ofsted (2010) *London Challenge*. London: Ofsted.

Schein, E.H. (2001) Clinical inquiry/research. In P. Reason and H. Bradbury (Eds.) *Handbook of action research*. London: Sage.

Skrtic, T.M. (1991) Students with special educational needs: Artifacts of the traditional curriculum. In M. Ainscow (Ed.), *Effective schools for all*. London: Fulton.

Tomlinson, S. (1982) *A sociology of special education*. London: Routledge.

West, M. and Ainscow, M. (2010) Improving schools in Hong Kong: A description of the improvement model and some reflections on its impact on schools, teachers and school principals. In S. Huber (Ed.) *School leadership: international perspectives*. London: Springer.

Wilkinson, R. and Pickett, K. (2009) *The spirit level*. London: Allen Lane.

RETHINKING THE AGENDA

Ainscow, M. (1999) *Understanding the development of inclusive schools*. London: Routledge (Chapter 2: Learning from experience)

Introduction

This book chapter summarises the changes in thinking that occurred following the publication of my first book, *Preventing Classroom Failure* (Wiley, 1979), not least as a result of developments in the Special Needs Action Programme in Coventry. A subsequent invitation from the publisher to update the book led to a crisis in my thinking and, indeed, that of my co-author, Dave Tweddle. As a result, we chose to write a different book, *Encouraging Classroom Success*, in which we revised our thinking and repositioned ourselves in relation to the field. The chapter explains the way our attention was refocused, away from a narrow perspective on individual learners towards the contexts in which learning takes place. This pointed us in the general direction of the approaches that are discussed in later readings in this book. It also signalled the importance of strengthening the capacity of mainstream schools to cater for learner diversity.

The development of my own thinking and practice is at the heart of the ideas presented in this book. Indeed, a central argument is about the importance of reflecting on and learning from experience. With this in mind, therefore, this chapter provides an outline of some of the changes in my thinking that had occurred in the years *prior* to the two projects that are the main focus of attention. These provide a theoretical context for the experiences that are described and the proposals that are made in subsequent chapters.

The retrospective account presented in this chapter helped me to define certain ideas and assumptions that seemed to be significant starting points for the two projects. In preparing the account extensive use was made of various of my previous articles and books. Where it seems helpful I quote verbatim from these publications. Having said, that I am also conscious of Weick's warning about the limitations of retrospective explanations. Specifically he warns that they:

> ". . . are poor guides to prospective action. We know relatively little about how we actually get things done. We don't know what works, because we misremember the process of accomplishment. We will always underestimate the number of false starts that went into the outcome. Furthermore, even though there were dead ends, we probably did learn from them – we learned more about the environment and about our capabilities".
>
> Weick (1985, page 132)

He goes on to suggest that keeping records during times of change may help to avoid glossing over difficult experiences whilst striving for a particular outcome. In some senses the publications that I have drawn on in preparing this chapter provide such a record. Certainly revisiting them helped me to identify alternative explanations over and beyond those that were articulated when the writing was originally carried out.

Looking back

Somebody said to me not so long ago, 'There are three kinds of people – people who make things happen; people who watch things happen; and people who wonder what the hell did happen!' If I look over my career in education I sense that I have at various stages been each of these.

My main professional interests have been and are with the difficulties that some children experience in school – and with attempts to find ways in which teachers can help all children to experience success in learning. Having worked as a teacher in secondary and special schools, I became a headteacher where my main role was to make things happen; I then worked as a local education authority adviser/inspector where I was able to spend more time observing practice in schools; and then, more recently, working in higher education, I have found myself looking back, reflecting on what I have learned from these experiences.

As I began work on the IQEA and UNESCO projects in the late 1980s, it was inevitably that these previous experiences would influence my decisions and actions. Whilst common sense suggests that everything that had occurred previously was likely to be an influence, two earlier experiences, in particular, seemed to be directly relevant to the task I faced. In this chapter, therefore, I provide reflective accounts of these experiences based upon my re-reading of my own writings during this time. The first of these experiences took the form of a curriculum development project in a special school; the other was an authority-wide staff development project related to the idea of special needs in ordinary schools. My accounts of these previous experiences provide the basis for an explanation of my thinking at the outset of the IQEA and UNESCO projects. They also indicate how this thinking had changed during the period of these earlier developments.

Curriculum development in a special school

During the 1970s I spent six years as headteacher of a special school in the Midlands for what were then referred to as ESN(M) (educationally subnormal, moderate) pupils (now designated as pupils with moderate learning difficulties). The population of the school consisted of pupils aged 5 to 16, most of whom were from economically poor families.

In collaboration with my colleagues in the school I attempted to develop an approach that would provide an educational experience suited to the needs of the pupils as we perceived them. We assumed that the children were in the school as a result of experiencing difficulties in ordinary schools and that in many instances these educational difficulties had come about, at least in part, as a result of social deprivation. Consequently, a strong influence on our thinking was a desire to compensate for the inadequacy of the children's experience. We were also keen to provide forms of intensive help that would accelerate their progress. Indeed, wherever possible our aim was to bring the pupils to a level of achievement that would enable them to return successfully to ordinary schools.

Informed by these assumptions and beliefs, I saw it as my task to co-ordinate a team of people in developing and providing a curriculum that emphasised consistency and continuity. My view was that the best way to help our pupils to learn successfully was to provide teaching that was carefully planned and which co-ordinated the efforts of each member of staff.

This work was going on during a period when the world of special education was subject to some criticism, particularly with respect to curriculum thinking and practices. This was part of a wider concern about the purposes and quality of schooling, leading to demands for greater accountability. There were, in addition, other more specific pressures that seemed to draw attention to the need for an examination of what happened in special schools. The Warnock Report had suggested that the quality of education offered to pupils in special provision was unsatisfactory, particularly with respect to the curriculum opportunities provided, and that many special schools underestimated their pupils' capabilities (DES, 1978). A number of other publications were also critical of existing practice (e.g. Brennan, 1979; Tomlinson, 1982).

Teachers in many special schools reacted to this new focus of attention on their work by taking a greater interest in the theoretical basis of their practice. Many became interested in curriculum theory, and in their search for guidance the staff in some special schools were influenced by the literature on planning with behavioural objectives, sometimes referred to as rational curriculum planning. This approach to planning, which was by no means new in the field of curriculum studies, had become popular in special education in North America, probably because of the strong influence of behavioural psychologists. Many of us working in special schools in the UK found the approach helpful as we sought ways of planning our teaching in a more systematic manner.

Initially this interest grew as a result of our own discussions within the school, building upon the previous experience of the staff. Gradually this became affected by ideas from elsewhere. Dave Tweddle, who at that time was the educational psychologist attached to the school, was one such influence.

Over a period of years the staff established a pattern of meeting together on a regular basis to plan the curriculum for the whole school. Recently this sort of approach has become quite familiar in many schools, particularly with the introduction of staff development days, but at that time it was not that common. To provide a framework within which these discussions could take place we devised a simple curriculum model which consisted of the following two aspects:

1. The Closed Curriculum. This was an attempt to define those areas of skill and knowledge that were regarded as essential learning for all pupils in the school.
2. The Open Curriculum. This was viewed as being more open-ended, allowing content to be modified to take account of the needs of individual pupils.

It is important to note that within the school there was considerable commitment to the idea of providing a broad and enriching programme for all pupils. Indeed, there was very good work in areas such as creativity, personal and social development, environmental studies and outdoor pursuits – an orientation rooted in our desire to provide compensatory education.

It is also important to recognise that whilst the Open/Closed framework was seen as a useful basis for planning, it was not the intention to use this distinction in planning actual classroom activities. In other words, it was acknowledged that pupils might well be engaged in tasks and activities related to Closed and Open Curriculum intentions at the same time.

Our detailed planning was based on agreed objectives. This involved taking broad goals and expressing them in terms of intended learning outcomes as a basis for planning and evaluating the teaching that was provided. It was also seen as a means of establishing the consistency and continuity to which we aspired. So, for example, a goal to do with teaching pupils to tell the time might lead to objectives such as

1.   Reads aloud hours from the clock
2.   Reads aloud minutes from the clock
3.   States that 60 minutes equals one hour
4.   Reads aloud time by half and quarter hours

Within the Closed Curriculum, objectives were stated as relatively precise statements of observable behaviour that could then be used as a means of observing and recording pupil progress. Furthermore, these objectives were arranged in hierarchies of learning steps in the belief that progress would be accelerated by teaching the pupils in a step-by-step manner. Figure 2.1 is an example of how this approach was used as a basis for planning and recording progress. Further examples of this format, based on the work carried out in the school, can be found in two books that were written as a result of our work (i.e. Ainscow and Tweddle, 1979 and 1984).

In the Open Curriculum, planning was carried out in a less precise way, thus allowing individual teachers to provide opportunities that took account of the interests and experiences of their pupils. Consequently a more flexible use of the objectives approach was encouraged, including the use of objectives that stated more general intentions and others which described experiences without predicting intended outcomes.

An area support centre

A further development of the work of the school grew out of the then novel idea of the special school establishing a role as area support centre. This involved the creation of links with local primary and secondary schools in order to provide advice and support on dealing with learning difficulties. One element of this initiative was a series of in-service workshops, held in the special school for teachers from primary schools, with a main focus on developing individual learning programmes based on objectives and task analysis.

Further publicity for the work at the school was provided by a range of publications written by members of staff, including the book *Preventing Classroom Failure* (Ainscow and Tweddle, 1979), and the participation of colleagues in various conferences and courses. This publicity had an impact on teachers in special and ordinary schools around the country. It also influenced the work of many educational psychologists and support services. I believe this influence was a positive one in a number of ways. It gave many teachers a means of talking about their work in ways that seemed practical and purposeful. It also had the effect of raising expectations about what certain pupils might achieve

Objective	Working	Mastered	Checked	Comments
1. Uses an identity statement of the form "This is a tree" in response to the question "What is this?"		25th Sept (assessed)	10th Oct	
2. Uses the negation of objective (1), i.e. "This is not a tree"	25th Sept	10th Oct		Lang Mast cards introduced 2nd October. David is responding v. well
3. Uses the identity statement "The dog is black" in response to the question "What colour is the dog?"		25th Sept (assessed)	10th Oct	
4. Uses the negation of objective (3), i.e. "The dog is not black".	12th Oct	18th Oct	19th Oct	Lang Mast cards used – prefers this to group puppet sessions.
5. Uses an action statement of the form "The boy is running" in response to the question "What is the boy doing?"		25th Sept (assessed)		
6. Uses the negation of objective (5), i.e. "The boy is not running".	19th Oct			Expect rapid progress (i.e. 26th Oct).

Figure 2.1 Format for recording progress using an objectives approach (from Ainscow & Tweddle, 1979)

by focusing attention on those factors that teachers could influence. The emphasis placed on observing pupil progress within the classroom as opposed to the previous over-use of norm-referenced tests was also a significant step forward in many schools.

On the other hand, I came to recognise that the approach had a number of limitations and, indeed, potential dangers, particularly if used inflexibly (Ainscow and Tweddle, 1988). These concerns can be summarised as follows:

1. Planning educational experiences based on sequences of pre-determined objectives tends to encourage a narrowing of the curriculum, thus reducing opportunities for learning.
2. Whilst the idea of individual programmes of objectives may be seen as a strategy for encouraging integration of pupils, it tends, in practice, to encourage segregation.
3. Where the approach is presented as a 'science of instruction' it tends to make teachers feel inadequate since it appears to give no value to their previous professional experience and expertise.
4. The idea of pre-planning leaves little or no room for pupils to participate in decisions about their own learning. Consequently they are encouraged to adopt a passive role.
5. Programmes of objectives can become static, leading to them being used even when they are found to be inadequate or even redundant as a result of unexpected circumstances occurring.

In reflecting upon the work that was carried out by my colleagues in this particular special school I came to the view that the successes that undoubtedly occurred were less to do with the idea of planning with objectives and more to do with group processes. In particular, I believe that the emphasis on staff discussion, leading to the creation of a common language that could be used to discuss matters of classroom practice, and the development of a more collaborative way of working in order to overcome difficulties, influenced the outlooks of individuals by raising their expectations and by providing a supportive social and professional environment. It also led to a strong sense of common purpose throughout the school, a factor which may be a common feature of all effective schools (see for example, Stoll, 1991). I should add that I have subsequently witnessed similar positive effects in other schools that have adopted this way of working (e.g. Ainscow and Hopkins, 1994; Hopkins et al, 1994).

A local authority staff development programme

In 1979 I became Adviser for Special Educational Needs in Coventry. As part of my duties there I instigated and helped co-ordinate the development of a staff development initiative, 'The Special Needs Action Programme' (SNAP). This project had arisen as a result of a review of the authority's special education provision which led to a recognition of the need for significant change. (A detailed account of the development of SNAP is provided in Ainscow and Muncey, 1989.) In general terms the aim was to redirect special education provision and services away from ways of working that encouraged segregation of pupils towards a much more integrated range of responses. It was not seen as a revolutionary strategy but as an attempt to bring about gradual change in ways that would limit the risk of damaging existing good practice.

The development of the project was influenced by a number of significant factors. As part of a wider movement aimed at protecting the rights of minority groups in the community, there had been an increased recognition that the rights of children are significantly reduced if they are excluded from all or part of the programme of experiences generally offered in schools. There was also the impact of Government legislation, particularly the 1981 Education Act. Whilst this had not come into effect at the outset of SNAP, the various consultative processes associated with its formulation helped to encourage the debate about special educational needs that had been fostered by the Warnock Report.

In addition the influence of parental opinion was having an increasing impact upon the education service. In the special needs field in particular, the idea of 'parents as partners', as promoted in the Warnock Report, had become widely accepted if not implemented.

Finally developments in educational thinking generally were also influential. New ideas about curriculum, teaching and learning styles, forms of assessment and recording, and staff development had all enriched the discussion about how schools might respond to pupils experiencing difficulty.

The aims of SNAP were to encourage headteachers of ordinary schools to develop procedures for the identification of pupils with special needs; to assist teachers in ordinary schools to provide an appropriate curriculum for such pupils; and to co-ordinate the work of the various special education support services and facilities in ordinary schools. We did not see SNAP as an attempt to impose one model of achieving these aims. We felt that each school should develop policies and practices compatible with its situation and usual ways of working. With this in mind, each school in the authority was asked to designate one member of staff as co-ordinator for special needs, a strategy that was later adopted as part of national policy. Emphasis was placed on this person's task in co-ordination all staff in sharing responsibility for the progress of all pupils. Meanwhile, we attempted to disseminate examples of good practice that schools could use as vehicles for reviewing and, where necessary, extending existing procedures. This last point is important since some of the publicity given to SNAP nationally was based upon a misunderstanding of the ways in which the project operated in Coventry. For example groups in some local authorities took some of the SNAP materials and used them as a means of imposing a particular way of working on teachers. Our emphasis was placed on helping schools to develop approaches that were consistent with their own traditions and philosophies.

Initially the project focused solely on primary schools, but subsequently it had an impact in the secondary phase. The central strategy in both sectors was a series of in-service courses related to special needs in ordinary schools which were developed by teams within the authority. These were presented initially to representatives from each school in the authority at the teachers' centre and then as part of school-based staff development programmes.

The early courses tended to be concerned with helping teachers to devise individualised teaching programmes, based very much on the ideas recommended in Ainscow and Tweddle (1979 and 1984). So, for example, the course for primary schools 'Teaching Children with Learning difficulties' involved a workshop guide, 'Small Steps'. This introduced procedures for developing individual programmes based upon planning with behavioural objectives in the form described earlier in this chapter. However, as SNAP developed the courses gradually took on a much broader perspective. The course 'Problem Behaviour in Primary Schools', for example, examined issues related to school management and organisation as well as examining principles of classroom organisation. Similarly, the course 'Special Needs in the Secondary School' attempted to get schools to review all aspects of policy and practice as a means of finding ways of meeting the individual needs of all pupils.

From starting in a small way as just another in-service initiative SNAP gradually grew until it became effectively the co-ordinating mechanism for the whole of the authority's policy on special needs. As such it was, in my view, an interesting example of how change can be facilitated provided the efforts of those involved are co-ordinated and supported over a period of years. Unfortunately too often sound initiatives aimed at bringing improvements in educational contexts are less successful because this long-term commitment is not sustained.

Evaluating SNAP

Since the main purpose of SNAP was to help schools to review and develop their policies and practice this had to be the main focus of its evaluation. Extensive evidence from a number of sources, including detailed case studies of the work in schools and follow up evaluations of particular courses (e.g. Ainscow and Muncey, 1989; Arthur, 1989; Moses et al, 1988) indicated that a series of features incorporated in the various courses developed as part of SNAP were particularly effective in encouraging staff development and change.

We found, for example, that the self-contained format of the course materials appeared to provide a relatively neutral stimulus that staff could use for reviewing existing practice. They did not imply that a school's existing approaches were redundant; but rather sought to build upon good practice. In addition the emphasis on active learning approaches and group problem-solving, as opposed to the traditional didactic teaching style of so much in-service education, encouraged participation and seemed to help overcome fear of change. Furthermore, involving all staff within a school in a process of review and development of policy helped facilitate a commitment to implement any changes that were agreed.

The courses attempted to present practical ideas and, in some cases, materials that could be used in the classroom. They also aimed to provide teachers with early success by getting them to try out strategies in their own classrooms. This was much appreciated by participants who suggested that too many in-service experiences provide theory without any attention to practical implications. The credibility of courses seemed to be enhanced by the fact that they were tutored by practising teachers. Furthermore considerable efforts were made to support teachers as they tried out new approaches in their classrooms. This was provided by members of the various advisory and support services. A further source of help was created by emphasising the importance of within-school support between teachers.

In reflecting upon the experience of SNAP in Coventry it seems to me that once again the major lesson to be learned relates to the importance of group processes. Whilst the in-service materials that developed were often quite impressive, the greatest impact may well have resulted from the collaborative problem-solving that they encouraged and the way in which this helped to foster creativity and experimentation. This collaboration seemed to occur at different levels within the service. First of all the teams of people who came together to develop materials gained much from the professional dialogues that this process demanded. Then, those who acted as tutors gained in terms of their own confidence and expertise as a result of working together with representatives from the schools. Finally, where schools were able to use the project materials to facilitate review and development of policy and practice, this seemed to be an effective strategy for encouraging more co-ordinated whole school approaches.

An interactive perspective

The period I spent in Coventry led me to change my views in a number of ways, particularly as a result of the many opportunities I had to observe teachers at work in primary and secondary schools. This gave me a much better understanding of the issues involved in attempting to respond to the needs of individual pupils in classes larger than those in the special schools in which I had previously taught.

My perspective was further influenced by my involvement in the planning of various other authority staff development initiatives (e.g. management, personal and social education). Consequently I was able to review my ideas about the nature of educational difficulties. I began to recognise that much of my earlier work had been based on the assumption that these difficulties were to a large extent a result of within-child factors. I had tended to exclude from consideration causal explanations that might lie in contextual processes that are external to the individual child. Furthermore I began to realise that this perspective leaves the organisation and practice of ordinary schools untouched since they are assumed to be appropriate for the great majority of children. In other words, the provision of special education tends to confirm the assumption that difficulties occur in schools because certain children are special and this becomes a justification for the maintenance of the *status quo* of schooling.

In the light of these arguments I increasingly found myself joining others at the time (e.g. Wedell, 1981; Dessent, 1987) in adopting an interactive perspective to the special needs tasks. This position was summarised in the first chapter of a book I completed in 1988 with my colleague from Coventry, Jim Muncey (i.e. Ainscow and Muncey, 1989). In that book we contrasted what we called pre- and post-Warnock thinking with regards to special needs, using the publication of the Warnock report into the future of special education as our reference point (DES, 1978). This led us to suggest what we referred to as a 'new approach based upon an acceptance of the Warnock argument that great numbers of children experience difficulties in the school system' (page 10). We went on to state that most of these children are already present in ordinary schools and that we could anticipate a continuing trend towards youngsters with more severe difficulties being educated in mainstream provision.

The thinking associated with this interactive perspective to special needs is well summarised by the 'new assumptions' that Muncey and I put forward. I quote from these in some detail since they give a clear statement of our agreed position at that time.

New assumption 1:

Any child may experience difficulties in school at some stage
"It has to be recognised that experiencing difficulty in learning is a normal part of schooling rather than an indication that there is something wrong

with a child. It is only when difficulties in learning cause anxiety to the child, the child's parents or teachers that particular attention needs to be paid. Furthermore, this can apply to any youngster whatever his or her overall attainments in comparison with others in the same class. So, for example, a child who is generally successful in learning may go through a period of boredom with the work presented by the class teacher. If this means that he or she is not applying effort to the task then it becomes a cause for concern. On the other hand, a child whose progress is generally slower than that of classmates may be getting on well and feeling generally positive about his or her work. The point is clear, therefore: our concern is with all children.

This notion that any child can experience difficulties with learning is not of course confined to children. This was brought home to one of us recently when we were talking to a group of advisers, who, to their credit, pointed out that just as any child can experience a difficulty in learning so can any adviser, or indeed any adult."

New assumption 2:

Help and support must be available to all pupils as necessary
"Given that any child may experience some difficulty that causes concern at some stage of their school life, it makes sense that forms of support should be available as and when necessary.

With a traditional approach this would be difficult to achieve since the focus was on providing help for designated groups of children . . . . this often necessitated complex and time-consuming processes of identification, which made it very difficult to make rapid and appropriate responses to pupils who might have a particular short-term difficulty in learning. In order to have a more responsive and flexible system we are now developing ways of providing support and extra attention through the normal and everyday processes of the life of the school – through the curriculum, through social encounters and relationships, and within the constraints and resources that are normally available. The aim is to make all the arrangements for teaching and learning as effective as possible. Indeed, since the principles of good practice for youngsters with special needs tend to be principles of good practice for all, a focus on special needs is a way of improving the delivery of education to all children."

New assumption 3:

Educational difficulties result from an interaction between what the child brings to the situation and the programme provided by the school
"In moving towards a new way of working it is important to recognise its theoretical basis . . . . In the traditional, pre-Warnock approach, the concern was with finding out what was wrong with the child. This approach, often characterised as a medical model, assumed that pinpointing the cause of the child's problems (i.e. diagnosis) would help us to determine an appropriate response (i.e. treatment or prescription). The new thinking, on the other hand, recognises that, whilst the individual differences of children must influence their progress, what we as teachers do is also very important. Difficulties in learning occur as a result of the decisions teachers make, the tasks teachers present, the resources teachers provide and the ways in which teachers choose to organise the classroom.

Consequently difficulties in learning can be created by teachers but, by the same token, can be avoided. This viewpoint is essentially an optimistic one since it points to areas of decision-making, over which we as teachers have reasonable control, that can help children to experience success in the classroom and overcome whatever disadvantages or impairments they bring with them into school."

New assumption 4:

Teachers should take responsibility for the progress of all the children in their classes
". . . the message of the past was that special education was for experts. When children were seen as being in some way exceptional or special, teachers were encouraged to look for outside experts who could solve the problem. Consequently they tended to assume that there were certain members of the class that they could not be expected to teach. Furthermore, the work of some of the special education experts often encouraged this viewpoint by giving the impression that they had methods of working that were exclusive to them. This had the effect of further undermining the confidence of primary school teachers and implying that they need not take responsibility for certain pupils. The new thinking requires each of us to retain responsibility for all members of the class."

New assumption 5:

Support must be available to staff as they attempt to meet their responsibilities
"Taking responsibility for all pupils does not mean that teachers should feel that they cannot look for help and advice. All of us are limited by our own previous experience and existing skills; all of us must expect to meet situations and challenges that we find difficult; and, indeed, all of us must be prepared to recognise our professional limitations. There is nothing to be gained by pretending to cope with something that is beyond our competence. So, in wishing to discourage the idea of special education experts who appear to take away certain of our responsibilities, we wish to argue that what is needed instead are approaches to teaching and learning that emphasise the sharing of expertise, energy and resources. Furthermore, as we argue in subsequent chapters, an emphasis on sharing and collaboration is a noticeable feature of successful schools."

Ainscow and Muncey (1989, pages 10–12)

In the light of these 'new assumptions' Muncey and I characterised the way in which we believed schools should respond to the post-Warnock approach. We argued that the pre-Warnock emphasis on 'categories, care and segregation' should be replaced by ways of working that paid attention to 'needs, curriculum and collaboration'. We then want to note that the abolition of the formal categories of handicap had left something of a gap in the language of the education service. If we were not to describe a child as being maladjusted or educationally subnormal, how might we describe his or her difficulties and ensure the provision of appropriate help and support?

The 1981 Education Act had incorporated the concept 'special educational need', as proposed in the Warnock Report. On first sight it was an attractive idea in that it seemed to mean that we should think positively about the sorts of arrangements that need to be made in order to help individual children to gain access to the curriculum. Unfortunately, in the period following the implementation of the legislation, it was possible to detect a serious distortion of the original concept. From being an approach that attempted to pay particular attention to individuality, the term 'special educational need' increasingly became a super-label used to designate a specific group of pupils thought to have problems. In fact, what we had seen was a tendency to return to the old perspective of interpreting educational difficulties purely in terms of within-child deficits. Even worse, the category 'special educational need' was now being used in a fairly indiscriminate way to refer to a large minority of the school population. Thus, from a policy that was intended to facilitate the integration of pupils experiencing difficulties in learning, we had effectively seen an increase in the proportion of pupils labelled and segregated, at least in the sense that they were perceived by their teachers as being different.

An influence on this development was the wide acceptance of the idea that up to 20 per cent of pupils have special educational needs. This estimate was used widely in the early 1980s as a means of arguing for greater resources and the sharing of responsibility across the service. Unfortunately, from being an estimate of the number of youngsters who may experience difficulties of some kind at some stage in their school career, it became a target. Even worse, in some schools it became linked to crude notions of low general ability, so that teachers perceived the 'bottom 20 per cent' as having special needs. Hence the increase in labelling and segregation.

Given these difficulties Muncey and I concluded that it probably made sense to part company with the term 'special educational need'. Instead we felt that the aim should be to find ways of making schools responsive to pupils' individual needs in the belief that **all** children are special.

In the light of this analysis we decided that the central question to be addressed in the book was, How do we take account of the needs of individual pupils? This being the case we went on to consider strategies and approaches for managing schools and classrooms that would enable all children to participate successfully in broadly the same range of experiences alongside others from their community. In this respect, we argued, our emphasis was on integration.

Encouraging classroom success

Meanwhile, almost ten years after completing the book *Preventing Classroom Failure*, Dave Tweddle and I met up again with a view to writing a revised second edition. After a series of meetings, over a period of months, we came to the view that this was now impossible. Our thinking had moved on so far as a result of our experiences and our assumptions had changed so fundamentally that we decided that it would be wiser to write a new book, *Encouraging Classroom Success* (Ainscow and Tweddle, 1988).

In this book we reflected on different approaches to the assessment of difficulties in learning. This led us to define two overall orientations that seemed to dominate practice. These were concerned with:

- Analysing the learner; and
- Analysing learning tasks.

Having considered the limitations and, indeed, potential dangers of each of these, we proposed a third possibility, that of:

- Analysing the learning context.

In this way our attention was refocused away from a narrow perspective on individual learners towards the contexts in which learning takes place. This pointed us in the general direction of many of the approaches that are discussed in the later chapters of this book. It also led us to suggest a framework for reviewing practice as a means of finding ways of helping all pupils to experience success. It was an approach that replaced the rather closed prescriptions of our earlier work with a more open agenda that is intended to encourage teachers to take responsibility for their own learning. Our aim became one of helping all teachers to be 'reflective practitioners' (Schon, 1987). Classroom evaluation was central to this orientation. This is a process of gathering information about how pupils respond to the curriculum as it is enacted. The focus, therefore, is on areas of decision making over which teachers have a significant influence. Broadly speaking these areas are:

- Objectives, i.e. Are objectives being achieved?
- Tasks and activities, i.e. Are tasks and activities being completed?
- Classroom arrangements, i.e. Do classroom arrangements make effective use of available resources?

Because of the complexity of classroom life and the importance of unintended outcomes, there is also a need to keep a further question in mind. This is:

- What else is happening? i.e. Are there other significant factors that need to be considered?

We recommended that the framework provided by these four broad questions be used by teachers and pupils to reflect upon the encounters in which they are engaged. In other words, the framework becomes an agenda for reflection. This approach was based upon our belief that success in the classroom is more likely to occur if objectives, tasks and activities, and classroom activities take account of individual pupils and are understood by all those involved. Thus classroom evaluation is seen as a continuous process, built into the normal life of the classroom. Furthermore it requires collaboration and negotiation if it is to be effective.

Proposing this wider perspective, we argued, has major implications for the ways in which the education service provides support to youngsters experiencing difficulties in learning. It requires that the focus of assessment and recording should be children in their normal classroom environment; that information should be collected on a continuous basis; that pupils should have a key role in reflecting upon their own learning; and that the overall aim should be to improve the quality of teaching and learning provided for all pupils. It is perhaps worth adding that it is a perspective that does not lend itself to the provision of 'quick-fix' solutions to educational difficulties.

Implications

The account presented in this chapter provides an outline of the changes in my thinking that had occurred in the years prior to the IQEA and UNESCO projects that are at the centre of discussions in this book. My commitment to an interactive perspective on educational difficulties, in particular, represented a significant change from the predominant view in the special needs field. It means that educational difficulties have to be seen as being context bound, arising out of the interaction of individual children with a particular educational programme at a certain moment in time.

Whilst being somewhat complex this definition has the advantage that it tends to encourage a sense of optimism. Unlike the traditional approach where the focus on child-centred causes of educational difficulty tended to create an air of despondency, the interactive perspective focuses attention on a range of factors that teachers can influence to encourage children's learning. It emphasises the fact that what teachers do, the decisions they make, their attitudes, the relationships they develop and their forms of classroom organisation, are all factors that can help children to experience success in school. By the same argument, of course, these factors can also help to **create** educational difficulties for some children.

This interactive approach to special education has major implications for the organisation of schools and the work of teachers. In particular it has implications for provision made in ordinary schools. It argues for the development of primary and secondary schools that are responsive to children with a wide range of needs (e.g. Thousand and Villa, 1991; Wang, 1991). Indeed special education, instead of being seen as a search by specialists for technical solutions to the problems of particular children becomes a curriculum challenge shared by all teachers within every school (Ainscow and Tweddle, 1988).

Partly as a result of the influence this type of argument schools and school systems in many countries began to review their policies and practices (Hegarty, 1990). In many cases the aim was to move towards what had come to be called 'a whole school approach' to special educational needs (Ainscow and Florek, 1989). The idea was that all teachers within a school should accept responsibility for the development and progress of all its pupils, including those with difficulties and disabilities.

Across the whole range of provision the changes that were taking place had specific implications for the work of individual teachers, particularly those perceived as being specialists. Many teachers who had traditionally spent much of their time working with small groups of children withdrawn from regular lessons for intensive instruction in basic skills, now found themselves having to work collaboratively with colleagues in mainstream education, either providing support or working on joint curriculum initiatives (Ainscow, 1989).

As we look back, this account of developments during the 1980s sounds positive, rational and encouraging. It gives the impression that education services were marching in unison towards new ways of working with agreement and understanding. Alas, this was far from being the case. As is usual with significant change, the service in many countries found it very difficult to come to terms with the new version of special education. In England, for example, Government documents continued to encourage confusion between traditional and newer perspectives, whilst at local authority level the implementation of policies based on interactive perspectives remained in some confusion (Goacher et al, 1988).

Inevitably this general confusion was reflected in the practice of schools. Despite the rhetoric of whole school approaches for responding to individual needs, traditional views of special education persisted and the policies of many schools remained an uneasy amalgam of old and new (Clark et al, 1997).

This created contradictions and tensions that could be a major source of stress for individual teachers. Indeed, using the terms of Schwab (1969), it can be argued that there was evidence of a crisis of thinking in the field.

If education systems were to find a way successfully through this difficult phase there was a need for those involved, at all levels, to become clearer about the rationale upon which the new ways of working are based. As we know, change, particularly when it involves new ways of thinking and behaving, is a difficult and time-consuming process. Michael Fullan (1991) argues that for it to be achieved successfully, a change has to be understood and accepted by those involved. Understanding and acceptance take time and need encouragement.

How then could this be achieved? How could teachers and others involved in schools be helped to come to terms with a version of special education that was, in essence, about the development of the mainstream? The message that emerged from the analysis in this chapter, which was to become central to my own thinking, was that one way forward was to encourage teachers to take a more positive approach by learning how to investigate and develop their own classroom practice. The aim should be to facilitate understanding and to encourage professional development through processes of classroom evaluation and reflection, as Tweddle and I had recommended in 1988. In this respect the emphasis on collaboration that had emerged also represented an important message.

References

Ainscow, M. and Florek, A. (eds.) (1989) *Special Educational Needs: Towards a Whole School Approach*. London: Fulton.

Ainscow, M. and Hopkins, D. (1992) Aboard the 'moving school'. *Educational Leadership* 50(3), 79–81.

Ainscow, M. and Hopkins, D. (1994) Understanding the moving school. In G. Southworth (ed.), *Readings in Primary School Development*. London: Falmer.

Ainscow, M., Hopkins, D., Southworth, G. and West, M. (1994) *Creating the Conditions for School Improvement*. London: Fulton.

Ainscow, M. and Muncey, J. (1989) *Meeting Individual Needs in the Primary School*. London: Fulton.

Ainscow, M. and Tweddle, D.A. (1979) *Preventing Classroom Failure: an objectives approach*. London: Fulton.

Ainscow, M. and Tweddle, D.A. (1984) *Early Learning Skills Analysis*. London: Fulton.

Ainscow, M. and Tweddle, D.A. (1988) *Encouraging Classroom Success* London: Fulton.

Arthur, H. (1989) Inset and whole school policies. In Ainscow, M. and Florek, A. (eds.), *Special Educational Needs: Towards a Whole School Approach*. London: Fulton.

Brennan, W. (1979) *Curricular Needs of Slow Learners*. Milton Keynes: Open University.

Burgess, R.G. (1982). Keeping a research diary. *Cambridge Journal of Education*. 11(1), 75–83.

Clark, C., Dyson, A., Millward, A. and Skidmore, D. (1997) *New Directions in Special Needs: Innovations in Mainstream Schools*. London: Cassell 152–157.

Department for Education and Science (1978) *Report of the Committee of Enquiry into Special Educational Needs (The Warnock Report)*. London: HMSO.

Dessent, T. (1987) *Making the Ordinary School Special*. London: Falmer.

Dyson, A. (1990) Special educational needs and the concept of change. *Oxford Review of Education* 16(1), 55–66.

Fullan, M. (1991) *The New Meaning of Educational Change*. London: Cassell.

Gipps, C., Gross, H. and Goldstein, H. (1987) *Warnock's 18%: Children with Special Needs in the Primary School*. London: Falmer.

Goacher, B., Evans, J., Welton, J. and Wedell, K. (1988) *Policy and provision for special educational needs*. London: Cassell.

Hegarty, S. (1990) *The Education of Children and Young People with Disabilities: Principles and Practice*. Paris: UNESCO.

Hopkins, D., Ainscow, M. and West, M. (1994) *School Improvement in an Era of Change*. London: Cassell.

Moses, D., Hegarty, S. and Jowett, S. (1988) *Supporting ordinary schools*. Windsor: NFER-Nelson.

Schwab, J.J. (1969) The practical: a language for the curriculum. *School Review* 78, 1–24.

Stoll, L. (1991) School effectiveness in action: supporting growth in schools and classrooms. In M. Ainscow (ed.), *Effective Schools for All*. London: Fulton.

Thousand, J.S. and Villa, R.A. (1991) Accommodating for greater student variance. In M. Ainscow (ed.), *Effective Schools for All*. London: Fulton.

Tomlinson, S. (1982) *A Sociology of Special Education*. London: Routledge.

Wang, M.C. (1991) Adaptive education: an alternative approach to providing for student diversity. In M. Ainscow (ed.), *Effective Schools for All*. London: Fulton.

Wedell, K. (1981) Concepts of special educational needs. *Education Today* 31(1), 3–9.

Weick, K.E. (1985) Sources of order in underorganised systems: Themes in recent organisational theory. In Y.S. Lincoln (ed.), *Organisational Theory and Inquiry*. Beverly Hills: Sage.

West, M. and Ainscow, M. (1991) *Managing School Development*. London: Fulton.

CHAPTER 3

AN OBJECTIVES APPROACH

Ainscow, M. and Tweddle, D.A. (1979) *Preventing classroom failure: an objectives approach*. London: Wiley/Fulton (Chapter 1: Peter; and Chapter 2: Teaching slow learners)

Introduction

Together, these two short, linked chapters explain the basis of the approach that emerged from my work in the special school where I was headteacher. Using the terminology of the time (e.g. 'children with learning difficulties'; 'slow learners'), my colleague Dave Tweddle and I argued for a move away from explanations of difficulties in learning that concentrate solely on the characteristics of individual pupils, to one that focuses attention on the tasks that they are asked to do to foster their learning. At a time when the field that was then usually called 'special and remedial education' was under considerable scrutiny in England, this book was widely quoted and was later published in a series of new editions. The approach it recommended – based around the idea of carefully sequenced learning objectives – gradually became common practice in special schools in the UK and, subsequently, in many other parts of the world. It also influenced ways of developing individualized education plans for pupils categorised as having special educational needs in mainstream schools.

This is the story of Peter Blakey's first year in the junior department of a primary school. Most teachers who have taught in a primary school will probably know a child like Peter – some may know many.

Peter moved into Mrs Jones's class in September. Fairly quickly she realized that Peter was some way behind the others and raised the subject in conversation with Miss Nolan, Peter's previous class teacher. Miss Nolan confirmed that this had always been the case, but said that Peter seemed happy enough and had made some progress during his year with her, albeit rather slow. Mrs Jones decided to keep a careful eye on the situation.

As time went on the problem seemed to grow steadily worse. It was true that Peter was making some progress, but it was painfully slow and the gap between him and the rest of the class seemed to be growing by the day. Perhaps even more worrying was that Peter's behaviour seemed to be deteriorating. He had been very rude once or twice when told to get on with his work, and was frequently finding excuses not to work. Books and pens had been lost, requests to go to the toilet had become more frequent, and Peter was always first to volunteer for any job that would take him out of the classroom.

Mrs Jones decided to ask the headteacher's advice. She described the problems she was having with Peter to Mr Walker, the headteacher, who decided first to talk to Miss Nolan and then later asked Mrs Jones to prepare a full written report over the Christmas holidays so that consideration could be given to Peter's needs. Mrs Jones presented the following report to the headteacher on the first day of the new term:

Report on Peter Blakey

Peter is a pleasant and likeable little lad, despite the fact that it is almost impossible to keep him working for more than a few minutes at a time. He needs constant one-to-one supervision. Otherwise his mind seems to wander and eventually he begins interrupting the other children. I feel as though I have tried absolutely everything. I have shouted at him and tried kindness, but it doesn't seem to make much difference to his attitude.

As far as work is concerned Peter can only read six or seven words on the Burt Word Recognition Test. He can recognize his own name and is currently reading Ladybird 2A, although he doesn't always seem to understand what the book is about. In arithmetic it is much the same story! He is a long way behind the rest of the class, he can count reasonably well and do simple sums (on a good day and provided he can use counters), but again he doesn't seem to really understand the processes involved. In group and class language lessons Peter rarely contributes.

I have thought a lot about Peter in an attempt to get to the bottom of his problem by finding what is really the matter with him. I have wondered whether he has difficulty hearing because his speech is still very immature and he invariably fails to carry out any instructions that I give him. I just cannot decide whether he has difficulty hearing properly, doesn't understand what is said to him, or is simply lazy.

I have not met Peter's mother as she did not turn up to the parents' meeting last term. Miss Nolan told me that Peter has no father – apparently he died before Peter was three. I have wondered whether this may have affected his work in some way.

Peter's favourite activities in school are painting and PE, and he says that he likes watching TV at home. He loves to paint or crayon and he will sit doing this all day if I let him.

I hope that some special help can be provided for Peter as soon as possible. I feel very sorry for him, but I am afraid I just don't understand his difficulties and don't know how best to help him. I think that it is an urgent problem because his behaviour in class is getting steadily worse.

Mrs P. Jones, Classteacher

The headteacher, who had met Mrs Blakey only once, decided to invite her to school to discuss Peter's problems. He wanted to find out more about the family background and thought he might persuade Mrs Blakey to do some work with Peter at home. In any event, he needed her permission to refer Peter to the Remedial Service and the school medical officer.

Eventually, a meeting was arranged between Mr Walker, Mrs Jones, and Mrs Blakey. Apparently, Mr Blakey had died in a road accident just before Peter's third birthday and whilst Mrs Blakey was pregnant. Susan, Peter's sister, was now nearly five and attended a local nursery school full-time. It appeared that Mrs

Blakey had not attended parents' evening because she had been let down by the baby-sitter at the last minute. Both Mr Walker and Mrs Jones were impressed by Mrs Blakey's genuine concern for Peter and her eagerness to help as much as possible at home. Mrs Blakey was not surprised to learn that Peter was some way behind the other children in his class because, in her words, he had 'always been slow to catch on'. She explained that he was one and a half before he could walk properly, and well over two before he could say more than two or three words clearly. Mr Walker was particularly interested to hear that Peter's birth had been a difficult one. Mrs Blakey said that forceps had been used and 'his head was a funny shape'. He wondered if mild brain damage had been sustained, or if Peter was suffering from dyslexia. He said nothing about this to Mrs Blakey, however, but decided to mention these details to whoever subsequently came to see Peter. Mrs Blakey agreed to Mr Walker's suggestions that advice should be sought from the Remedial Service. She was less happy about referring him to the school medical officer, since she was sure that Peter's hearing was normal and felt that the exercise was rather pointless. Nevertheless, consent for the referral was given.

Afterwards, Mrs Jones and Mr Walker discussed the interview, which they both felt had been helpful. A number of points had been raised which might at least partly explain Peter's problems. It was possible that Mr Blakey's death had had some kind of long-lasting effect upon Peter, and Mrs Blakey had said that 'Peter often asks about him'. Mr Walker felt sure that the difficult birth was an important factor and thought that mild brain damage had probably been sustained. And finally, while Mrs Blakey seemed a caring and well-intentioned mother, she clearly was not very bright herself, and maybe this was a factor. Whatever the cause of the problem, Mr Walker agreed with Mrs Jones that expert help should be sought immediately, and so he wrote to the Remedial Service and asked the school medical officer to check Peter's hearing.

Whilst Mr Walker received prompt acknowledgements to his requests, it was some time before he heard anything further. He knew that the school medical officer and the Remedial Service had quite long waiting lists and therefore did not expect Peter to be seen by either much before Easter. Eventually, Mrs Blakey was asked to take Peter to the school clinic for a hearing test. This she did, and the results of a thorough audiometric investigation indicated, as Mrs Blakey had anticipated, that Peter's hearing was normal. A letter confirming these findings was sent to the school.

In the meantime a speech therapist had visited the school to see another child and Mr Walker took the opportunity of mentioning Peter. The speech therapist kindly agreed to see him that morning and, after talking to him for some time, reported back to the headteacher that, although Peter's speech was rather immature for an eight-year-old, there was certainly no sign of any abnormal articulation. The problem would solve itself with time, she said, and she could not justify giving him regular, individual, speech therapy.

Just before the Easter holidays, Mr Thompson, a teacher from the Remedial Service, visited the school to see Peter. He took him into the medical room and administered a number of tests. Throughout the session Peter worked well for Mr Thompson and showed no signs of distractibility. This did not surprise Mrs Jones because she knew that Peter was capable of concentrating for quite long periods if he was really interested and she was prepared to give him her individual attention. This was one of the main problems – she had thirty-two children in her class and she could not ignore them to deal with Peter.

Before leaving, Mr Thompson discussed his findings with Mr Walker and Mrs Jones, and later submitted a detailed written report. A number of interesting points came out of the discussion. First of all, test results indicated that Peter might be in need of special education. Mr Thompson had administered the English Picture Vocabulary Test (Full Range), and Peter had a standard score of 76. Mr Thompson explained that sophisticated intelligence tests could be administered only by a psychologist but the EPVT, which measures 'receptive vocabulary', 'correlates' highly with IQ. If Peter's IQ was also 75–80 he would be very close to the range of IQ which was usually associated with educationally subnormal children. He therefore suggested that a referral for a full psychological assessment should be made immediately, but pointed out that this could only be done with parental consent.

Mr Thompson listened to Mr Walker's information about Peter's home circumstances and the difficult birth. He agreed that these factors might well be the cause of Peter's learning difficulties, but again felt that an educational psychologist would be better qualified to judge.

A number of useful suggestions were made by Mr Thompson. He had used Stephen Jackson's Phonic Skills Test with Peter. This test attempts to identify which of a wide range of phonic skills have been acquired, and which have not. In actual fact, Peter could not manage much of the test and most of the information it yielded was already known to Mrs Jones. Nevertheless, a booklet is supplied with the test which contains a variety of teaching suggestions as well as instructions for administration, and Mr Walker felt that the test would be useful with other children who had reading difficulties. In addition, Mr Thompson suggested that D. H. Stott's Programmed Reading Kit contained a wide range of materials which would be appropriate for Peter, and said that he would loan one to the school so that they could evaluate its usefulness.

By now Mrs Jones had mixed feelings about all that had happened. On the one hand the school medical officer, the speech therapist and the remedial teacher had presumably acted as promptly as their work load had permitted, and each had done their job properly. The medical officer and the speech therapist had answered the questions they had been asked about Peter's hearing and speech, and Mr Thompson had made a number of useful and practical suggestions. On the other hand, Mrs Jones was aware that Peter's problems still existed, the gap between him and the rest of the class was still growing, and his behaviour, if anything, had further deteriorated. Peter's name was now to be placed on yet another waiting list. In all probability, by the time he was seen by the psychologist the end of the Summer Term would be in sight, and then Peter would be moving into someone else's class. She was frustrated, believing that more should be done for Peter but not knowing who to blame.

It was late June before the psychologist arrived at the school. Mrs Blakey had consented to the referral which was made in writing by Mr Walker soon after the Easter holidays. Mrs Armitage, the educational psychologist, saw Peter in the medical room and the interview lasted most of the morning. A meeting was held that afternoon after school between Mrs Armitage, Mr Walker and Mrs Jones to discuss the results of the assessment. The first important point to come out of the discussion was that Peter apparently did not need special education. He was not educationally subnormal. Mrs Armitage had used the Wechsler Intelligence Scale for Children, a test which provides a Verbal Scale IQ and a Performance Scale IQ. Peter's VS IQ was 79. The Verbal Scale, the psychologist explained, consists of a number of subtests which involve the child's using and understanding language. Hence the close correlation between the VS IQ and the EPVT standard score produced by Mr Thompson. However, Peter's PS IQ was

94, nearly average. The Performance Scale consists of the same number of subtests but requires the child to respond non-verbally by doing puzzles, coding exercises and so on. Peter's Full Scale IQ was 'well within the normal range', Mrs Armitage felt that segregating Peter would not be in his best interests. She pointed out that 'sending Peter to a special school would deprive him of the opportunity to interact with normal children'. Peter was apparently a good deal brighter than the children at the local ESN school and anyway, 'his reading age is now over six, and so he is obviously making some progress'.

The recommendation not to transfer Peter to a special school was not contested by either Mr Walker or Mrs Jones. After all, they were not wanting to off-load their problems, but were more concerned to learn what could be done to help Peter within their school.

Mrs Armitage asked about Peter's home circumstances, and Mr Walker provided the background information he had collected during his interview with Mrs Blakey six months earlier. The psychologist then explained that it was difficult to determine exactly *why* a child was having learning difficulties in the same way as a doctor, for example, might diagnose a physical ailment. The truth was, she explained, that all of these factors were probably involved in some way.

Mrs Jones then raised the question of dyslexia. Was Peter dyslexic? Mrs Armitage explained that she had reservations about the use of this term, again because it was difficult to know exactly what people meant by it, and in any event, she said, 'there are no special teaching methods which are particularly suitable for the treatment of dyslexia'.

Three practical suggestions were made by Mrs Armitage before she left. First, she said that she could probably arrange for a peripatetic remedial teacher to visit the school once a week from September to take Peter out of his class for individual reading lessons. Secondly, she suggested that language work for Peter was as important as reading, and in a subsequent written report to Mr Walker she listed three books containing useful suggestions and a language development programme which she felt would be appropriate. And, finally, regarding Peter's deteriorating classroom behaviour, Mrs Armitage emphasized that the classteacher should praise Peter's efforts generously, no matter how modest his achievements were, compared to his peers. Mr Walker ordered the books and the language programme immediately in the hope that they would arrive before Peter began his second year in the junior department.

Mrs Jones ended the year as she had started it – worried about Peter. The remedial teacher, the school medical officer, the speech therapist, and the psychologist had all seen him. They had all either answered the questions they had been asked, or made useful suggestions about what might be done with him in the classroom. Various books, a language programme and a test had been recommended and ordered, and a remedial teacher was to visit Peter once a week from the start of the following term. Although Peter had made some progress during his year with her and was still manageable in the classroom, albeit at times rather awkward and most of the time easily distracted, Mrs Jones was still apprehensive about his future.

Teaching slow learners

What happened to Peter Blakey is probably not unlike what happens to many other slow-learning children in primary schools throughout the country. It represents the accepted approach to the identification and assessment of children with learning difficulties, and provides some insights into the special efforts which are made on their behalf. There are, no doubt, considerable variations in approaches to this problem from area to area, and even from school to school, but the case study of Peter represents what might typically happen in many areas to a young child who is seen to be having serious learning problems.

It must be stressed at this point that there is no intended criticism of any of the characters who are involved in the case or, for that matter, the professional groups they represent. The teachers and specialists are all seen to be conscientious and well-intentioned persons who respond to Peter's problems in a caring and professional manner. Stating that a child has to wait to be seen by a psychologist, for example, represents what is usually the case in most areas. No criticism is intended, and none should be inferred.

Despite the conscientious attention of the classteacher, the prompt and proper attention of the headteacher, and the helpful suggestions from all those who eventually become involved, our system for dealing with slow learners seems somehow to fail Peter Blakey. Is Peter's case typical or exceptional in terms of the success of this form of intervention? Unfortunately, there is a lamentable lack of objective data on the effectiveness of this traditional approach, but the limited evidence which exists (e.g. Collins, 1961) seems to support the impression that, despite the skill and commitment of teachers and specialists involved in this kind of work, the success rate is suprisingly low. While it is, of course, undeniable that successes do occur, readers with extensive teaching experience, who have seen young children resist special attempts to accelerate progress, will probably support this conclusion.

The purpose of this chapter is to look closely at some of the important features of the approach adopted in the case study, with a view to identifying those aspects that might be improved. In order to do this, a distinction will be made between those factors which are *within* the teacher's control and those which are *outside* the teacher's control. There are clearly certain factors which influence a child's educational progress over which the teacher can have little or no influence. Since nothing can be done about these, there seems to be little point in focusing too much attention in their direction. It is factors which are within teacher-control that must be our primary concern. This is a practical classification with which to structure the development of the argument, and one which leads to interesting conclusions.

Factors outside the teacher's control

There is a natural desire among those who teach slow learners to know *why* a particular child is having learning problems. The discussion between Mrs Jones and Mr Walker was probably fairly typical in that they were speculating about the reasons for Peter's difficulties. The death of Mr Blakey, Mrs Blakey's subsequent struggle to raise two children, her own limited ability, the difficult birth and the possibility of mild brain damage were all mentioned as possible contributory factors. It will also be recalled that the issue was never clearly resolved, the psychologist suggesting that probably *all* these factors in some way influenced Peter's development.

What if Mrs Armitage had been able to solve the riddle and specify which of the suggested possible causes was largely responsible for Peter's difficulties? How useful would this information have been? Certainly the staff of the school could do little to improve Mrs Blakey's domestic situation, and significantly influencing Mrs Blakey's intellectual competence was also outside their control. Although parent–teacher co-operation can, to some extent, influence a domestic situation or parental attitudes towards schools, it is unrealistic to have expected Mr Walker to do much more than he had already done in that direction. There already existed good parent–teacher liaison and special efforts had been made to have Mrs Blakey continue at home the work which Mrs Jones was doing in her classroom. It seems that in Peter's case at least, if family history or domestic circumstances were a significant causal factor, there was little more that Mr Walker or his colleagues could do about it.

What about the question of mild brain damage, or 'minimal cerebral dysfunction' as it is sometimes called, possibly caused in Peter's case by the forceps delivery? If Mrs Armitage could have confirmed that this was at the root of his difficulties, would any particular action or treatment necessarily follow from the diagnosis? The condition is a difficult one to diagnose reliably, it is not something which can be rectified surgically, and there is no evidence to suggest that children with minimal cerebral dysfunction should be taught differently from those without it (Bateman, 1974). Even if we were able to confirm that this was the root cause of Peter's problem, therefore, we would still be no further forward in knowing how best to help him. In other words, brain damage might or might not be a significant causal factor, but in any event it is beyond the control of the classteacher.

It would appear that the causes, or aetiology, of Peter's problems in particular, and of mild to moderate learning difficulties generally, are elusive. Furthermore, in the search for a cause, there seems to be a tendency to speculate about factors which are largely beyond teacher control and consequently have minimal prescriptive value. If this is true, why do teachers persist in seeking the cause? It is as if there is an implicit assumption that a knowledge of the cause will lead directly to an understanding of what to do about it. This kind of approach resembles the medical model of diagnosis and prescription, and in fact may have derived from that source. Whilst it may suit medicine admirably, it seems to lead teachers up a series of blind alleys, and succeeds only in setting questions to which invariably there are no definitive answers and in inadvertently focusing attention on factors which are outside teacher influence.

A medical-style approach is apparent too in other ways. Mrs Jones thought that Peter might be dyslexic, and Mrs Armitage addressed herself to the question of whether or not he was educationally subnormal. Classifying children's difficulties by the use of descriptive labels, such as 'dyslexia', 'ESN', 'maladjusted' or whatever, is not unlike the medical labelling of physical ailments. But again there are problems, since what seems to work in medicine is not automatically useful in the field of education. First of all, there are enormous problems of definition. Very often there exists no commonly agreed, specific definition of terms such as 'dyslexia' or 'educationally subnormal'. Consequently, a child classified as ESN by one psychologist may not be so deemed by another. And the same is true of dyslexia. Secondly, and perhaps more important, there are no specific prescriptive implications associated with either diagnosis. That is to say, there is no evidence that ESN children learn, or should be taught, in a fundamentally different way from children who are not ESN. And the same with dyslexia. In fact Keogh (1975) wrote '. . . with the possible exception of children with sensory deficits or severe physical conditions, where modification of curricular materials is required to enhance availability of information, there is little evidence that exceptional children learn differently from normal children, or that they require dramatically modified instructional techniques.'

To sum up, therefore, what are the practical implications of labelling a child with terms such as 'ESN' or 'dyslexic'? First, it seems that there may be considerable differences of opinion between experts as to what constitutes an ESN or dyslexic child. And secondly, it seems to tell us little or nothing about how best to help the child. There is another important repercussion of the labelling process. The work of Rosenthal and Jacobsen (1968), Pidgeon (1970), and Nash (1973) seems to indicate that providing teachers with information about a child's *predicted* progress may influence the progress that is *actually* made. It has been demonstrated that children described to their prospective teacher as 'bright' seem to make more progress than those described as 'rather dull' – even when no such differences exist. If this is so, describing a child as ESN, dyslexic or brain-damaged not only has the disadvantage of telling us little or nothing about what or how he should be taught, but may also establish expectations of slow progress and limited achievement.

In Peter's case, attention was focused on the likely causes and possible classifications of his difficulties, and a number of factors were identified as being of possible significance. There was the social history and domestic circumstances, the question of the difficult birth and possible mild brain damage, and the question of whether he was 'ESN' or 'dyslexic'. Throughout this chapter the usefulness of this orientation has been questioned and it has been argued that the reason for the apparent dearth of prescriptive implications is simply that teachers are tending to focus on aspects of the problem that are largely, or even totally, beyond their control. The same criticism is sometimes made of intelligence tests. Mrs Armitage used an intelligence test with Peter, and, as a result, stated that he was not educationally subnormal. It is important, therefore, to spend some time examining this aspect of the psychologist's contribution.

The fortunes of intelligence tests have varied dramatically during the past 30 years, and inexplicably continue to be the subject of heated debate. An intelligence test usually consists of a wide range of tasks that have been standardized on a large number of randomly selected children of various ages. The purpose of doing an intelligence test with a child is to see how he or she performs on those tasks compared to all the other children of a similar age who were tested during the standardization. IQ scores, therefore, are a fairly reliable means of comparing children's general mental ability, and were consequently useful to Mrs Armitage in deciding whether or not Peter would be better placed in a special school. It is important to realize, however, that this is all an IQ can do. It does not purport to indicate what, or how, a child should be taught, and again there is no evidence to suggest that a child with an IQ of 69 learns, or should be taught, differently from a child with an IQ of 91.

It seems, therefore, that IQ is another factor beyond the teacher's control. In this case Mrs Armitage noticed that there was a considerable discrepancy between Peter's performance on verbal and non-verbal tasks and, as a result, recommended intensive language work. However it must be said that, although this is probably a reasonable interpretation of those test results, it is using the test for a purpose for which it was not designed, and in any event does not provide any detailed or specific indication of the *kind* of language work required.

So far a number of important aspects of the approach used with Peter have been examined. They have been found to have one important feature in common in that none of them seem to provide any detailed indication of what, or how,

Peter Blakey should be taught, and it has been suggested that the reason for this is that they involve focusing on factors which are outside the teacher's control. Is it reasonable to assume, therefore, that the efforts of Mrs Jones and the specialists who eventually became involved would have been no less effective if these factors had been ignored?

Factors within the teacher's control

The analogy between medicine and the traditional remedial style of intervention can be extended a little further. Both approaches are curative. When a child is seen to be having difficulties the remedial expert or psychologist is called in to diagnose the problem and prescribe appropriate remedial treatment, rather like the GP who is called in to the sick patient to diagnose the complaint and prescribe a treatment. Both situations represent a curative orientation in that the expert waits for the complaint to develop and then tries to cure it. There are considerable dangers involved in exposing children to prolonged classroom failure. Peter was starting to avoid that which he found difficult and his classroom conduct was beginning to deteriorate in other ways. Those readers who have taught slow learners will no doubt confirm this tendency from their own experiences.

Slow learners often develop a poor opinion of themselves, lose confidence and bring an expectation of failure with them into the classroom. Experienced teachers will recall dealing with children who hesitate at every step, who seek constant reassurance from the teacher and seem almost to know that they will fail. Keogh (1975) quotes research indicating that '. . . children with long histories of school failure . . . bring a generalized expectation of failure to new problem-solving tasks. Self-perceived inadequacy and a "set" for failure may explain at least part of their school problems'.

If a complaint can be made against Peter's school it would be that it was two years before help was called, and almost a further year before any practical change occurred in Peter's circumstances. For almost three years he made 'painfully slow' progress, and was exposed to the failures and frustrations which that involved. This is a factor over which it is possible to have complete control. The headteacher could have referred the problem at least a year earlier, and it is even possible that the reception classteacher may have been able to predict that these difficulties were likely to occur. The point being made is that whatever provision is made for the slow learner, it is better for the intervention to occur as early as possible, thus eliminating unnecessary exposure to failure.

Considerable attention has recently been paid to procedures for identifying 'educationally at risk' pupils at an early age, and it has been consistently found that the most reliable system for spotting children liable to have learning difficulties is to structure the classroom observations of experienced teachers (Wedell and Raybould, 1976; Marshall, 1976). The material presented later in this book will provide a basis for this kind of observation. Meanwhile, teachers in primary schools should be aware that it is their responsibility to be on the look out for children who display signs of having difficulty with any aspect of the curriculum. Had this been the prevalent orientation in Peter's area, what eventually happened to him could have occurred at least one, and maybe even two or three, years earlier. This then represents the first fundamental difference between the approach used with Peter and the approach described in later chapters of this book. Instead of waiting for failure to occur and using external support services to formulate curative strategies, the intervention should be geared toward preventing failure by taking immediate action as soon as it is seen that a child is having difficulty.

It must be mentioned that the notion of early identification has been criticized because this too can influence teacher expectation, the prediction of failure becoming a self-fulfilling prophecy and actually limiting the child's prospect of success. This is a real danger, but one which can be overcome. It is being suggested that children with learning difficulties should be spotted as early as possible in order that subsequent classroom failure can be averted. It is certainly *not* suggested that we predict educational failure and then wait to assess the accuracy of our predictions.

A good tip that can be gained from Peter's story concerns the question of his possible hearing loss. The headteacher's swift action in calling for Peter's hearing to be checked must be applauded. Very often problems of learning can be avoided if an observant teacher, or parent, can pick out possible signs of hearing difficulty and an early investigation is made. The same, of course, applies with regard to possible visual abnormalities. It is vital that even a slight doubt in these directions should always be followed up.

Thus, the timing of the intervention is within the control of the teacher and might be modified to good effect, and possible problems of hearing or vision can be investigated. What are the other important factors which are within teacher-control and might be manipulated to benefit the child with learning difficulties? There is one which perhaps supersedes all others in importance. Look into most primary school classrooms and you will find a wide range of ability, with a few children working very quickly and accurately, the majority working steadily despite occasional problems, and a few, like Peter, experiencing difficulties in most subjects. Most class work is geared to the large middle group, their needs, interests, and rate of progress. As a result, while some children find their work easy, there are others who work and learn at a slower rate and find it increasingly difficult to produce the level of work required. As time goes on these children fall further and further behind, as the deficiency accumulates. The problem is amplified in some subject areas where a mastery of the first step is required before progressing to the next. If the first step has not been successfully accomplished, failure at subsequent stages becomes almost inevitable.

An influence on the thinking of many teachers is the notion of the natural distribution of ability which assumes that, given children of a full range of ability for whom a standard lesson is prepared, some will succeed with ease, some will steadily plod through, and others will be largely incapable of success. This kind of thinking is detrimental to the child with learning difficulties in many schools, where subjects are taught for a set amount of time, at a predetermined point in the child's primary school career. Given this kind of organization the natural distribution of ability does, in fact, become a 'natural distribution of attainment', where some children achieve a great deal, most children learn more or less what the teacher sets out to teach, and the likes of Peter are not given sufficient time to master much of the provided material.

Bloom (1975), at the University of Chicago, has developed the idea of 'mastery learning'. It is an approach which is helpful in producing learning programmes geared to the individual pupil. It recognizes that children have different aptitudes for learning. In other words, children need different periods of time to master a particular topic. Bloom suggests that we should *not* teach a topic for a predetermined time, assuming that all the children in the class will learn it to a varying degree of competence. Instead, in mastery learning, the amount of material to be learnt thoroughly is held *constant* and teaching time becomes the *variable* which is manipulated. Thus the emphasis is switched from consideration of ability, and other factors which imply limited potential, to that of aptitude, which suggests that all the children will achieve mastery of the topic provided the teacher allows sufficient time and matches other classroom conditions to the needs of the individual child.

This is the second factor over which teachers have a direct control and which might be manipulated to benefit the child with learning difficulties. He can be given enough time to master essential areas of learning.

Not a great deal was said about Mrs Jones's classroom, and so we are unaware of the extent to which the idea of mastery learning featured in her planning. In fact, not a great deal was said about any of a multitude of classroom variables which may have been influencing Peter's progress. Let us look even closer at Mrs Jones's classroom and consider other aspects of her methods and organization which might be modified to good effect.

If Peter was beginning to improvise strategies to avoid work, it may be that too much was being asked of him. Perhaps the tasks he was being set were too difficult, involving skills or knowledge which he did not possess. If this was the case then Peter's distractability and deteriorating classroom conduct were actually being caused, albeit inadvertently, by the teacher. This is certainly a potentially fruitful line of enquiry, but again one which was largely overlooked by the people in the case study.

What about the way in which Mrs Jones introduced the work and presented the tasks to Peter? Very often children who have difficulty with learning do so because, for whatever reason, they fail to understand the instructions that are given. It will be recalled that Mrs Jones was worried about Peter's hearing because of his apparent lack of understanding or oral instructions. Understanding of language is an area of crucial difference from pupil to pupil. Therefore, it is vital that teachers pay careful attention to the way that tasks are explained, ensuring that each pupil understands the vocabulary used.

What records were being kept in the classroom about Peter's progress? Again there was no mention of this in the case study. If there existed an accurate record of the work set, the teaching methods used, the skills already acquired, the areas of particular difficulty to Peter, it could provide invaluable data for the formulation of an appropriate programme of intervention. What about Mrs Jones's management of Peter on those occasions when he was being rude, interrupting other children or avoiding settling down to do his work? Could praise be used more effectively to maintain Peter's interest for longer periods and encourage his efforts?

This brief discussion of aspects of Mrs Jones's classroom is not intended to imply that she was necessarily doing anything wrong. It is merely suggested that her planning, teaching methods, and classroom organization are within her control but were not considered in any detail when Peter was being investigated. Instead there was a preoccupation with Peter himself, the state of his brain, his family background, test results, diagnosis, and classification – none of which provided Mrs Jones with any specific and detailed practical advice.

Summary

Throughout the analysis of the identification and assessment of, and the intervention in, Peter Blakey's difficulties an attempt has been made to vindicate the personalities and professional groups involved. Each was seen to act professionally and properly with Peter's best interests in mind, and in some way each contributed positively to the situation. The fault lies in the general approach which seems, in a number of ways, to emulate a medical model quite unsuitable for the treatment of children with learning difficulties. It allows children to fail before action is taken and is then preoccupied with factors outside the classteacher's control in an attempt to ascertain the cause of the problem or to fit the child to a descriptive label or category of handicap. In so doing attention is taken away from the multitude of variables within the teacher's control which might be manipulated to the benefit of the child.

The rest of this book attempts to focus on controllable classroom factors and ignores those things which are beyond teacher-influence. It is not denied that brain damage, a broken home, or a low IQ may have a direct and detrimental effect on a child's educational achievements. However, these things are largely, or entirely, beyond the teacher's control, and consequently provide no specific prescriptive information. Therefore there seems to be no point in focusing attention upon them. Instead, the theme throughout is on manipulating aspects of classroom organization and teaching methods in an attempt to prevent educational failure. Hopefully, the ideas and suggestions presented will help teachers to do a better job for the slow learner.

References

Bateman, B. (1974). Educational implications of minimal brain dysfunction, *Reading Teacher*, 27, 662–668.
    Argues that there are *no* educational implications in a diagnosis of minimal brain dysfunction.
Bloom, B. S. (1975). Mastery learning and its implication for curriculum development in Golby, M., Greenwald, J., and West, R. (Eds), *Curriculum Development*. London: Croom Helm.
    Outlines the fundamental issues involved in mastery learning.
Brophy, J. E., and Good, T. L. (1974). *Teacher-Student Relationships*. New York: Holt, Rinehart & Winston.
    Reviews recent research that has demonstrated the effects of teacher expectation.
Delamont, S. (1976). *Interaction in the Classroom*. London: Methuen.
    Includes an introduction to teacher and pupil expectations and the notion of the self-fulfilling prophecy.
Holt, J. (1964). *How Children Fail*. Harmondsworth: Penguin.
    Uses classroom observation to argue that 'school is a place where children learn to be stupid'.
Nash, R. (1973). *Classrooms Observed*. London: Routledge and Kegan Paul.
    The behaviour of teachers and pupils observed in an attempt to demonstrate and explain how teacher expectations can act as self-fulfilling prophecies.

CHAPTER 4

A NEW PERSPECTIVE

Ainscow, M. and Tweddle, D.A. (1988) *Encouraging classroom success*. London: Fulton (Chapter 1: Success in the classroom)

Introduction

Published almost ten years after *Preventing Classroom Failure*, this book reflected on the experiences of using the approach we had recommended in many schools across the Coventry local authority. This led us to argue that the major goal must be to increase the effectiveness of teaching in mainstream schools as a means of helping all pupils to participate and experience success in the classroom. This meant a move away from carefully structured education plans for individual pupils, an approach that was by this time standard practice across the English education system and in many other countries. Instead, we proposed a framework that could be used to evaluate the quality of teaching and learning available for all pupils within a school. In this way we were moving the agenda towards the core business of school improvement. This also signalled a move from the idea of integration – focused on finding ways of supporting individual pupils seen as having special needs – towards inclusive education, a new conceptualisation that was to shape international thinking over the next two decades.

During the last twenty or thirty years, there has been a major growth in the range of provision and services for pupils with 'special educational needs' – whatever that term means. A great deal has changed over this period, not least the names we use to describe youngsters who are thought to have problems of one kind or another. The nature and style of the provision has also changed. In particular, recent years have seen an increased emphasis on providing services for such pupils within the ordinary class.

Despite increases in resources, changing fashions in terminology and the recent switch to supporting children in mainstream schools, one assumption has remained unchallenged. Whenever learning difficulties occur, it is assumed that there is a deficiency within the pupil. Learning difficulties are thought to be something which the pupil 'has'. As a result, we become preoccupied with an in-depth investigation of the child in an attempt to locate the 'fault'.

There is comfort and security in this assumption. As teachers, it will always let us off the hook! If there is something wrong with the pupil, it cannot possibly be our fault. What we teach, and the way we teach it, can continue as before. We can't lose.

We want to challenge this assumption. This does not necessarily imply assuming blame and guilt for each pupil's difficulties. The outcome can be much more positive and optimistic by switching the emphasis to factors over which we, as teachers, have influence. Instead of focusing on the pupil's limitations, let's concentrate on those things which we can do something about – *namely, our own teaching*.

Every day we make dozens of decisions in the classroom. By and large, *we* decide what's going to happen. These are the factors over which we have influence. This should be the focus of our attention. In this book we provide a framework for evaluating the quality of teaching and learning. It is intended to be applicable to teachers of *all* children and young people, and it is rooted in the assumption that the most important source of learning – for pupils and teachers – is personal experience.

Traditional approaches

The approaches that have been common to what was known as remedial and special education, but which is now more usually referred to as the field of special educational needs, have rightly emphasised the importance of considering pupils as individuals. Unfortunately this focus on individuality, linked as it often is with the assumption that learning difficulties occur mainly because of the limitations of particular pupils, has led us to adopt a narrow perspective. This narrowness has had a negative influence on the attitudes and practice of many teachers which, in turn, has been to the disadvantage of their pupils.

For example, the emphasis that has been placed on the need to identify particular pupils who have learning difficulties (or, more often these days, 'special needs') may have a significant effect on the expectations we have of what they can achieve. As a result, arrangements are made in order that they will not have to face experiences or challenges that are seen as being beyond them. This perceived need to protect 'special children' may be extended into the curriculum, which is then reduced to provide a diet that is felt to be more appropriate.

In addition, there is a tendency for teachers to doubt their own professional competence to deal with children who are 'special'. These children are felt to need special teaching, different methods of learning, and materials which have been designed to help them overcome their problems. Feelings of inadequacy may be reinforced by the presence of experts working with children who have special needs, who seem prepared to take responsibility for those pupils who create most anxiety for the teacher. Matters may be made even worse if the expert offers advice or special materials that seem so complex or time consuming that they cannot be used by a teacher who has to give attention to a full class.

An almost inevitable outcome of this focus on individual children is that they find themselves dealt with separately. This may mean that they are placed at least for part of the time in a separate class or group where they can be offered additional help, or they may be provided with separate tasks or materials to work with in the classroom. As a result they may spend long periods working in isolation from their fellow classmates, perhaps feeling somewhat rejected, and certainly gaining none of the potential educational and social benefits that can accrue from working closely with those who are more successful. It may also be the case that their tasks and activities are less challenging or even trivial in comparison with those in which the rest of the class are engaged.

The hidden message that is being given to the pupil as a result of what was intended as a form of positive discrimination is that he or she is inadequate and different. This often has a damaging effect on morale and confidence.

A more positive orientation

Recognising the potential dangers of this traditional approach to learning difficulties, we intend to adopt a radical view that is more optimistic, realistic and rational.

We believe that every adult and child, without exception, experiences learning difficulties in particular circumstances. Listening to, but failing to understand, a lecture; being able to complete less than half of the *Guardian* crossword; and becoming utterly confused as a result of reading a users' guide for a word processor, are all examples of learning difficulties experienced recently by the authors. Similarly, every reader will recall instances from the recent past, and possibly also from their childhood, when the presented task was apparently impossible.

If the tasks and activities in which the learner is engaged are not matched to the learner's existing capabilities, or are not understood by the learner, then learning difficulties are likely to occur. Thus, learning difficulties are context-specific and are, from time to time, experienced by everybody – teachers, pupils, parents and even writers of books about education.

We believe that this definition is:

- **Realistic**
  It recognises the real problem faced by all teachers – that of teaching a large class of pupils who may all, occasionally at least, experience learning difficulties. It is not simply a case of providing some extra help for one or two.
- **Rational**
  It does not automatically include or exclude academically successful pupils, those for whom English is a second language, adolescents who seem difficult to motivate, or 'middle of the road' pupils who have no obvious strengths or weaknesses.
- **Optimistic**
  If learning difficulties are 'context-bound', in other words associated with particular tasks or circumstances, then they can be prevented or, indeed, created by teachers. Moreover, when they occur, as they inevitably will, they can be resolved.

This working definition of learning difficulties leads us to focus attention on the context within which teaching and learning take place – the classroom. It also means that we must give attention to the purpose and nature of the tasks and activities that pupils encounter. Our concern is with improving the quality of our teaching in ways that will help all pupils to do well.

The agenda for this book can, therefore, be summarised as a single question. It is:

> How can we help all pupils to
> succeed in the classroom?

In any classroom some pupils will experience difficulties in learning what the teacher is trying to teach. For some pupils this occurs very rarely, for others rather more often, and sadly some seem to experience difficulties much of the time. This is true irrespective of the context. It applies to examination classes in secondary schools as much as it does to a class of 6 and 7 year olds, or even students in higher education.

In addressing the question we will try to remain within the confines of typical classroom conditions. That is, we recognise that most teachers work with thirty pupils or more, and that usually they teach their classes alone. All the ideas and strategies discussed, therefore, can be applied in a general way with a full class; they do not assume that a disproportionate amount of time can, or should, be spent with one or two pupils. We also assume that most teachers are normal people and have better things to do with their time than spend four hours each evening preparing the next day's work.

Finally the book does not set out to provide simple solutions to complicated problems of curriculum and classroom organisation. The uniqueness of each encounter between teacher and pupils is such that prescriptions rarely fit and leave the reader either irritated or, even worse, feeling inadequate. Instead what is provided here is a framework that can be used to review and, we hope, extend and develop our thinking and practice in relation to the central question – how can we help all pupils to succeed in the classroom? We believe that this question is the concern of all teachers and that the framework we provide is equally applicable wherever they work.

Defining success

First of all then we must begin by explaining what we mean when we say 'success'. It is a difficult idea to define precisely not least because it tends to mean different things to different people. In some ways it is easier to state what we don't mean. For example, we don't mean passing examinations. This is, of course, important but, given the narrow focus of the forms of examination used in schools, such a restricted definition consigns vast numbers of youngsters to almost inevitable failure.

For similar reasons we don't mean doing better than the next pupil. Obviously competition for jobs or places in higher education is a fact of life. If, however, learning becomes characterised as solely a matter of competition in which there are winners and losers, some pupils will almost always end up as the losers who therefore have no possibility of success.

And finally, we don't mean never making mistakes. Such a definition would make 'success' both unachievable and, indeed, undesirable.

So, what do we mean by success? There are two strands to our definition. The first of these concerns *self-confidence*. We want pupils to develop a positive and optimistic attitude towards learning and a willingness to tackle unfamiliar challenges in the classroom. As John Holt (1964) said, 'The scared learner is always a poor learner'. The second strand to our definition of success concerns *independence*. By this we mean encouraging pupils to learn more about themselves as learners and to become sensitive to their preferred methods of learning.

In a sense, nurturing self-confidence and independence is a means to an end. The ultimate goal is *to help pupils to take responsibility for their own learning*. Much of the book is influenced by this single idea, which we believe should guide the process of learning from when children first attend school and continue throughout their education. It is unreasonable and foolish to foist this responsibility upon youngsters at some arbitrarily selected age and expect them to cope.

In summary, therefore, our definition of 'success' is bound up with the pupils' own perceptions of, and subsequent attitudes towards, classroom experiences. Pupils are succeeding if they are becoming more self-confident, better able and more willing to tackle unfamiliar problems independently, and taking an increasing responsibility for their own learning.

Key factors

To recap. We have explained that this book examines ways of helping all pupils to succeed in the classroom. We have defined success in terms of pupils' willingness and ability to take responsibility for their own learning. In the same way that success is attainable for all pupils, all pupils may from time to time experience learning difficulties.

What follows is a framework which is intended to provide readers with a means of reviewing their own thinking and practice. We believe that teachers, like their pupils, should take responsibility for their own learning. The framework provides an indication of those aspects of teaching that we feel should be kept under review. These have been chosen in the belief that it makes sense to pay particular attention to those factors over which we have some significant influence.

The idea of de-emphasising factors and information over which we have little or no influence represents a departure from current thinking for many of us. An example will perhaps illustrate what it means. Some children grow up in a happy, caring and stimulating home; others do not. Some children are taught, by all that is said and done at home, that school is important and teachers are nice, approachable people; others are not. The influence of the home is considerable, and it works both ways.

As teachers we can all think of pupils whose difficulties at school are linked, obviously and directly, to circumstances at home. However, whilst we may be convinced that the cause of learning problems is in the home, the solution – if there is one – is seldom to be found there. Why? Simply because the social and domestic circumstances of the pupils we teach are usually outside our sphere of influence.

In presenting this argument we are certainly not seeking to undermine the importance of effective communication and liaison between school and home. We would also agree that it is helpful for teachers to be aware of important domestic changes and upheavals which may be upsetting pupils in school. We are simply warning against a preoccupation with background domestic information, past or present, which is of neither legitimate concern nor practical relevance to teachers. Concentrating on factors over which we have significant influence rarely, if ever, means concentrating on the domestic affairs of our pupils.

Similarly we need to resist the temptation to seek explanations and solutions to children's difficulties by speculating about the inside of their brains. How often do we hear of pupils having a 'learning blockage', 'mild brain damage', a 'specific learning disability' or 'low intelligence'? Even if it was agreed what any of these phrases mean, which is doubtful, what are we supposed to do about it? Such attempts to explain the causes of children's problems were very much the fashion amongst remedial and special education experts until recently, but are now generally recognised to have been a wild goose chase.

So what are the important factors over which we have an influence? Quite simply, the decisions we take that determine what happens in the classroom. This is not to deny that children's performance in the classroom is affected by other dimensions which may be of a social, emotional, medical or intellectual nature. If, however, these factors are largely beyond our influence they can become a distraction, leading us to underestimate the importance of what happens in school, in our own classrooms.

Our attention, therefore, will be on examining and monitoring the effects of decisions that are made about the curriculum. For the purposes of this discussion we use the term 'curriculum' to refer to all the planned experiences that are provided for the pupils.

Framework for review

The process of reflection which we are keen to encourage teachers to adopt is based on our assumption that the most significant source of learning is personal experience. So, in trying to improve our professional practice as teachers we suggest that all of us need to keep our ways of working under continual review in order to identify areas that are worthy of development. In particular, the aim should be to improve skills in planning and implementing the curriculum in ways that will encourage success for all pupils.

Central to this approach is what we call classroom evaluation, a continuous process of monitoring and reviewing important decisions about what happens in the classroom.

Our framework for review provides a map of the three areas to be considered. Together they are a comprehensive agenda for keeping under review those factors over which we have substantial influence. They are summarised in the table on page 53.

The three broad areas – objectives, tasks and activities, and classroom arrangements – are not discrete and independent. Decisions about one cannot be taken without reference to the others. For example, the design of tasks and activities must be linked to pupils' objectives and take account of the arrangement of resources in the classroom. Neither are we suggesting that decisions have to be taken in any particular order. The three areas of decision-making are so inextricably interlinked that often they are made at the same time. They are examined separately here merely for the convenience of writers and reader.

(1) Objectives

The amount of freedom teachers have in making decisions about curriculum objectives varies considerably. Some, whether they like it or not, seem to have virtual autonomy; others have to teach within a curriculum framework that has been adopted as a departmental, school or local authority policy. As we write, this whole area is a matter of considerable debate as a result of government legislation which requires the introduction of a National Curriculum.

Nevertheless, as things stand, we all still have considerable influence over the choice of objectives for our pupils. Even teaching older pupils who are working towards public examinations provides some scope for deciding what is taught and how.

A later Chapter discusses the issues involved in determining objectives for all pupils. It stresses the importance of clarifying intentions, taking account of the needs of individual pupils, flexibility and keeping objectives under review. Emphasis is placed on pupil involvement as part of a planned policy for helping all pupils to take responsibility for their own learning.

(2) *Tasks and activities*

For the purposes of discussion we have distinguished between objectives and tasks and activities. 'Tasks and activities' describe what pupils do in the classroom; 'objectives' define the purpose of tasks and activities.

ENCOURAGING CLASSROOM SUCCESS: FRAMEWORK FOR REVIEW

Through the process of *classroom evaluation* the following broad areas of decision-making are kept under review:

OBJECTIVES

- How can we determine appropriate objectives for all our pupils?

TASKS AND ACTIVITIES

- How can we help pupils to be actively engaged in the tasks and activities that are set?

CLASSROOM ARRANGEMENTS

- How do we make effective use of the resources available to facilitate learning?

The key issue here is that tasks and activities should be designed in ways that will encourage pupil participation. Important features of teaching that is successful in this respect are the clarification of the nature and purpose of what is planned, the matching of tasks and materials to individual pupils, an emphasis on interest, and the provision of support and feedback.

In later Chapters examines these issues, emphasising the value of setting tasks and activities in ways that encourage pupils to work cooperatively.

(3) *Classroom arrangements*

The concern here is with the use of available resources. By resources we are not referring solely, or even mainly, to books and equipment. We are using the term in its broadest sense. For example, pupils can learn from and be supported by one another; pupils are a resource. Some schools enjoy the benefits of encouraging active parental involvement and even using parents as classroom helpers; parents are a resource. Perhaps the most valuable resource, however, is the teacher's own time. All of these resources, if they are to be used to the greatest benefit of all pupils, need to be managed effectively. This is our third area of decision-making.

A later Chapter looks at these issues with particular reference to the use of time. The need to arrange the classroom in ways that increase the amount of time available for pupils and teachers to interact in ways that facilitate learning is stressed.

Two final points

As we use the framework to consider important areas of decision-making, we will emphasise two points which we believe to be crucial if teaching is to enable pupils to experience feelings of success. These points apply equally to each aspect of our framework – objectives, tasks and activities, and classroom arrangements.

First of all, we must recognise the importance of achieving a reasonable match between the attainments and interests of individual pupils and the activities they are asked to do. Our concern is to take account of their individual differences, particularly with respect to their:

- **Previous experience**
  Every pupil brings to school a unique range of personal experience. Looked at from our perspective as teachers the experience of some may seem limited or distorted, perhaps, for example, as a result of the economic circumstances of their families. Nevertheless each pupil has personal knowledge and preferences that can and should be used as a basis for enhancing their learning.
- **Existing skills and knowledge**
  Setting tasks at an appropriate level for each pupil is a fundamental skill of being an effective teacher. Essentially this is a matter of knowing what the child can already do in order to decide what he or she should be asked to do next. This might be at a very obvious level, for example, when a child must be able to count before carrying out tasks involving addition and subtraction of numbers. More often, however, the skills and knowledge necessary for progression to some new educational tasks are complex and difficult to determine.
- **Attitudes**
  On first admission to school most children are eager to learn and explore new experiences. It is sad that this initial enthusiasm and confidence seems to die away in some cases. In considering pupils as individuals we need to be sensitive to their attitudes towards various types of learning tasks. Some may have a negative view of themselves as learners based upon previous experiences of failure; some may also have little confidence in teachers as people who can help them to succeed in learning.

The overall message of all of this, therefore, is that we need to know our pupils as well as possible.

The second point to be kept in mind as we make decisions about the curriculum is the vital importance of understanding. Learning will occur only if those involved have a sense of personal meaning about what is to happen, why and how. Without meaning, classroom tasks and activities simply become routines to be followed because they are required by the teacher. We have to find effective ways of ensuring that our pupils share an understanding of what we have planned in order that they can engage in these activities in a manner that will facilitate their learning.

This leads us to place particular emphasis on the importance of negotiation in the classroom. We believe that where teachers and pupils work collaboratively, sharing in decision-making to a reasonable degree, a greater sense of understanding is likely to be achieved. In considering decisions about classroom evaluation, objectives, tasks and activities and classroom arrangements, therefore, we stress the point that collaboration is an effective means of facilitating understanding.

In summary, then, the aspects of teaching that feature in the framework for self-review presented in this book were selected because they are areas of decision-making over which we have significant influence. In considering these aspects we will stress the importance of taking account of pupils' individual differences and finding ways of ensuring understanding, since these are critical features of classroom activity which encourage success.

Summary

The growth of remedial and special education provision over the last twenty-five years has been influenced by the assumption that learning difficulties arise largely as a result of the limitations and disabilities of children. Consequently the approaches that have developed have tended to focus attention on individual children, taking little or no account of the contexts within which teaching and learning take place. This orientation has had negative effects on the attitudes and practices of many teachers and has worked to the disadvantage of some of their pupils.

A new orientation is proposed which emphasises the importance of making teaching more effective. The overall aim is to find ways of helping all pupils to experience success in the classroom. Attention is focused on key decisions over which teachers have influence, particularly with respect to the planning and implementation of the curriculum. It is assumed that the most significant source of learning is personal experience. This has implications for the learning of pupils and teachers.

The rest of this book provides a framework that can be used by teachers to review their existing practice. Central to this is the process of classroom evaluation, which involves the monitoring of decisions about objectives, tasks and activities, and classroom arrangements. Throughout, two points are emphasised: first of all the need to take account of each pupil's existing skills, knowledge and interest, and their previous experience; secondly, the importance of ensuring that pupils have an understanding of the purpose and nature of classroom activities.

References

Ainscow, M. and Tweddle, D. A. (1979). *Preventing Classroom Failure: An Objectives Approach,* London: David Fulton Publishers.

Ainscow, M. and Tweddle, D. A. (1984). *Early Learning Skills Analysis,* Chichester: London: David Fulton Publishers.

Barrow, R. (1984). *Giving Teaching Back to Teachers,* Brighton: Wheatsheaf.

Bennett, N., Desforges, C., Cockburn, A. and Wilkinson, B. (1984). *The Quality of Pupil Learning Experiences,* London: Lawrence Erlbaum.

Brennan, W. K. (1974). *Shaping the Education of Slow Learners,* London: Routledge & Kegan Paul.

Broadfoot, P. (ed.) (1986). *Profiles and Records of Achievement,* London: Holt, Rinehart & Winston.

Brophy, J. E. (1983). Classroom organisation and management, *The Elementary School Journal*, **83** (4), 264–285.

Fullan, M. (1982). *The Meaning of Educational Change*, New York: Teachers College Press.

Galton, M. and Simon, B. (eds) (1980). *Progress and Performance in the Primary School*, London: Routledge & Kegan Paul.

Holt, J. (1964). *How Children Fail*, London: Penguin.

Hopkins, D. (1987). The new initiatives: An overview, *British Journal of Special Education*, **14** (4), 137–140.

Johnson, D. W. and Johnson, R. T. (1986). Mainstreaming and co-operative learning strategies, *Exceptional Children*, **52** (6), 553–561.

Kounin, J. (1970). *Discipline and Group Management in Classrooms*, New York: Holt, Rinehart & Winston.

Lunzer, E. and Gardner, K. (eds) (1979). *The Effective Use of Reading*, London: Heinemann.

Lunzer, E., Gardner, K., Davies, F. and Greene, T. (1984). *Learning from the Written Word*, Edinburgh: Oliver & Boyd.

Popham, W. J. (1975). *Educational Evaluation*, Englewood Cliffs, NJ: Prentice Hall.

Rosenshine, B. (1983). Teacher functions in instructional programmes, *The Elementary School Journal*, **83** (4), 335–351.

Slavin, R. E. (1983). *Co-operative Learning*, London: Longman.

Thomas, G. (1986). Integrating personnel in order to integrate children, *Support for Learning*, **1** (1), 19–26.

Tomlinson, S. (1982). *A Sociology of Special Education*, London: Routledge & Kegan Paul.

CHAPTER 5

IMPROVING THE QUALITY OF EDUCATION FOR ALL

Ainscow, M. and Hopkins, D. (1994) Understanding the moving school. In G. Southworth (ed.), *Readings in primary school development.* London: Falmer

Introduction

In repositioning myself around the idea of inclusive education, I increasingly worked with colleagues with expertise in the fields of school effectiveness and school improvement. These links were explored in an edited book, *Effective Schools for All* (Fulton, 1991) that included contributions from some key international authorities. Building on their ideas, this chapter illustrates the approach my colleagues and I developed in the school improvement project, 'Improving the Quality of Education for All (IQEA)', which was widely influential in the UK and internationally. The project involved teams of university academics collaborating with schools during what proved to be an unprecedented period of national educational reform. These experiences led my colleagues and me to rethink many of our assumptions as to how school improvement can be achieved, noting in particular the way local histories and circumstances bear upon the improvement efforts of individual schools.

In recent years primary schools have faced an enormous range of demands for change. Despite these pressures some schools find opportunities for improvement in this new context. This chapter will describe a school improvement project that involves groups of schools collaborating to develop ways of working that enable the current reform agenda to be turned to advantage. Specifically the chapter will focus on developments going on in three primary schools that are participants in the project, drawing out some lessons that have emerged from an analysis of their activities.

Improving the Quality of Education for All

During the past three years or so we and a team of colleagues have been working closely with some thirty schools on a school improvement project known as Improving the Quality of Education for All (IQEA). This project has involved the schools and us in a collaborative enterprise designed to strengthen their ability to manage change, to enhance the work of teachers, and ultimately to improve the outcomes, however broadly defined, of pupils. At a time of great change in the educational system, the schools we are working with are using the impetus of external reform for internal purpose. In other words they are attempting to become what Susan Rosenholtz (1989) has called *moving schools*.

IQEA works from an assumption that schools are most likely to strengthen their ability to provide enhanced outcomes for all pupils when they adopt ways of working that are consistent with their own aspirations as well as the current reform agenda. This involves building confidence and capacity within the school, rather than reliance on externally produced packages—although good ideas from the outside are never rejected out of hand.

The project in each school is based upon a contract between the staff of the school, the local education authority and the Cambridge team. This contract is intended to clarify expectations and ensure the conditions necessary for success. For our part, we co-ordinate the project; provide training for the school co-ordinators and representatives; make regular school visits and contribute to staff training; provide staff development materials; and monitor the implementation of the project. For the schools on the other hand, involvement in the project requires the following commitments:

- The decision to participate in the project is made as a result of consultation amongst *all staff* in the school.
- Each school designates a minimum of two members of staff as project co-ordinators (one of whom is the headteacher or deputy head) who attend ten days of training and support meetings (the group of co-ordinators is known as the *project cadre*).
- At least 40 per cent of teachers (representing a cross-section of staff) take part in specified staff development activities in their own and each others' classrooms. Each participating teacher is regularly released from teaching in order to participate in these classroom based aspects of the project.
- Teachers are able to use their participation in the project as a basis for accrediting their professional development work.
- Each school participates in the evaluation of the project and shares findings with other participants in the project.
- The whole school allocates substantial staff development time to activities related to the project.

The style adopted in the project is to develop a strategy for improvement that allows each school considerable autonomy to determine its own priorities for development and, indeed, its own methods for achieving these priorities. In this sense we (all the partners in the project) are involved in one project within which individual schools devise their own projects.

Within IQEA we place considerable importance on the need for inquiry, reflection and evaluation. The collecting of school-based data of various kinds for purposes of informing planning and development is seen as a powerful element within each school's strategy. Consequently the schools are expected to collect data about progress in establishing conditions for improvement, and, of course, about student and teacher outcomes. Agreement that these data would be shared is one of the specifications of the project contract.

The journals kept by the project co-ordinators provide a common approach to recording relevant information. In general terms the journals provide a detailed account of events, decisions and processes that occur, as well as summaries of significant outcomes that are noted. Co-ordinators are also requested to write reflective comments, indicating their personal reactions to what occurs and map their involvement in the project over time. In this way individuals can monitor the progress of their school's project and, at the same time, record developments in their own thinking and practice.

Throughout the period of the project the project team make regular visits to each school to support co-ordinators in their work and, at the same time, to collect additional data. All these data are systematically processed on a continuous basis in order to build up a clearer picture of the activities going on in each school. These findings are also being fed back to the school in order to inform development processes. In this respect the project can correctly be characterized as a process of collaborative inquiry within which all partners are contributing to its evolution.

From data collected through these processes we are gradually gaining a greater understanding of what goes on in schools that are successful in managing change during a period of intensive innovation. In what follows we draw out some lessons from three primary schools that seem to us to have made significant progress in providing a quality education for all their children.

Establishing a climate

Our experience has been that it is vital to establish a climate in a school that encourages all colleagues to participate in improvement activities. Ideally, the aim should be to create a feeling amongst staff that they can contribute to the leadership of such developments. A commitment to participate in the leadership process seems to grow from the headteacher's commitment to secure participation—once staff believe the invitation is authentic then the quality of individual involvement increases. However, the building of openness and trust hinges on the quality of communication which is established alongside and around the decentralization of decisions. This communication needs to flow upwards and sideways as well as down, and to be seen as an important part of the influence process—where information replaces authority as the basis for decision-making then additional information inevitably changes the equation and sometimes the decision. Nurturing such an influence pattern is difficult in the larger school, where groups and individuals do not always meet one another regularly; it may be even harder in the smaller school where staff see each other daily and patterns of headteacher patronage are well established.

Within the IQEA project we have observed a number of schools that have moved towards a much more participatory climate. One of these schools, we will call it Eastside, is a particularly good example in that it involved a newly appointed headteacher in transforming staff expectations of leader behaviour.

Eastside is a large junior school serving a working-class district on the outskirts of a large city. The headteacher, Christine Jones, joined the school about four years ago at the same time as a new deputy head who had been appointed by the previous headteacher. Christine's previous experience had been as a teaching head in a very small primary school where she had been used to a relaxed atmosphere within which it was a tradition for all staff to contribute to development activities. When Christine met the staff for the first time she began to realize how different this school was from her previous experience. She knew, for example, that previously staff had addressed the head by her full title and there were real expectations of a formal and hierarchical structure being maintained. At that stage, therefore, she decided that her chief aim must be to gain their trust and respect. She also felt that she would have to take time to appraise the school as well as support her staff. Like many new heads, therefore, she faced many dilemmas about how quickly to act in introducing proposed changes.

Christine found that the leadership pattern established in the school was of a pyramid type, with ideas and decisions passed to the staff via the deputy and senior management team. She also gradually found that there were a small number of very influential teachers (not necessarily members of the SMT) but that the majority saw themselves as being powerless. Except in one particular year group team, planning was very much carried out by individuals for their own classes.

Early on Christine and her new deputy head colleague decided to adopt a different approach to staff meetings in order to make it possible for everyone to participate. Indeed, the first step was to establish a pattern of regular weekly staff meetings. Before the meetings, information was circulated so that everybody knew what was to be discussed, and Christine chaired the meetings in ways that attempted to avoid undue pressure.

After some time there was evidence of increased staff participation. Teachers with responsible posts were encouraged to take on non-specific management tasks and were given opportunities to decide on resources in their own areas. As the power of the majority of staff gradually increased, however, the small group of teachers who had previously been influential experienced some loss of status. Consequently a level of distrust and uncertainty continued.

At the start of her second year in the school Christine decided to emphasize the idea that planning should take place within year groups. About the same time she produced a draft school development plan and submitted it to the staff for comments. In addition, use was made of various LEA advisers as part of the school's staff development programme. The main aim was to enable class teachers to develop their expertise in the light of new curriculum requirements.

In the spring of that second year the whole staff set out their priorities for the development plan and a system of working groups was established. Time was also allocated in order that year group teams could meet to plan for the following term. At first the whole staff worked on the core subjects, English, Maths and Science, but then people began to feel that this was taking too long. Working groups or subject co-ordinators, with advice and help from the authority, now prepared policies and schemes of work, which were presented to the whole staff for discussion and adoption as working documents. Much was achieved in a relatively short time as staff worked to get the best for the children. The ethos gradually became one of commitment and enthusiasm although this also led to occasional periods of exhaustion.

As the staff became empowered it became necessary to respond to their requests knowing that any demands that were made were for the benefit of the children. Christine felt that the recognition that no one person had all of the answers, even if theoretically they had the power, changed the way decisions were made. The belief that a team committed to working together with the same aim has more to offer than an individual wielding power is a very basic belief. It is also very uncomfortable at times because the team can propose some things that the head does not totally agree with and yet the style of management means that it must be tried out.

This account of what happened at Eastside underlines the importance of relationship building. The mutual trust which is needed for genuine empowerment hinges on the quality of the relationship between head and staff. The account also shows how trust builds once relationships are right. Communication is clearly important here too: new opportunities were created for staff to meet and talk about what is happening—occasions when the formal communications hierarchy gave way to whole school meetings where horizontal, vertical and, most importantly, upward communication were possible. But, better quality communication does not mean universal agreement—indeed, it was very uncomfortable at times. What is important is that although certain issues or discussions create discomfort, the staff feel able to raise them. This leads to a much healthier environment for handling conflict (i.e. by acknowledging and exploring it) than is usually the case in leader-dependent cultures, where differences in view tend to be minimized or hidden, rather than viewed as opportunities for growth.

This account also demonstrates the motivational potential of shared leadership—the staff feel more enthusiasm and commitment to their jobs because they are actively involved in decisions about them, creating a strong sense of personal identification with organizational jobs. It also shows how school leaders can, by transforming their ways of working, encourage the creation of a culture that is, to some degree at least, shaped by the values and expectations of the teachers themselves. These transformations represent the first steps towards a more empowered and autonomous staff group.

Clearly, to devise management arrangements that empower is a challenging task. Yet this challenge is already being attended to in many schools, since the pressures for change are creating a strain on the existing arrangements, and are leading governors, heads and staff to review traditional ways of managing and leading the school. Governors in particular are looking for new ways of working with the head and staff which build upon the good relationships already established. Teachers are also realizing that the management of classrooms cannot be isolated from the management arrangements for the school as a whole. As budgets are delegated to schools, systems for managing finance and resources have to be created to complement or replace existing arrangements. The National Curriculum is leading to a new approach to the whole curriculum, to the deployment of teachers and to the organization of teaching, learning and assessment.

Schools that are more successful in coming to terms with change will clearly need more leadership. There will be visions to be identified, agendas to be built; new ways of working to be designed, and climates of problem-solving and learning to be nurtured—among the many other major tasks—but there will be a need for better management as well. The school will inevitably become a more complex organization. More day-to-day interventions will be needed to make sure that the relevant teams have the resources to function effectively. Although the roles of teachers may expand and develop considerably, the head's role will be no less central. It seems, therefore, that all heads need to become better versed in creating climates that support staff in the process of change.

Creating development structures

Day-to-day maintenance has to be the priority of any school. Organizing large groups of children and adults requires a set of structures that ensure that order is maintained and tasks completed. In times of massive innovation, however, it is also necessary to build in systems by which the school can allocate resources to support staff in responding to new requirements.

Within the IQEA project we have many excellent examples of schools that have been able to establish successful structures for supporting development activities. These often involve the creation of temporary systems, such as staff task groups to get things done. The success of such groups requires a degree of sophistication and an emphasis on co-ordination and communication. Riverside primary school is a good example of how this can be achieved.

The school has twenty-four teachers. The use of staff groups has developed as an effective way of enabling teachers to focus on planning and be engaged in the development of specific curriculum areas, while, at the same time, maintaining their involvement in the development of the whole curriculum and whole school issues. There are three parallel, mixed-ability classes in each year group. Each year team of teachers is released for one-half day towards the end of the summer term so that they can make an overall plan of work for the coming year. The school has an overall curriculum framework that outlines the content for their plans. The year team decide how to group the subjects effectively, making use of their expertise. They can also ask other subject co-ordinators for advice. At the end of each term they are also released to make detailed plans for the coming term. One hour per week is included in the time budget for Year Team meetings. This enables them to refine and adjust their plans as well as to discuss any problems. The strength of the Year Team is in mutual support and inspiration.

The time spent on planning is valued as enabling the more efficient use of time and resources during the term. It is also seen as helping to raise the standard of work produced in the classroom. Monday is the regular staff meeting time. There is a sequence of staff meetings, middle management meetings (year co-ordinators and senior staff), staff INSET and curriculum groups. All staff are members of curriculum groups. Each year co-ordinator is also a subject co-ordinator. These groups change according to the current priorities for development. The Mathematics, Science and Language co-ordinators continue to develop their subject areas and these curriculum groups are reconvened when necessary.

In the current climate of change, staff are working to implement and monitor National Curriculum requirements. The use of groups means that a few staff can concentrate on developing one subject area and construct policy statements and school guidelines to ensure continuity and progression. All policies and documents produced by any group must be discussed by the whole staff and amended if necessary before being passed to the Governors for approval.

Recently there was concern with the time gap which was occurring between groups producing draft policies or guidelines and staff meeting time for discussion. Also, with a large staff, there was a worry that all staff might not feel able to contribute to the discussion through pressure of time and items on the agenda. It was, therefore, decided to give draft copies of the policies to the year co-ordinator for discussion within their year team. Each team can then scribble their comments on the draft version, either during a team meeting or individually, at a convenient time.

This proved to be an effective way of getting useful responses from all members of staff. The revised draft is again given to year teams for comments. The senior staff approve the final version before submitting it to the governors. This process also emphasizes the management role of year co-ordinators and ensures that all staff are fully involved in the decision making process.

All staff are involved in producing the school development plan. The curriculum groups and subject co-ordinators produce their own plans for the coming year. Whole school issues can be raised by any member of staff. All staff discuss all aspects of the development plan. This is regarded as essential if all staff are going to be committed to implementing the plan. After the whole staff discussion, the plans are discussed by the senior management team and the middle management team so that the advantages and disadvantages of each element can be discussed and prioritized.

The school development plan is organized on a financial year basis as many aspects are dependent on an allocation of money. Each co-ordinator is then allocated a budget to support their subject area. The use of staff groups enables staff to work more efficiently and effectively, to maximize the expertise available within the school and to develop their own professional skills. This format is not static but developing. Each year refinements or changes are made, either in response to staff requests or in anticipation of future needs.

Riverside is an excellent example of a well thought through development structure. Particular features that should be noted are:

- the way in which groups are constructed to ensure that all staff are involved;
- the allocation of time to support staff as they take on additional responsibilities;
- accountability of individuals who are designated to take on co-ordination tasks;
- attention to ensuring good communication between the various groups.

Improving classroom practice

Our experience has been that the establishment of a participatory climate and development structures can make a significant impact upon the quality of work going on in a school. However, this is only part of the story. A much greater impact can be achieved if these overall improvements can be made to influence what happens in the classrooms. Ultimately it is the interactions between pupils and teachers that have the greatest effect upon learning outcomes. Consequently real movement towards quality will only be achieved where there is attention to the improvement of classroom practice.

We could quote many examples of schools that have used staff development as a central strategy for supporting teachers as they have attempted to engage in improvement activities. All of them work from an assumption that attention to teacher learning is likely to have direct spin-offs in terms of pupil learning. All of them demonstrate the pay-off of investment of time and resources in teacher development.

An excellent example is that of Sunnyside Infants School. There, over the last few years, a sophisticated strategy has been adopted to create conditions in the school that support the development of the staff. At the outset was a concern with how to find time to observe children in the classroom for the purposes of new assessment requirements. With this in mind a staff development day was led by an external consultant. This event had an enormous impact on staff thinking. Specifically, the consultant led the staff through a series of problem-solving processes focusing on the arrangement of one classroom. Gradually the teachers rearranged furniture and resources in order to make the classroom more autonomous. Subsequently similar activities have been carried out in other rooms. It does seem that the impact of this approach had to do with the tangible nature of the task (i.e. rearranging equipment, etc.) and the context (i.e. the classroom).

Following on from this day the staff explored classroom management issues. This led to the formulation of a house style involving the use of learning centres in which pupils carry out assignments. By the end of the first year there was clear evidence of increased pupil autonomy in the classroom.

During the second year staff began to question the quality of learning going on in the learning centres. Their concern was that pupils might simply be completing tasks without any significant learning taking place. With this in mind they decided to work in small teams to observe in one another's classrooms. Observation focused on the quality of engagement in the learning centres. To facilitate these observations the Headteacher covered classes to free teachers. She asked them to plan the observations and also allocated time to debrief what had occurred.

The evidence suggests that the strategy has had a significant impact. Specific changes in teaching style are evident in all classrooms; there is clear evidence of increased pupil autonomy in learning, even with very young pupils; and the quality of dialogue about teaching and learning amongst staff is very striking to the outsider. Indeed it does seem that the adopted strategy has brought about a significant change in the culture of the school.

A crucial element of the Sunnyside strategy is the importance placed on locating staff development in classrooms. This seems an obvious point and yet it is one that is usually overlooked. So much of in-service education occurs away from the usual context in which teaching takes place and, indeed, is led by people who have not visited the specific contexts in which their participants have to operate. Eisner suggests that this is 'akin to a basketball coach providing advice to a team he has never seen play' (1990: 102).

In recent years the work of Bruce Joyce and Beverley Showers (1988) on staff development, in particular their peer coaching strategy, has transformed thinking on staff development. Joyce and Showers identified a number of key components which when used in combination have much greater power than when they are used alone.

These major components are:

- presentation of theory or description of skill or strategy;
- modelling or demonstration of skill or models of teaching;
- practice in simulated and classroom settings;
- structured and open-ended feedback (provision of information about performance);
- coaching for application (hands-on, in-classroom assistance with the transfer of skills and strategies to the classroom).

Based on this analysis, Joyce and Showers (1988: 85) summarized their 'best knowledge' on staff development like this:

- the use of the integrated theory-demonstration-practice-feedback training programme to ensure skill development;
- the use of considerable amounts of practice in simulated conditions to ensure fluid control of new skills;
- the employment of regular on-site coaching to facilitate vertical transfer— the development of new learning in the process of transfer;
- the preparation of teachers who can provide one another with the needed coaching.

More recently Joyce (1991) has distinguished, helpfully in our opinion, between the two key elements of staff development: the workshop and the workplace.

The *workshop,* which is equivalent to the best practice on the traditional INSET course, is where we gain understanding, see demonstrations of the teaching strategy we may wish to acquire, and have the opportunity to practice them in a non-threatening environment.

If however we wish to transfer these skills that the workshop has introduced to us back into the *workplace* (i.e. the classroom and school) then merely attending the workshop is insufficient. The research evidence is very clear that skill acquisition and the ability to transfer vertically to a range of situations requires on-the-job support. This implies changes to the workplace and the way in which we organize staff development in our schools. In particular this means the opportunity for immediate and sustained practice, collaboration and peer coaching, and studying development and implementation. We cannot achieve these changes in the workplace without, in most cases, drastic alterations in the ways in which we organize our schools.

Patterns of development

From our work with schools such as the three we have described in the IQEA project, we can begin to put together a picture of what happens in moving schools and, in so doing, point to certain patterns that seem to be connected to their success. IQEA schools are encouraged to use the school development planning process to express their developmental aspirations in the form of *priorities.* The school's development plan contains a series of priorities which are ideally supported by action plans. These are the working documents for teachers. In them the priority is subdivided into targets and tasks, responsibilities are allocated, a time frame established, and evaluation or progress checks identified (Hargreaves and Hopkins, 1991).

Through this approach to planning, priorities are then reformulated within a *strategy.* A strategy typically involves teachers in some form of collaborative classroom based action. The exact nature of the strategy, or combination of strategies, is peculiar to each school. Strategies need to take account of the priorities that have been agreed, existing conditions and the resources that are available.

Most primary schools are, of course, used to planning in this way and to establishing working groups for developmental tasks. But, as we saw in the account of Eastside School, it is as they move into action that problems tend to arise. Beginning to work on something new, to change, inevitably creates some difficulties, both for individuals and the institution. Teachers are faced with acquiring new teaching skills or mastering new curriculum material; the school is often faced with new ways of working that are incompatible with existing organizational structures.

This phase of destabilization or *internal turbulence,* as Michael Huberman (1992) calls it, is as predictable as it is uncomfortable. Many research studies have found that, without a period of destabilization, successful, long lasting change is unlikely to occur (see Louis and Miles, 1990). Yet it is at this point that most change fails to progress beyond early implementation. In these cases, when the change hits the wall of individual learning or institutional resistance, internal turbulence begins to occur and developmental work begins to impact on all staff. Often the working group continues for a while, but eventually it fragments, or another priority is found on which they can focus. The change circles back on itself and nothing much is achieved—so we start something new. This is the cycle of educational failure so well documented by Slavin (1989) in his article on faddism in education. This, we find, is the predictable pathology of educational change.

Many of the schools that we have been working with seem to survive this period of destabilization by either consciously or intuitively adapting or accommodating the *internal conditions* in the school to meet the demands of the agreed on change or priority. In order to overcome the wall, we encourage schools to diagnose their internal conditions in relation to their chosen change *before* they begin developmental work. They can then begin to build these modifications to the school's internal conditions into the strategies they are going to adopt (Hopkins *et al.*, 1994; Ainscow *et al.*, 1994).

When this happens we begin to detect changes in the culture of the school of the sort described in the story of Eastside. In this way a school's change capacity increases and the ground-work is laid for future change efforts. Instead of rebounding against the wall, a virtuous circle of change began to be established. Our experience is that schools like Riverside that have been through similar change cycles experience less internal turbulence because they have progressively enhanced their capacity to change as a result of this developmental process.

Headteachers who adopt this type of approach to the management of change seem to agree with Schein when he wrote, 'that the only thing of real importance that leaders do is to create and manage culture' (1985: 2). They realize that the impact of successful change needs to be on the culture of the school, for it is culture that sustains change and consequently enhances the achievement of students. They therefore focus on culture first. It is almost as if they begin by asking 'What cultural changes are required?' and then, 'What priorities, strategies, and changes in conditions can bring this about?' The link between setting priorities and the culture of the school is therefore of some importance. Sequencing priorities over time can help the successive shaping of school culture. In recognition of this many school leaders 'start small and think big' in their planning for development, they also sequence priorities in such a way that they build on initial good practice and then on subsequent success (see Fullan, 1991). They manipulate strategy and conditions in order to affect culture, in the pursuit of enhancing the quality of educational out-comes and experience for all pupils.

Although the conditions may be eased and the internal turbulence reduced at the school level, the pressure of individual learning on the part of teachers remain the same. The conditions in and the culture of the school are increasingly supportive of their developmental efforts. As was noted at Sunnyside School, teachers who experience a more supportive environment within the school feel more able to endure the threat of new learning. As they adapt the teaching and learning practices in their classrooms, they begin to see that the learning of their pupils is enhanced and this evidence gives them confidence in the change and increases their commitment to the new approach.

In this discussion it is the strategy chosen by the school that not only links the priority to the conditions, but also has the impact on culture and student outcomes. In the schools we are working with we have seen many strategies and combinations of strategies. The following list is not exhaustive. It is simply a composite of those strategies used by schools in the early phases of the project. Obviously no school used them all, but also no school relied on just one:

Staff development

- staff development processes are used to support individual teacher and school development;
- teachers are involved in each other's teaching;
- where appropriate, external consultants are used to support teacher development.

Inquiry and reflection

- there is a search for increased clarity and shared meanings;
- reflection and review activities are used to monitor progress and enhance the professional judgment of teachers.

Leadership

- staff throughout the school are encouraged to adopt leadership roles;
- temporary systems or working groups are created;
- individuals take on key roles in initiating change and supporting development work.

Involvement

- pupils, staff and parents are encouraged to be involved in school development;
- a climate that encourages access is created;
- effective use is made of external consultants.

Coordination

- efforts are made to maintain momentum;
- links are made between formal and informal structures;
- images of success are created.

Planning

- planning processes are used to legitimize and coordinate action;
- resources for school improvement are specifically allocated.

Although it may be helpful conceptually and strategically to think of these aspects of school improvement as distinct, in reality they coalesce. In practice, the priority or curriculum focus and the strategy combine in the minds of teachers to present a uniform reality. On a day-to-day basis school improvement is an amalgam of broad strategies such as self-review, action planning, staff development which link together the classroom and the school, as well as the more dynamic aspects of the change process.

In this section of the chapter we have tried to tease out the process of development as we have seen it in the schools in which we have been working. The analytical and conceptual distinctions we have made may be a necessary element in setting out the territory of school development, but they are insufficient to tell us why the process works in the way it does. In order to get a better understanding of movement in schools, therefore, we have to examine how one development cycle leads on to another.

Moving on

Schools that are successful in their improvement initiatives seem to move from one cycle of development to another through the creation of what we have called earlier *a development structure*. However, this is easier said than done. Schools often seem to find it difficult to draw a line under certain developments and to move on to something new. It certainly helps to have a clear idea of what the school wants to achieve by when and to build evaluation into the end of the work on a particular priority. What must be avoided is development work on a priority just 'fizzling out', and then the school searching around for something else to work on.

The transition from one cycle to another is greatly assisted by the creation of a development structure. Perhaps the most crucial challenge facing schools today is how to balance change and stability effectively; how on the one hand to preserve what is already successful in a school, and how on the other, to respond positively to innovation and the challenge of change. We believe that the school's internal conditions are crucial in achieving the correct balance. We are also realizing from our current work that by adapting their structural arrangements, many successful schools, such as Riverside, are finding it easier to move from one developmental sequence to another.

Schools are finding out quite rapidly, or eventually more painfully, that procedures established to organize teaching, learning and assessment cannot also cope with developmental activities which inevitably cut across established hierarchies, curriculum areas, meeting patterns, and timetables. What is required are complementary structures each with their own purpose, budget and ways of working. Our experience is that the innovative responses required for sustained development are likely to involve:

- delegation;
- task groups;
- high levels of specific staff development;
- quality time for planning;
- collaborative classroom activity.

Obviously the majority of a school's time and resources will go on its day-to-day activities, but unless there is also an element dedicated to development, the school is unlikely to progress in times of change. Decisions can then be made as to what aspect of the school requires development, and it is that priority which gets the treatment for a specified period of time. In practice, therefore, the development structure acts as a support system for the rest of the school's activities. A priority on teaching and learning, for example, will inevitably spread itself across a school's curriculum if carefully managed. After work on a particular development is completed, another aspect of the school's operation is selected, and so on. In this way, over time, most aspects of the school will have been subject to some form of development activity.

Concluding remarks

In our experience it is in these ways that successful schools respond to the challenge of imposed reform within a decentralized system. Schools will embrace some changes immediately. This will be because the school either has no other legal option, or because it has a particular expertise or penchant for that change. Other changes, where experience is perhaps lacking, are selected as development priorities and sequenced over time. Some centralized initiatives, however, are resisted, either because they are incompatible with the school's central purpose, or because they may be regarded as being wrong.

This discussion and the various examples given in this chapter go some way to explain what happens in moving schools. This analysis suggests that unless schools are able to take a more assertive approach towards external policy initiatives they will continue to suffer from 'innovation overload' and gradually lose control of their own educational agenda. It is the integration of phases of action such as those described in this chapter into the daily life of the school that keeps the process of development going.

Acknowledgements

We would like to acknowledge the contributions of our many colleagues in the IQEA project, particularly Geoff Southworth and Mel West, to the ideas presented in this chapter.

References

Ainscow, M., Hopkins, D., Southworth, G. and West, M. (1994) *Creating the Conditions for School Improvement*, London, Fulton.

Eisner, E.W. (1990) 'The meaning of alternative paradigms for practice', in Guba, E.G. (Ed) *The Paradigm Dialog*, London, Sage.

Fullan, M.G. (1991) *The New Meaning of Educational Change*, London, Cassell.

Hargreaves, D.H. and Hopkins, D. (1991) *The Empowered School*, London, Cassell.

Hopkins, D., Ainscow, M. and West, M. (1994) *School Improvement in an Era of Change*, London, Cassell.

Huberman, M. (1992) 'Critical introduction', in Fullan, M.G. *Successful School Improvement*, Milton Keynes, Open University Press.

Joyce, B. (1991) 'Cooperative learning and staff development; teaching the method with the method', *Cooperative Learning*, **12**, 2, pp. 10–13.

Joyce, B. and Showers, B. (1988) *Student Achievement Through Staff Development*, London, Longman.

Louis, K.S. and Miles, M. (1992) *Improving the Urban High School*, London, Cassell.

Rosenholtz, S. (1989) *Teachers' Workplace: The Social Organization of Schools*, New York, Longman.

Schein, E. (1985) *Organizational Cultures and Leadership: A Dynamic View*, San Francisco, Jossey-Bass.

Slavin, R. (1989) 'PET and the pendulum: Faddism in education and how to stop it', *Phi Delta Kappan*, June, 752–8.

CHAPTER 6

LEARNING FROM DIFFERENCES

Ainscow, M. (2000) Reaching out to all learners: some lessons from international experience. *School Effectiveness and School Improvement* 11(1), 1–9

Introduction

This paper links the lessons from our involvement with schools involved in IQEA with the work I had been doing internationally as a result of the UNESCO teacher education project, 'Special Needs in the Classroom', which I directed during the 1990s. This took place within the context of the groundbreaking Salamanca Statement on Special Needs Education, agreed by representatives of 92 governments and 25 international organisations in June 1994. The paper uses examples of developments in different parts of the world to illustrate ways of learning from differences. This leads me to argue that the power of comparison for the development of practice comes not from lifting approaches and moving them from place to place, but from using the stimulus of more exotic environments to reconsider thinking and practice in familiar settings. It is about making what is strange familiar and what is familiar strange, as when seeing your own town in a new light when showing a visitor around. Features that are normally ignored become clearer, possibilities that have been overlooked are reconsidered, and things that have become taken for granted are subjected to new scrutiny.

In this article I set out to encourage teachers and others interested in school improvement to think about the possibilities we can create for ourselves when we attempt to reach out to *all* learners. My suggestions arise, in the main, as a result of reflections on the experience of working with schools over many years in my own country and overseas. In particular they arise from my involvement over the last 10 years in a UNESCO teacher education initiative to do with the development of more inclusive forms of schooling. This project originally involved research in eight countries but has subsequently led to dissemination activities of various kinds throughout the world (more detailed accounts of the project can be found in Ainscow, 1994, 1999).

During the early phases of the project it was assumed that materials and methods would be developed that could be distributed in a straightforward way for use in different parts of the world. Gradually those of us leading the project came to realise that schooling is so closely tied into local conditions and cultures that the importation of practices from elsewhere is fraught with difficulties. In other words, learning from other people, particularly those who live their lives

in far away places, is by no means straight forward. Clearly this has major implications for international cooperation within the education research community.

Keeping this in mind, I will use some of my own experiences to illustrate
ways in which an engagement with the issue of how to respond to pupil
differences can stimulate our thinking about the issue of school improvement.
The approach I will use is to present short vignettes based on observations made
in schools and classrooms in various parts of the world to show how such
experiences have stimulated a reconsideration of my thinking about practice
in my own country. This leads me to argue that the power of international
comparison for the development of more effective schools comes not from
lifting approaches and moving them from place to place, but from using the
stimulus of more exotic environments to reconsider thinking and practice in
familiar settings (Delamont, 1992). It is about making what is familiar strange,
as when seeing your own town in a new light when showing a visitor round.
Features that are normally ignored become clearer, possibilities that have been
overlooked are reconsidered, and things that have become taken for granted are
subject to new scrutiny.

Stories and reflections

The shifts in thinking that took place within our UNESCO project involved a
reconceptualisation of how some children come to be marginalised within or
even excluded from schools. This, in turn, pointed us towards many possibilities
for the development of schools that might otherwise have been overlooked. It
also helped us to realise that a concern with local context had to be at the heart
of development activities. In this way we became aware of the importance of
existing practice as the essential starting point for our efforts. Indeed, as we
looked more closely at what was going on in the classrooms in which we worked
we realised that very often much of the expertise that was needed in order to
reach out to all learners was already there. Thus the strategy becomes less about
importing ideas from elsewhere and more to do with finding ways of making
better use of local knowledge. Put simply, therefore, our experience has been
that teachers frequently know more than they use! The task, therefore, becomes
essentially one of helping teachers to analyse their own practice as a basis for
experimentation.

In what follows I illustrate what I have in mind by using stories from my
learning journal to show the potential of using local thinking and practice as a
foundation for school improvement. These accounts also demonstrate some
ways in which we might learn from the experiences of others.

Vignette 1 – China

*A primary school classroom in Inner Mongolia. There are approximately
75 children, sitting in rows of desks packed into a long, rather bleak looking
room. The teacher stands at one end of the room on a narrow stage in front of
a blackboard. Lessons are 40 minutes long and, although each is taught by a
different teacher, mostly follow a common pattern. Typically this involves
a process by which the teacher talks or reads and, frequently, uses questions to
stimulate choral or individual responses from the class. Throughout the lesson
the pace is fast and the engagement of pupils appears to be intense. Afterwards
the teacher explains how she tries to help those who experience difficulties by*

directing many more questions to them and by encouraging their classmates to go over the lesson content with them during the breaktimes.

What, then, does an English observer make of such an experience? Does it suggest patterns of practice that might be relevant to teachers in my country where, despite much smaller classes, it is not uncommon to find groups of children whose participation in lessons is marginal to say the least? Why are these Chinese pupils so quiet and obedient throughout a day of lessons that appear so repetitive? It would be so easy to jump to simple conclusions that might appear to offer strategies that could be exported to other parts of the world. On the other hand there are so many factors to consider. It is apparent, for example, that many other influences help to shape the events observed in this classroom. We are told that teachers are held in high esteem in Chinese society, although this is changing as a result of current economic reforms. It also seems that children are often under considerable pressure from their families to achieve success at school. Such community attitudes are but a part of a range of influences that help to shape the interactions that occur in local schools but which are difficult for the foreign visitor to determine.

Having said that, the Chinese story does point to the importance of teachers planning their lessons with all members of the class in mind. Here we bring into focus a central dilemma that confronts any teacher faced with their class. Put simply it is this: how do I work with the whole group and, at the same time, reach out to each member of the class as an individual?

It has taken me a long time to appreciate that existing practice represents the best starting point for development activities, not least because of my previous experience and training in the field of special education. Specifically it took me many years to recognise that the ways in which earlier attempts to develop integrated arrangements for pupils said to have special needs had often, unintentionally, undermined our efforts. As we tried to integrate such pupils into mainstream schools, we imported practices derived from earlier experience in special provision. What we learned was that many of these approaches were simply not feasible in primary and secondary schools. Here I am thinking, in particular, of the individualised responses, based on careful assessments and systematic programmes of interventions, that have been the predominant orientation within the special needs world. For many years this was very much the orientation that shaped my own work (e.g., Ainscow & Tweddle, 1979, 1984). Gradually, however, experience has taught me that such approaches do not fit with the ways in which mainstream teachers plan and go about their work. For all sorts of sensible and understandable reasons the planning frame of such teachers has to be that of the whole class. Apart from any other considerations, the sheer numbers of children in the class and the intensity of the teacher's day makes this inevitable.

The gradual recognition that schools for all will not be achieved by transplanting special education thinking and practice into mainstream contexts has opened my mind to many new possibilities that I had previously failed to recognise. Many of these relate to the need to move from the individualised planning frame, referred to above, to a perspective that emphasises a concern for and an engagement with the whole class. Thus as one teacher explained, what is needed are strategies that *personalise* learning rather than individualise the lesson. An understanding of what these might involve can be gained from the study of practice, particularly the practice of classteachers in primary schools and subject teachers in secondary schools. As my awareness of the value of such studies has developed, so my interest in observing and trying to understand practice has grown. Put simply, I am arguing that a scrutiny of the practice of what we sometimes call 'ordinary teachers' provides the best starting point for understanding how classrooms can be made more inclusive.

My own observations of planning processes used by teachers who seem to be effective in responding to diversity suggest certain patterns that might be born in mind (Ainscow, 1999). Usually experienced teachers have developed a range of lesson formats that become their repertoire and from which they create arrangements that they judge to be appropriate to a particular purpose. Here they seem to take account of a range of interconnected factors, such as the subject to be taught, the age and experience of the class, the environmental conditions of the classroom, the available resources and their own mood, in order to adapt one of their usual lesson outlines. Such planning tends to be rather idiosyncratic and, indeed, often seems to be conducted at a largely intuitive level. In this sense it is unlike the rather rational procedure introduced to student teachers in that it consists, to a large degree, of an on-going process of designing and redesigning established patterns.

All of this may sound rather informal, even hit and miss, but observations indicate that for many experienced teachers it involves an intellectually demanding process of self-dialogue about how best to stimulate the learning of the class. Attempts to encourage and support further improvements in practice in this area must, therefore, take account of the nature of this complex approach to planning.

It is also essential to recognise that planning does not conclude when the lesson commences. Indeed, often the most significant decisions are those that are made as the lesson proceeds, through what I have characterised as a process of improvisation that is somewhat analogous to the practice of jazz musicians (Ainscow, 1996). In this respect one researcher compares the work of teachers to that of artisans (Huberman, 1993). An example will illustrate the point he makes. Faced with a leak in a sink an experienced plumber sets about the task in the certain knowledge that he (or she) has the way-with-all to solve the problem. Since he has fixed many similar leaks before he is confident that one of his usual responses will do the trick. Occasionally, however, he experiences a surprise – his usual repertoire proves to be inadequate. What does he do? Does he go on a course? Call for help? Read a manual? More likely he will 'tinker' with the problem pipes until he is able to invent a solution. In this way he adds a new way of working to his repertoire, which, of course, he can then take with him to the next leaking sink.

The suggestion is that this is something like the way in which teachers develop their practices. Arguably the key difference is that teaching is far less predictable than plumbing; so much so that during each lesson there are many 'surprises' to be dealt with and, therefore, far more possibilities for 'tinkering'. For example, there is the pupil who suddenly wants to tell the teacher about something interesting that happened the previous night; another who asks a question about the subject of the lesson that the teacher has never thought of; and, inevitably, those who lose interest or misbehave in some way. All of these unexpected events require an instant decision. Just like the plumber, the teacher has no opportunity to take advice. In this way new responses are trialled and, where they are found to be of value, added to the teacher's range of usual approaches. Through this form of 'planning in action' teachers learn how to create classroom arrangements that can be more effective in responding to individuals within their classes.

Vignette 2 – Ghana

A primary school in a rural district in West Africa. Here class sizes are much more manageable than those observed in the Chinese school. Typically there are 50 or so children in each class. On the other hand, the physical resources are noticeably poorer. Many of the children arrive in the morning carrying stools on their heads. It seems that for these children this is the equivalent of children in the West bringing a pen and a ruler from home. Apparently each evening the stools are taken home so that they can be used for domestic purposes. It may also be that some families are reluctant to leave them in school where they might be stolen, since the classrooms are open, having few walls. One of the teachers explains that his biggest problem is the lack of textbooks. In fact, for most lessons he only has one copy of the book and so frequently he has to write the text on the blackboard.

A surprising feature of the school from an English perspective is the presence of a number of pupils who are noticeably disabled. Further inquiries confirm that the headteacher assumes that it is his responsibility to admit all children in the district. 'Where else would they go?', he remarks. Apparently such examples of what Miles (1989) refers to as 'casual integration' can be found in a number of so-called developing countries, particularly in rural districts. Once again, however, there is the danger of jumping to simplistic conclusions and in so doing, perhaps, ignoring other factors that may well be influential in the context of Ghana? Can foreign visitors be sure of the conclusions they draw as they interpret their observations in the light of their previous experiences and existing frames of reference? Writing about the development of special education in Africa generally, Kisanji (1993) explains that there is evidence that the nature of provision is influenced by community perceptions of disabled children. He notes, for example, that in some countries disability is seen to arise as a result of the influence of factors such as witchcraft, curses or punishment from God, and anger of ancestral spirits. This being the case it may be that some children will be hidden away from sight by the family in order to avoid feelings of shame.

It seems, then, that attempts to reach out to all learners will be influenced by the ways in which student differences are perceived. At the risk of oversimplifying what is undoubtedly a complicated issue, two possibilities come to mind. On the one hand differences may be seen in a normative way. This means that students are defined in terms of certain taken-for-granted criteria of normality, against which some come to be seen as being abnormal. Within such an orientation those who do not fit into existing arrangements are seen as needing attention elsewhere or, at least, assimilating into the status quo. Alternatively, perceptions may be guided by a view that all students are unique, with their own experiences, interests and aptitudes. Associated with this second orientation is a belief that schools have to be developed in ways that can take advantage of this diversity which is, therefore, seen as a stimulus for learning.

Here some of the traditional practices of many Western countries, including my own, may have encouraged a particular type of response. Specifically the tradition has been to perceive some pupil's differences as requiring a technical intervention of some kind (Ainscow, 1998a; Heshusius, 1989; Iano, 1986). This leads to a concern with finding the 'right' response; that is different teaching methods or materials for pupils who do not respond to existing arrangements. Implicit in this formulation is a view that schools are rational organisations offering an appropriate range of opportunities; that those pupils who experience difficulties do so because of their limitations or disadvantages; and that *they*, therefore, are in need of some form of special intervention (Skrtic, 1991). It is my argument that through such assumptions, leading to a search for effective responses to those children perceived as being 'different', vast opportunities for developments in practice are overlooked.

I accept, of course, that it is important to identify useful and promising strategies. However, I believe that it is erroneous to assume that systematic replication of particular methods in themselves, will generate successful learning, especially when we are considering populations that historically have been marginalised or even excluded from schools. This over-emphasis on a search for 'quick-fix' methods often serves to obscure attention from more significant questions such as, why do we fail to teach some pupils successfully?

Consequently, it is necessary to shift from a narrow and mechanistic view of teaching to one that is broader in scope and takes into account wider contextual factors (Skrtic, 1991). In particular it is important to resist the temptation of what Bartolome (1994) refers to as the 'methods fetish' in order to create learning environments that are informed by both action and reflection. In this way, by freeing themselves from the uncritical adoption of so-called effective strategies, teachers can begin the reflective process which will allow them to recreate and reinvent teaching methods and materials, taking into account contextual realities that can either limit or expand possibilities for improvements in learning.

Teaching methods are neither devised nor implemented in a vacuum. Design, selection and use of particular teaching approaches and strategies arise from perceptions about learning and learners. In this respect even the most pedagogically advanced methods are likely to be ineffective in the hands of those who implicitly or explicitly subscribe to a belief system that regards some pupils, at best, as disadvantaged and in need of fixing, or, worse, as deficient and, therefore, beyond fixing.

Vignette 3 – Austria

This example is set in a very different context, that of a primary school in Austria where class sizes are small and resources luxurious by any standards. Like a number of other European countries Austria has been moving towards a greater emphasis on the integration of children described as having special needs. As a result of recent legislation, the number of pupils in an integration class is limited to 20: a maximum of 4 with disabilities and 16 others. A wide range of support personnel is also available to such classes. The school is in a small town in the eastern part of the country. There are 17 children sitting mainly in pairs at tables that are arranged informally, some pointing to the front of the room, others directed towards the centre of the room. One boy sits alone at a desk towards the rear of the room. There is thick snow outside and all the children wear slippers. The lesson is about Christmas and all the children have on their desks in front of them a worksheet that has been prepared on a computer by the class teacher. After a short introductory presentation by the teacher the children carry out tasks on the worksheet, chatting to one another as they work. Meanwhile, the boy sitting at the back of the room is being addressed by another teacher in a way that suggests that she perceives him as experiencing significant difficulties in understanding the spoken word. It seems that she is there to provide support to two pupils, who are seen as having special needs, one of whom is absent. This support teacher has her own desk, also located at the rear of the room. On this occasion she has designed a separate worksheet for the children she supports, one that deals with similar content but in a less demanding way.

This experience, like the earlier two, raises many questions. Certainly the boy in question is present in a regular classroom and, given his apparent learning difficulties, this would possibly not be the case in a number of other European countries. He also has the advantage of a large amount of individual attention of the sort for which parents in other countries have to fight. On the other hand his physical location at the back of the room suggests that he remains somewhat marginalised, not least because the support teacher tends to stand between him and the rest of the class as she addresses him. So is he integrated or not? Can we take lessons from this encounter that might inform the development of more inclusive practices in other parts of the world?

The approach to inclusion that I am suggesting involves 'a process of increasing the participation of pupils in, and reducing their exclusion from, school curricula, cultures and communities' (Booth & Ainscow, 1998). In this way the notions of inclusion and exclusion are linked together, because the process of increasing participation of pupils entails the reduction of pressures to exclude. This link also encourages us to look at the various constellations of pressures acting on different groups of pupils and acting on the same pupils from different sources.

Often the processes that lead to some pupils feeling excluded are subtle ones that occur within the classroom. So, for example, as I watched lessons in one English school recently I noted how 'throw away' remarks by teachers appeared to suggest that a low level of participation was anticipated. One teacher appeared to have targeted one boy as somebody who was unlikely to make much of a contribution: 'Grant, homework, I assume you didn't do it – you never do, despite letters home to your mum.' Similarly, an English teacher on calling the class register remarked, 'Amazingly we have Shula here.' It can be argued that such interactions help to reduce expectations and, in so doing, discourage participation and learning.

For these reasons, therefore, I am suggesting that yet another starting point for the development of practice within a school has to be with a close scrutiny of how existing practices may be acting as barriers to learning. With this in mind, the Centre for Educational Needs at the University of Manchester is currently carrying out a study in cooperation with the Centre for Studies on Inclusive Education, the aim of which is to develop, evaluate and disseminate an index that can be used to review and improve current practice with respect to inclusion and exclusion in schools (Ainscow, 1998b). The 'Index for Inclusive Schools' sets out to build on existing good practice within a school in order to encourage ways of working that will facilitate the learning of all pupils; minimise the need for exclusions; and support a school's efforts to widen its capacity for responding to diversity.

Vignette 4 – Laos

Laos is said to be one of the economically poorest countries in the world. Certainly this classroom has few material resources. The teacher spends the first 10 minutes of the lesson talking to the children about a topic to do with nature. His presentation is illustrated by a lovely drawing he has done which is pinned to the blackboard. Suddenly the children move into groups of three to five and begin discussions. My interpreter explains that the teacher has set a question for them to address arising from his initial presentation. It is apparent from the speed with which all of this happens that the class is used to working in this way. What is also rather noticeable is the change in the atmosphere. The body language and facial expressions suggest that these children who had previously seemed rather passive were now much more engaged in the agenda that the teacher had set.

A feature of lessons like this that seem to be effective in encouraging pupil participation is the way available resources, particularly human resources, are used to support learning. In particular I am referring to a range of resources that is available in all classrooms and yet is often poorly used, that of the pupils themselves. Within any classroom the pupils represent a rich source of experiences, inspiration, challenge and support which, if utilised, can inject an enormous supply of additional energy into the tasks and activities that are set. However, all of this is dependent upon the skills of the teacher in harnessing this energy. This is, in part, a matter of attitude, depending upon a recognition that pupils have the capacity to contribute to one another's learning; recognising also that, in fact, learning is to a large degree a social process. It can be facilitated by helping teachers to develop the skills necessary to organise classrooms that encourage this social process of learning. Here we can learn much from countries of the South where limitations of resources have led to a recognition of the potential of 'peer power', through the development of 'child-to-child' programmes (Hawes, 1988). The recent interest in co-operative group work in a number of Western countries has also led to the development of teaching specifications that have enormous potential to create richer learning environments (e.g., Johnson & Johnson, 1994).

For example, a history teacher in an English secondary school described to me how he had been using highly structured group learning methods in order to improve achievement in his lessons. He explained how he had planned one particular lesson around the idea of the 'jigsaw classroom' (Johnson & Johnson, 1994). Briefly, this involves the use of small 'expert groups' that each study separate texts. Then new groups are formed consisting of at least one member of each of the expert groups and they pool their material and ideas.

When he arrived at the classroom the teacher was surprised to find that the classroom assistant who was usually there to help communication with a deaf boy in the class was absent. Despite this he pressed ahead with his carefully planned lesson. His evaluation was that not only had the lesson been successful in facilitating the learning of the class but that also it had been the first occasion in which the deaf pupil had really seemed to be fully involved. Apparently the carefully planned social processes of his plan had opened up opportunities for the other pupils to overcome communication barriers that had previously left this individual rather marginalised during lessons.

There is strong evidence to suggest that where teachers are skilful at planning and managing the use of cooperative group learning activities as part of their repertoire, this can lead to improved outcomes in terms of academic, social and psychological development (Johnson & Johnson, 1994). Furthermore, they have also been found to be an effective means of supporting the participation of 'exceptional pupils', for example those who are new to a class; children from different cultural backgrounds; and those with disabilities. However, it is important to stress again the need for skill in orchestrating this type of classroom practice. Poorly managed group approaches usually involve considerable waste of time and, indeed, present many opportunities for increased disruption.

Vignette 5 – Nicaragua

A class of forty-five 12- and 13-year-olds. Standing at the front of the classroom, five students are holding large posters that summarise conclusions about the local history projects they have been doing in groups. They take it in turn to present their ideas to the rest of the class. The teacher, a young male, comments on their presentations. Sitting at the back of the room is an older woman who, from her dress, is a nun; later I am told she is the deputy headteacher. After a time she interrupts the discussion to suggest to the teacher that he was perhaps placing too much emphasis on the ways in which the groups had been working. More attention needed to be given, she argued, to the actual content of the group discussions. They discussed this point across the room and, eventually, the teacher drew some of the students into a consideration of the deputy head's point. There was no impression given that the teacher or the students found these discussions in any way disturbing. Indeed, they seemed to be rather taken for granted as being part of normal activities.

Later I was told that this type of interaction is part of the school's overall strategy for encouraging improvements in teaching. The experience reminded me of some of the ideas my colleagues and I have been exploring within our school improvement work here in England. Much of our early work in schools involved attempts to introduce particular policies and, in so doing, to strengthen the schools' capacity to handle change (Ainscow, Hopkins, Southworth, & West, 1994; Hopkins, Ainscow, & West, 1994). Gradually we recognised, however, that even where such initiatives were successful they did not necessarily lead to changes in classroom practice. Other studies have pointed to similar conclusions (e.g., Elmore, Peterson, & McCarthy, 1996). It seems that developments of practice, particularly amongst more experienced teachers, are unlikely to occur without some exposure to what teaching actually looks like when it is being done differently, and assistance from someone who can help teachers understand the difference between what they are doing and what they aspire to do (Elmore et al., 1996). It also seems that this sort of problem has to be solved at the individual level before it can be solved at the organisational level. Indeed, there is evidence that increasing collegiality without some more specific attention to change at the individual level can simply result in teachers coming together to reinforce existing practices rather than confronting the difficulties they face in different ways (Lipman, 1997).

Given these arguments it is important to look closely at schools where improvement efforts have led to changes in practice to see what lessons might be learned from their experiences. In stating that, however, I stress that I am not suggesting that our engagement with such a school will help to devise blueprints that can point the way forward for all schools. What I have learnt as a result of many years of working in schools, trying to support a variety of innovations, is that they are complex and idiosyncratic places. What seems to help development in one school may have no impact or even a negative effect in another. So, whilst we can, I believe, learn through vicarious experience, this learning has to be respected for its own qualities. Essentially it is a form of learning that provides a stimulus to reflect on existing experience and current understandings, rather than a means of providing prescriptions that can be transposed to other environments.

Recently I spent some time looking closely at one urban primary school in England where practices had been developed that have facilitated the participation of pupils with a range of disabilities and from a large variety of minority ethnic cultures (Ainscow, 1996). As a result of my observations and discussions in the school I noted the ways in which things were structured in order to facilitate teamwork. Indeed, enormous amounts of time were given over to this process. Staff met in their working teams many times during the school week for planning and in-service activities. Their formal planning processes seemed to have two main elements. First of all, there was the planning of the overall learning environment. This involved taking the programmes of study outlined in the National Curriculum and turning these into appropriate activities, materials and classroom arrangements. The second element was concerned with planning for individuals. This required the creation of individual curriculum plans for each child based upon the best available knowledge amongst the staff team working with the child.

This formal planning, carried out in a collaborative way within the teams, provided a basis for yet a third form of planning. Influenced by the ideas of Schon (1987), I characterised this as 'planning-in-action'. It is the decision-making that individual teachers in this particular school make throughout the school day in the light of their interpretations of the observations they are making. This has to take account of the decisions that individual children make as they engage with the opportunities that are provided. It is, I believe, guided by the knowledge, principles and sensitivities that members of staff develop as they take part in the more formal planning procedures that I have described. However, all of this takes place in what can best be described as a 'hothouse' atmosphere within which all staff are subject to the continual scrutiny of their colleagues (Hargreaves, 1995). In this context, planning-in-action becomes a demanding requirement on those who work in the school. Fortunately, the evidence indicates that these pressures are, to a degree, alleviated by the heavy emphasis placed on team work and collaboration which, in effect, provides on-going support and encouragement for individual members of staff. As one teacher noted, 'having to justify yourself to your colleagues helps you to think about what you do in the classroom.'

At the heart of the processes in schools like this, where changes in practice do occur in response to pupil feedback, is the development of a common language with which colleagues can talk to one another and indeed to themselves about detailed aspects of their practice. It seems that without such a language teachers find it very difficult to experiment with new possibilities. Frequently when I report to teachers what I have seen during their lessons they express surprise. It seems that much of what they do during the intensive encounters that occur is carried out at an automatic, intuitive level. Furthermore there is little time to stop and think. This is why having the opportunity to see colleagues at work is so crucial to attempts to develop practice. It is through shared experiences that colleagues can help one another to articulate what they currently do and define what they might like to do. It is also the means whereby taken-for-granted assumptions about particular groups of pupils can be subjected to mutual critique.

Vignette 6 – India

The school serves a poor community in New Delhi. Having watched a wonderful lesson in which the children engaged in a role play activity about families I ask a couple of the teachers how this had been planned. They explain how for the previous year or so the headteacher had instigated occasional Saturday morning meetings to discuss their work. Around the walls of the school are beautiful posters developed during these gatherings. It was these discussions, the teachers explained, that had stimulated them to try out different approaches to teaching. However, they explained that it was not just the meetings. They had also developed the idea of what they called 'partnership teaching', whereby they would occasionally have opportunities to work together in one another's classrooms. It was this, more than anything, they argued, that had stimulated their experimentation. I asked about how they found time given the numbers of children in each class. They explained that sometimes the headteacher would take a class to release a teacher to work with a colleague. Other times they might put two classes together but this usually meant that they would have to work outside since the classrooms were too crowded.

As can be seen, my interest in studying practice takes me beyond just a consideration of the work of individual teachers. Much of my research over the last few years convinces me of the importance of the school context in creating a climate within which more effective practices can be developed. The nature of such positive contexts can take many forms and, therefore, attempts at generalisations are very difficult. Nevertheless, the monitoring of developments in particular schools over time suggests certain patterns that are at least worthy of consideration.

There is now considerable evidence showing how norms of teaching are socially negotiated within the everyday context of schooling (e.g., Keddie, 1971; Rosenholtz, 1989; Talbert & McLaughlin, 1994). It seems that the culture of the workplace impacts upon how teachers see their work and, indeed, their pupils. However, the concept of culture is rather difficult to define. Schein (1985) suggests that it is about the deeper levels of basic assumptions and beliefs that are shared by members of an organisation, operating unconsciously to define an organisation's view of itself and its environment. It manifests itself in norms that suggest to people what they should do and how. In a similar way Hargreaves (1995) argues that school cultures can be seen as having a reality-defining function, enabling those within an institution to make sense of themselves, their actions and their environment. A current reality-defining function of culture, he suggests, is often a problem-solving function inherited from the past. In this way today's cultural form created to solve an emergent problem often becomes tomorrow's taken-for-granted recipe for dealing with matters shorn of their novelty.

Certainly my impression is that when schools are successful in moving their practice forward this tends to have a more general impact upon how teachers perceive themselves and their work. In this way the school begins to take on some of the features of what Senge (1990) calls a learning organisation, that is 'an organisation that is continually expanding its capacity to create its future' (p. 14). Or, to borrow a useful phrase from Rosenholtz (1989), it becomes 'a moving school', one that is continually seeking to develop and refine its responses to the challenges it meets.

It seems possible that as schools move in such directions the cultural changes that occur can also impact upon the ways in which teachers perceive pupils in their classes whose progress is a matter of concern. What may happen is that as the overall climate in a school improves, such children are gradually seen in a more positive light. Rather than simply presenting problems that have to be overcome or, possibly, referred elsewhere for separate attention, such pupils may be perceived as providing feedback on existing classroom arrangements. Indeed they may be seen as sources of understanding as to how these arrangements might be improved in ways that would be of benefit to all pupils.

It is important to recognise, of course, that the cultural changes necessary to achieve schools that are able to hear and respond to the 'hidden voices' are in many cases profound ones. Traditional school cultures, supported by rigid organisational arrangements, teacher isolation and high levels of specialisms amongst staff who are geared to predetermined tasks, are often in trouble when faced with unexpected circumstances. On the other hand, the presence of children who are not suited to the existing 'menu' of the school provides some encouragement to explore a more collegiate culture within which teachers are supported in experimenting with new teaching responses. In this way problem-solving activities may gradually become the reality-defining, taken-for-granted functions that are the culture of an inclusive school.

How, then, can schools be helped to organise themselves in ways that encourage the development of such a culture? Here I will draw on findings from a series of our school improvement studies (e.g., Ainscow et al., 1994; Ainscow & Southworth, 1996; Hopkins et al., 1994). All of these findings point to ways in which the restructuring of schools in order to support development activities can impact upon organisational culture and, in turn, the development of classroom practice.

By and large schools find it difficult to cope with change (Fullan, 1991). In this respect they face a double problem: they cannot remain as they now are if they are to respond to new challenges, but at the same time they also need to maintain some continuity between their present and their previous practices. There is, therefore, a tension between *development and maintenance*. The problem is that schools tend to generate organisational structures that predispose them towards one or the other. Schools (or parts of schools) at the development extreme may be so over-confident of their innovative capacities that they take on too much too quickly, thus damaging the quality of what already exists. On the other hand, schools at the maintenance extreme may either see little purpose in change or have a poor history of managing innovation. Moving practice forward, therefore, necessitates a careful balance of maintenance and development.

Attempting to move practice forward also leads to a further area of difficulty which is experienced at both an individual and organisational level. This involves forms of *turbulence* that arise as attempts are made to change the status quo. Turbulence may take a number of different forms, involving organisational, psychological, technical or micro-political dimensions. At its heart, however, it is frequently about the dissonance that occurs as experienced people struggle to make sense of new ideas.

From our experience of a range of English schools that have made tangible progress towards more inclusive policies we note the existence of certain arrangements that seem to be helpful in dealing with periods of turbulence. These provide structures for supporting teachers in exploring their ideas and ways of working whilst, at the same time, ensuring that maintenance arrangements are not sacrificed. More specifically they support the creation of a climate of risk-taking within which these explorations can take place. In attempting to make sense of such arrangements my colleagues and I have formulated a typology of six 'conditions' that seem to be a feature of moving schools. These are: effective leadership, not only by the headteacher but spread throughout the school; involvement of staff, students and community in school policies and decisions; a commitment to collaborative planning; coordination strategies, particularly in relation to the use of time; a policy for staff development that focuses on classroom practices; and, attention to the potential benefits of inquiry and reflection.

Drawing out the lessons

My hope is that this article will enhance an interest in the shaping effect on practice, of national and local policies, and cultural and linguistic histories. Too often there is a failure to describe the way practice is to be understood within its local and national context. This is all part of a positivist view of social science in which research in one country can be amalgamated with that of another. The problem is compounded by differences of meaning of terms. Often this leads to the presentation of deceptively misleading international statistics, as in the case, for example, of special education, where data are frequently used to imply that the actual numbers of disabled children are the problem, leading to an assumption that solutions must focus on prevention, cure, and taking steps to make these children as normal as possible. In this way the statistics distract our attention from the ways in which attitudes, policies and institutions marginalise certain groups of children (Stubbs, 1995).

All of this is in marked contrast to studies where there is a deliberate attempt to draw out nuances of meaning. An important contribution here is provided by the work of Susan Peters (1995). Speaking as both a disabled person and a professional, she argues that educational concepts are by no means self evident in that they are culturally and context bound. Similarly, Miles and Miles (1993) use their experiences in Pakistan to outline how concepts such as childhood differ substantially between cultures; and Stubbs (1995) reports accounts that indicate that the concept of childhood does not even exist under Lesotho law. Rather, the population is divided into 'majors and minors', the latter being unmarried males and females who are not heads of families. As a result Lesothan primary school pupils may be in their late teens or even early twenties, having spent their younger years herding animals.

Such careful analyses of differences in perspective, context and meaning enhance rather than reduce the contribution that an examination of unfamiliar contexts can make to local practice, though they invalidate any attempt at simple imitation (Fuller & Clarke, 1994). As I have suggested, the power of comparison involves using the stimulus of more exotic environments to reconsider thinking and practice in familiar settings. In this way accounts of practice in other countries can present some of the opportunities afforded to travellers, particularly if they provide sufficient information to make practice transparent.

Bearing these concerns very much in mind, this article has attempted to illustrate how an engagement with less familiar contexts can stimulate a process of critical reflection, thus enabling previous experiences to be reconsidered and new possibilities for school improvement to be recognised. In my own case this has drawn attention to a series of ideas that I am currently using to guide my school improvement efforts (Ainscow, 1999). For the reasons I have outlined, these do not represent a recipe that can be applied in any context. Rather they might be seen as a series of possible 'ingredients' that may also be of use to others who are interested in the development of schools that can become more effective in reaching out to all learners.

Acknowledgements

I would like to thank the many colleagues around the world who have contributed to the development of ideas in this article. Particular thanks to my close colleagues Tony Booth, Alan Dyson, Michael Fielding, David Hargreaves, David Hopkins, Susan Hart, Lena Saleh, Judy Sebba, Geoff Southworth and Mel West, all of whom helped me to see possibilities previously overlooked.

An earlier version of this article was presented as a keynote address at the International Congress for School Effectiveness and Improvement, Manchester, January, 1998.

References

Ainscow, M. (1994). *Special needs in the classroom: A teacher education guide*. London: Jessica Kingsley/UNESCO.

Ainscow, M. (1996). The development of inclusive practices in an English primary school: Constraints and influences. Paper presented at the Annual Meeting of the American Educational Research Association, New York.

Ainscow, M. (1998a). Would it work in theory? Arguments for practitioner research and theorising in the special needs field. In C. Clark, A. Dyson, & A. Millward (Eds.), *Theorising Special Education* (pp. 63–77). London: Routledge.

Ainscow, M. (1998b). Developing links between special needs and school improvement. *Support for Learning, 13*, 70–75.

Ainscow, M. (1999). *Understanding the development of inclusive schools*. London: Falmer.

Ainscow, M., Hopkins, D., Southworth, G., & West, M. (1994). *Creating the conditions for school improvement*. London: Fulton.

Ainscow, M., & Southworth, G. (1996). School improvement: A study of the roles of leaders and external consultants. *School Effectiveness and School Improvement, 7*, 229–251.

Ainscow, M., & Tweddle, D.A. (1979). *Preventing classroom failure*. London: Fulton.

Ainscow, M., & Tweddle, D.A. (1984). *Early learning skills analysis*. London: Fulton.

Bartolome, L.I. (1994). Beyond the methods fetish: Towards a humanizing pedagogy. *Harvard Education Review, 64*(2), 173–194.

Booth, T., & Ainscow, M. (Eds.). (1998). *From them to us: An international study of inclusion in education*. London: Routledge.

Delamont, S. (1992). *Fieldwork in educational settings*. London: Falmer.

Elmore, R.F., Peterson, P.L., & McCarthy, S.J. (1996). *Restructuring in the classroom: Teaching, learning and school organisation*. San Francisco: Jossey-Bass.

Fullan, M. (1991). *The new meaning of educational change*. London: Cassell.

Fuller, B., & Clarke, P. (1994). Raising school effects while ignoring culture? Local conditions and the influence of classroom tools, rules and pedagogy. *Review of Educational Research, 64*(1), 119–157.

Hargreaves, D.H. (1995). School culture, school effectiveness and school improvement. *School Effectiveness and School Improvement, 6*, 23–46.

Hawes, H. (1988). *Child-to-child: Another path to learning*. Hamburg: UNESCO Institute for Education.

Heshusius, L. (1989). The Newtonian mechanistic paradigm, special education and contours of alternatives. *Journal of Learning Disabilities, 22*(7), 403–421.

Hopkins, D., Ainscow, M., & West, M. (1994). *School improvement in an era of change*. London: Cassell.

Huberman, M. (1993). The model of the independent artisan in teachers' professional relations. In J.W. Little & M.W. McLaughlin (Eds.), *Teachers' work: Individuals, colleagues and contexts* (pp. 11–50). New York: Teachers' College Press.

Iano, R.P. (1986). The study and development of teaching: With implications for the advancement of special education. *Remedial and Special Education, 7*(5), 50–61.

Johnson, D.W., & Johnson, R.T. (1994). *Learning together and alone*. Boston: Allyn and Bacon.

Keddie, N. (1971). Classroom knowledge. In M. F. D. Young (Ed.), *Knowledge and control* (pp. 132–172). London: Macmillan.

Kisanji, J. (1993). Special education in Africa. In P. Mittler, R. Brouillette, & D. Harris (Eds.), *World yearbook of education: Special education* (pp. 158–172). London: Kogan Page.

Lipman, P. (1997). Restructuring in context: A case study of teacher participation and the dynamics of ideology, race and power. *American Educational Research Journal, 34*(1), 3–37.

Miles, M. (1989). The role of special education in information based rehabilitation. *International Journal of Special Education, 4*(2), 111–118.

Miles M., & Miles, C. (1993). Education and disability in cross-cultural perspective: Pakistan. In S. J. Peters (Ed.), *Education and disability in cross-cultural perspective*. (pp. 53–64). London: Garland.

Peters, S.J. (1995). Disabling baggage: Changing the education research terrain. In P. Clough & L. Barton (Eds.), *Making difficulties: Research and the construction of SEN* (pp. 19–38). Paul Chapman.

Rozenholtz, S. (1989). *Teachers' workplace: The social organisation of schools*. New York: Longman.

Schein, E. (1985). *Organisational culture and leadership*. San Francisco: Jossey-Bass.

Schon, D.A. (1987). *Educating the reflective practitioner*. San Francisco: Jossey-Bass.

Senge, P.M. (1990). *The fifth discipline: The art and practice of the learning organisation*. London: Century.

Skrtic, T.M. (1991). Students with special educational needs: Artifacts of the traditional curriculum. In M. Ainscow (Ed.), *Effective Schools for All* (pp. 20–42). London: Fulton.

Stubbs, S. (1995). *The Lesotho National Integrated Education Programme: A case study of implementation*. MEd thesis, University of Cambridge.

Talbert, J.E., & McLaughlin, M.W. (1994). Teacher professionalism in local school contexts. *American Journal of Education, 102*, 120–159.

CHAPTER 7

THE INDEX FOR INCLUSION

Ainscow, M. (2002) Using research to encourage the development of inclusive practices. In P. Farrell and M. Ainscow (eds.), *Making special education inclusive*. London: Fulton

Introduction

This chapter illustrates the way my own work attempts to contribute *directly* to thinking and practice in relation to inclusive developments in schools. It illustrates how this requires me to work closely with educational practitioners. Acting as a critical friend, I see my task as helping them to learn from their experiences and, in so doing, to point to patterns and examples of practice that might be instructive to others who are addressing similar agendas. In this sense my aim is not to propose recipes that can be applied universally but, rather, to suggest ingredients that might be worthy of further consideration within particular contexts. The analysis of what is involved in the development of inclusive schools has pointed to the connections between *policies, practices and cultures*. It has also shown that such developments involve an essentially social process within which those within a school learn how to live with differences and, indeed, learn from differences. This orientation underpins the 'Index for Inclusion', a school development instrument that was developed as a result of a collaborative inquiry project. It involved a team of teachers, parents, governors, researchers and a representative of disability groups, with wide experience of attempts to develop more inclusive ways of working. The chapter illustrates the use of the Index in different countries.

The field that has been known as special education or, more recently, special needs education, is involved in a period of considerable uncertainty. In particular, the emphasis on inclusive education that is now evident in many countries challenges special needs practitioners to reconsider their own thinking and practice. This context of uncertainty provides the special education field with new opportunities for continuing its historical purpose of representing the interests of those learners who become marginalised within existing educational arrangements. At the same time, many of the assumptions that have guided special education practice are, in my view, no longer relevant to the task (Ainscow 1999).

A brief look at history reminds us that in the nineteenth century special educators in this country argued for and helped develop provision for children and young people who were excluded from educational plans. Only much later did this provision become adopted by national governments and local authorities. It is also worth remembering that it was only as recently as 1971 that one group of learners, those categorised as 'having severe learning difficulties', was deemed to be even worthy of education.

Similarly, provision for children experiencing difficulties within mainstream schools grew as a result of a gradual recognition that some pupils were marginalised within and, in some instances, excluded from existing arrangements for providing education. As this provision developed during the latter part of the twentieth century, there was also increased emphasis on notions of integration, as special educators explored ways of supporting previously segregated groups in order that they could find a place in mainstream schools.

It can be argued, therefore, that the current emphasis on inclusive education is but a further step along this historical road. It is, however, a major step, in that the aim is to transform the mainstream in ways that will increase its capacity for responding to all learners. And, of course, such a project requires the participation of many stakeholders in ways that challenge much of the status quo.

My own work attempts to contribute *directly* to thinking and practice in relation to such developments, at the classroom, school and systems levels. For many years I have worked closely with educational practitioners, in this country and overseas, as they have attempted to move towards more inclusive ways of working (Ainscow 1999). Acting as a critical friend, I see my task as helping them to learn from their experiences and, in so doing, to point to patterns and examples of practice that might be instructive to others who are addressing similar agendas. In this sense my aim is not to propose recipes that can be applied universally but rather to suggest ingredients that might be worthy of further consideration within particular contexts.

In this chapter I illustrate the nature and potential of this approach, focusing on research that is concerned with the development of inclusive practices in schools. An important issue within this work focuses on the identification of factors that help to generate a momentum for change. In other words, what are the 'levers', or incentives, that are most effective in changing existing practice?

Collaborative inquiry

My research has involved a search for forms of inquiry that have the flexibility to deal with the uniqueness of particular educational occurrences and contexts; that allow social organisations, such as schools and classrooms, to be understood from the perspectives of different participants, not least children themselves; and that encourage stakeholders to investigate their own situations and practices with a view to bringing about improvements (e.g. Ainscow, Hargreaves and Hopkins 1995; Ainscow, Barrs and Martin 1998; Ainscow 1999). It has involved the development of a form of action research, an approach to inquiry that in its original form sought to use the experimental approach of social science with programmes of social action in response to social problems (Lewin 1946). More recently action research has come to refer to a process of inquiry undertaken by practitioners in their own workplaces. Here the aim is to improve practice and understanding through a combination of systematic reflection and strategic innovation (Kemmis and McTaggart 1982).

Action research is sometimes dismissed as not being 'proper' research by researchers working within more traditional research paradigms. Others, while acknowledging it as a worthwhile activity for practitioners, are anxious that claims for the validity of findings should not be made beyond the particular contexts in which the investigation is carried out (e.g. Hammersley 1992).

Proponents of action research, on the other hand, have responded to these criticisms by rejecting the conceptions of rigour imposed by traditional social science, and by mounting their own counter-criticism of the methodology and assumptions about knowledge upon which these conceptions of rigour are dependent (e.g. Winter 1989). They claim, for example, that the notions of rigour to which both positivist and interpretative researchers aspire are oppressive, restrictive and prescriptive, designed to perpetuate the hierarchical divisions between the producers and users of research (Iano 1986).

In devising a suitable methodology I have been aware of others who have attempted to follow a similar path. For example, Poplin and Weeres (1992) report a study called 'Voices From the Inside', carried out by students, teachers, administrators and parents in four schools. Here the aim was 'to create strategies that allowed everyone at the school site to speak and insured that everyone be heard'. Thus the research allowed all participants to be both the researchers and, at the same time, the subjects of the research. Since the study began with the assumption that academics had already 'misnamed the problems of schooling', the roles of outsiders had to be rethought so that those on the inside could come to know and articulate the problems they experience. The use of this process was reported to have led to many changes in the schools, although it was also found to be extremely time-consuming.

In developing my own approach I have been keen to pursue a similar, participatory orientation, along the lines of what has been defined as 'collaborative inquiry' (Reason and Rowan 1981; Reason 1988). Such approaches emphasise the value of group processes and the use of varied methods of recording. Here my own thinking has been influenced by experience of using collaborative inquiry methods in English schools (e.g. Ainscow, Hopkins, Southworth and West 1994; Ainscow *et al.* 1995; Ainscow *et al.* 1998), and approaches developed for use in countries of the South, such as 'participatory rural appraisal' (PRA), as developed by Chambers (1992) and refined by Stubbs (1995) and Ainscow (1999) for use in educational contexts.

From these earlier experiences I have found it useful to take account of four principles as I seek to involve colleagues in the research process. These are that it should:

- be of direct help to people in the contexts involved;
- demonstrate rigour and trustworthiness such that the findings are worthy of wider attention;
- contribute to the development of policies and practices elsewhere;
- inform the thinking of the 'outsider' research team.

As a result of earlier experiences of using this orientation I have become clearer about both the advantages and, of course, the difficulties involved in carrying out such a study.

In terms of advantages, from the point of view of the research contexts, there was strong evidence that those involved often found the process to be both informative and stimulating. Specifically they found that the need to engage with multiple interpretations of events forced them to think much more deeply about their own perceptions. Furthermore, exploring ways of valuing points of view that they might more usually ignore, or even oppose, also seemed to stimulate them to consider previously ignored possibilities for the development of thinking and practice. At the same time they found the process to be affirming, giving them an opportunity to celebrate many achievements in their working contexts.

Turning to difficulties, these earlier experiences highlight some of the problems that can occur when practitioners take on the task of carrying out what might be referred to as 'insider' research. We found, for example, that despite a commitment to reporting a wide range of opinions, some accounts revealed little evidence of alternative voices, thus giving the impression of what seemed to be most unlikely levels of consensus. Sometimes there was very little evidence presented from children and parents, gaps that seem particularly regrettable when I read the findings of the Poplin and Weeres study, reported earlier. Finally there remain some concerns about confidentiality. Specifically, as the accounts are read by more people in a particular context, can we be sure that the views of certain individuals will remain anonymous?

Overall, then, the methodology described here can be characterised as essentially a social process. It requires a newly formed group of stakeholders within a particular context to engage in a search for a common agenda to guide their enquiries and, at much the same time, a series of struggles to establish ways of working that enable them to collect and find meaning in different types of information. They also have to find ways of reporting their conclusions. All of this has to be carried out in a way that will be of direct benefit to those in the contexts under consideration. In so doing the members of the group are exposed to manifestations of one another's perspectives and assumptions. At its best all of this provides wonderful opportunities for developing new understandings. However, such possibilities can only be utilised if potential social, cultural, linguistic and micro-political barriers are overcome.

It seems to me that such an orientation helps to overcome the traditional gap between research and practice. As Robinson (1998) argues, it has generally been assumed that this gap has resulted from inadequate dissemination strategies. The implication being that educational research *does* speak to issues of practice, if only the right people would listen. She suggests an alternative explanation, pointing out that research findings may well continue to be ignored, regardless of how well they are communicated, because they bypass the ways in which practitioners formulate the problems they face and the constraints within which they have to work. As I have noted, participatory research is fraught with difficulties. On the other hand, the potential benefits are enormous, not least in that the understandings gained can have an immediate impact on the development of thinking and practice.

In what follows I use examples of collaborative inquiry from our Manchester research programme in order to illustrate the nature of the process and the types of outcomes that are generated. As I have suggested, these studies do not set out to develop understandings that can tell practitioners what to do. Rather they provide frameworks that practitioners can use to reflect on their own contexts and their own ways of working in order to formulate relevant ways of moving their practices forward.

Developing more inclusive schools

In recent years my colleagues and I have been involved in a series of collaborative research activities in relation to the development of more inclusive schools (e.g. Ainscow *et al.* 1994; Hopkins, Ainscow and West 1994; Ainscow 1999; Ainscow, Booth and Dyson 2001). In essence this work seeks to address the question, how do we create educational contexts that 'reach out to all learners'?

This research indicates that schools that do make progress in this respect do so by developing conditions within which every member of the school community is encouraged to be a learner. All of this helps to throw further light on what is meant by inclusion in education. It suggests that it involves the creation of a school culture that encourages a preoccupation with the development of ways of working that attempt to reduce barriers to learner participation. In this sense, moves towards greater inclusion can be seen as a significant contribution to overall school improvement.

Our analysis of what is involved in the development of inclusive schools has pointed to the connections between *policies, practices and cultures*. It has also shown that such developments involve an essentially social process within which those within a school learn how to live with differences and, indeed, learn from differences. This orientation underpins the 'Index for Inclusion', a school development instrument that was developed as a result of a collaborative inquiry project (Booth and Ainscow 2000). This project was carried out on behalf of the Centre for Studies on Inclusive Education, over a three-year period. It involved a team of teachers, parents, governors, researchers and a representative of disability groups, with wide experience of attempts to develop more inclusive ways of working. They carried out two phases of action research, in partnership with a total of 22 schools, in six different LEAs.

The Index involves schools in a process of inclusive school development, drawing on the views of staff, governors, pupils, parents/carers and other community members. It is concerned with improving educational attainments through inclusive practices and thus provides an attempt to redress a balance in those schools that have concentrated on raising attainment at the expense of the development of a supportive school community for staff and pupils.

The process of working with the Index is itself designed to contribute to the inclusive development of schools. It encourages staff to share and build on their existing knowledge about what impedes learning and participation. It assists them in a detailed examination of the possibilities for increasing learning and participation in all aspects of their school for all their pupils. This is not seen as an additional initiative for schools but rather as a systematic way of engaging in school development planning, setting priorities for change, implementing developments and reviewing progress.

It is important to understand that the view of inclusion presented in the Index is a broad one, which goes well beyond many of the formulations that have been previously used. It is concerned with minimising barriers to learning and participation, whoever experiences them and wherever they are located within the cultures, policies and practices of a school. It involves an emphasis on mobilising under-used resources within staff, pupils, governors, parents and other members of the school's communities. In this context diversity is seen as a rich resource for supporting the development of teaching and learning.

The Index materials guide the exploration of the school along three interconnected dimensions:

- 'creating inclusive cultures'
- 'producing inclusive policies'
- 'evolving inclusive practices'.

They cover all aspects of school life, from collaboration and values, to induction and learning support policies, to classroom practices and resource planning.

The dimensions have been chosen to direct thinking about school change and represent relatively distinct areas of school activity. In the past, too little attention has been given to the potential of school cultures to support or undermine developments in teaching and learning. It is through inclusive school cultures that those changes in policies and practices, achieved by a school community, can be sustained and passed on to new staff and students (Ainscow 1999). However, our experience indicates that sustainable development depends on change occurring in all the dimensions.

The materials contain a branching tree structure allowing progressively more detailed examination of all aspects of the school. The three dimensions are expressed in terms of 45 indicators and the meaning of each of these is clarified by a series of questions. The indicators are statements of inclusive aspiration against which existing arrangements in a school can be compared in order to set priorities for development. The detailed questions ensure that the materials can challenge the thinking in any school, whatever its current state of development. Together, the dimensions, indicators and questions provide a progressively more detailed map to guide the exploration of the current position of a school and to plot future possibilities.

Using the index

Considerable work has already gone on in relation to the use of the Index for school development purposes, including current projects that are going on in countries as diverse as Australia, Brazil, India, Norway, Portugal, Romania and South Africa. Nevertheless, there is still much more that needs to be done in order that we can develop deeper understandings as to how this complex and challenging document can be used effectively within different contexts.

Some examples provide illustrations of how the Index is being used in relation to particular circumstances. They illustrate how those within schools are choosing to select relevant areas of the Index and adjust the materials, including its wording, in order to make them appropriate. So, for example, the coordinating group in one English primary school carried out a survey of the views of pupils, staff and parents, using the indicators as the basis of rating scales. From the analysis of their data it was decided to concentrate on the development of aspects of classroom practice, focusing specifically on the following indicators:

- Lessons are responsive to pupil diversity.
- Lessons are made accessible to all pupils.
- Children are actively involved in their own learning.
- Children's differences are used as a resource for teaching and learning.

Over the period of a school year efforts were made to use these indicators during lesson planning. Eventually it was decided that something more specific was needed in order to stimulate developments in practice. The school was able to mobilise some extra resources so that pairs of teachers could be freed to work in one another's classrooms. Using the four indicators as the basis of a mutual observation schedule, the teachers made a record of what they saw as 'golden moments'. These were examples of classroom interactions that illustrated how the indicators could be turned into action.

Eventually, after every teacher in the school had been involved in these observation activities, a staff meeting was held during which each pair of colleagues talked about their experiences. A document was produced as a result of these discussions which summarised what had been learnt. It focused on issues such as the use of questions and how to respond to disruptive behaviour. In commenting on the document, however, the head teacher explained that it was a poor record of what had been discussed during the meeting. She commented, 'You would have to have been there to appreciate the richness of the professional learning that was going on.' It seems that through shared experiences within classrooms the teachers were stimulated to reflect on one another's styles of teaching. The story suggests that groups of teachers can use elements of the Index to focus investigations into their practice in ways that enable discussions to focus on important details that are often overlooked.

In a large urban secondary school in Portugal a team of eight teachers, including the principal, also carried out surveys of staff, students and parents. As a result of analysing their findings they recommended to their colleagues that efforts needed to be made to address what they saw as three interconnected priority areas in order to make their school more inclusive. These areas were summarised as follows:

Priority 1: During lessons students are encouraged to work together.
1.1 Do lesson activities require students to collaborate?
1.2 Do teachers ask students to discuss the content of lessons?
1.3 Do teachers help students to learn the skills of working together?

Priority 2: Students support one another.
2.1 Do students talk to each other about their learning tasks?
2.2 Do students feel that their classmates help them?
2.3 Are any students ignored by other members of their class?

Priority 3: Staff development policies support teachers in responding to student diversity.
3.1 Are there meetings where teachers can share their ideas?
3.2 Do teachers have opportunities to observe one another's practices?
3.3 Do teachers feel that they are supported in dealing with difficulties?

Over a period of a year the whole school used these indicators and questions as a framework for moving practice forward. They also provided a means of collecting more detailed evidence through mutual classroom observations, including group analysis of video recordings.

Possibly the most powerful strategy they used involved a series of group interviews with groups of students. These were carried out by an advisory team from outside the school. The school coordinating team spent a whole day analysing transcripts from these interviews. They went to use extracts as the basis of staff development activities in the school. Some extracts were also used on posters that were displayed in the staff room. These invited teachers to write their reactions to comments made by the students.

An adapted version of the Index is being used in Romania, in the context of a Unicef-funded project, 'The Development of Inclusive School Environments in the Community'. Here considerable use has been made of visual recording systems in order to encourage participatory inquiry processes in reviewing processes and outcomes of action research in the schools. These approaches have worked well in terms of helping colleagues within networks of schools to share their experiences and perceptions, and to summarise their learning.

Each school has focused on a small number of indicators chosen by their coordinating groups (e.g. 'Students are valued equally'; 'The school has an efficient policy for decreasing student absences'). They have been encouraged to collect and analyse various forms of evidence in relation to these indicators. For example, the idea of 'mindmaps' was used to help school groups to carry out an audit of evidence in order to review progress. The technique was demonstrated on the board and groups were asked to be creative in finding visual ways of illustrating their ideas. Each indicator was written in a circle on a poster. These were spaced apart. Groups then noted any evidence they had that suggested progress towards this indicator. No guidance was given as to what was meant by 'evidence' so as to encourage creative thinking. It was suggested that the relative 'strength' of evidence should be indicated in some way and that efforts should be made to illustrate how particular evidence might relate to more than one indicator. The posters were displayed on the wall and colleagues were asked to go and look at the work of other schools. Here it was emphasised that schools might borrow ideas from one another. Finally, school groups discussed the following questions:

- 'What other evidence do we need to evaluate our work?'
- 'Do we need to change our indicators for the next phase of action research?'

The Romanian schools also used 'timelines' in order to construct both group and individual records of processes used in their schools (Ainscow *et al.* 1995). During the first stage, groups designed a 12-month timeline on a large sheet of paper, noting key events in their schools. This was introduced using an example drawn on the board. Once the overall timeline was designed, each group member was asked to draw a summary version of their own on a small piece of paper. Then pairs of participants were formed from different schools. Before the individuals talked to each other they were asked to record their personal 'highs and lows' along their school timeline. Again, this was illustrated with an example on the board. No talking was allowed while individuals completed this step. Then each person talked to their partner about their personal experience and feelings during the year. It was stressed that active listening was required, only interrupting if it was necessary to seek clarification. Each person had five minutes to explain their timeline. The next stage involved school groups in entering their 'highs and lows' lines on the school poster version of the timeline. Here attention was placed on the need to recognise that school learning involved personal learning. It was also noted that differences can be a useful resource for facilitating deeper understanding of change processes. The final stage in the activity involved the school groups in summarising the outcomes of these processes by completing two sentences, as follows: 'We make progress when . . .', and 'Things are difficult when . . .' During a plenary session each school group read out their two completed sentences.

Learning from difference

In using these types of approaches in schools we have noted that they can lead to a degree of collusion among those involved, such that unwelcome ideas or evidence may be overlooked. Consequently, within our research network

'Understanding and Developing Inclusive Practices in Schools', we have been working with partner schools in order to explore ways of introducing a more critical dimension to the process (Ainscow *et al.* 2001). In particular we have been considering what types of 'levers' can be used to encourage those within a school to question their practices and, indeed, the assumptions behind these practices. So far a number of approaches are proving to be promising. These are:

- mutual observation of classroom practices, followed by structured discussion of what happened;
- group discussion of a video recording of one colleague teaching;
- discussion of statistical evidence regarding test results, attendance registers or exclusion records;
- data from interviews with pupils;
- staff development exercises based on case study material or interview data.

Through these approaches we are seeking to encourage discussions within the schools that are both supportive and yet challenging. In particular, we are trying to 'make the familiar unfamiliar' in order to stimulate self-questioning, creativity and action.

So, for example, in a number of the schools our discussions have challenged existing assumptions as to the nature of educational difficulties experienced by students. Specifically, we have been questioning the assumption that some students' characteristics are such that they require a different form of teaching from that offered to the majority of students. Such an orientation leads to a concern with finding the 'right' response, i.e. different teaching methods or materials for pupils who do not respond to existing arrangements. Implicit in this formulation is a view that schools are rational organisations offering an appropriate range of opportunities; that those students who experience difficulties do so because of their limitations or disadvantages; and that they, therefore, are in need of some form of special intervention (Skrtic 1991). Our concern is that through such assumptions, leading to a search for effective responses to those children perceived as being 'different', vast opportunities for developments in practice may be overlooked.

In introducing a critical perspective to the process of action research we recognise that schools, like other social institutions, are influenced by perceptions of socio-economic status, race, language and gender. This being the case, we feel that it is essential to question how such perceptions influence classroom interactions. In this way we set out to reveal and challenge deeply entrenched deficit views of 'difference', which define certain types of students as 'lacking something' (Trent, Artiles and Englert 1998). Specifically we believe that it is necessary to be vigilant in scrutinising how deficit assumptions may be influencing perceptions of certain students.

As Bartolome (1994) explains, teaching methods are neither devised nor implemented in a vacuum. Design, selection and use of particular teaching approaches and strategies arise from perceptions about learning and learners. In this respect even the most pedagogically advanced methods are likely to be ineffective in the hands of those who implicitly or explicitly subscribe to a belief system that regards some students, at best, as disadvantaged and in need of fixing, or, worse, as deficient and, therefore, beyond fixing.

We should add that all of this is challenging to the thinking of everybody within the Network, not least those of us from universities. Our assumptions are also challenged; we too have to find ways of dealing with and, hopefully, learning from one another's perspectives. We are also finding that we have a lot more learning to do in order to develop our skills in challenging our teacher colleagues in a supportive way.

Final thoughts

No doubt some who read this chapter will be disappointed that despite all the years of efforts, involving so many people, few definitive conclusions are reached. Surely, they might argue, educational research has a responsibility to provide practitioners with direct answers to the problems they face in their day-to-day work. My own view is that it is through such assumptions and expectations that possibilities for using research more effectively are masked. What I have tried to illustrate in this chapter is that by working together practitioners and researchers can use their different skills and perspectives in order to collect and engage with evidence in ways that can have a direct and immediate impact on thinking and practice in the field. Furthermore, I argue that such an approach is particularly important in relation to the development of inclusive practices. As we have seen, this is essentially about those within a given context learning how to work together in order to identify and address barriers to participation and learning experienced by members of their communities. Logic suggests that this requires the use of collaborative inquiry.

So then, returning to the question that I raised at the start of this chapter, what are the implications for those of us who have made our careers in the field of special education? Do we have a role in the development of inclusive practice and, if so, what might it be? I believe that we do have an important contribution to make and it is one that requires us to become more centrally involved in the development of the education system. This is what I meant when I referred to the 'major step' towards the idea of inclusive practice.

Within this formulation the field of special education has a particular tradition which is of importance. If I think of the best special education contexts I have known, including some excellent special schools that I have and do work with, they always seem to involve a particular way of working. In essence this means the creation of a problem-solving culture within which those involved learn how to use one another's experiences and resources in order to invent better ways of overcoming barriers to learning. My view is that this is the most important gift that the special education community can offer to the movement towards more inclusive forms of education.

Note

Part of the research reported in this chapter is funded by Award L139 25 1001 and, as such, is part of the Teaching and Learning Research Programme of the Economic and Social Research Council. Further information about the research can be found at: http://man.ac.uk/include

References

Ainscow, M. (1999) *Understanding the Development of Inclusive Schools*. London: Falmer Press.

Ainscow, M., Barrs, D. and Martin, J. (1998) 'Taking school improvement into the classroom'. Paper presented at the International Conference on School Effectiveness and Improvement, Manchester, UK, January 1998.

Ainscow, M., Booth, T. and Dyson, A. (2001) 'Understanding and developing inclusive practices in schools'. Paper presented at the American Educational Research Association Conference, Seattle, USA, April.

Ainscow, M., Hargreaves, D. H. and Hopkins, D. (1995) 'Mapping the process of change in schools: the development of six new research techniques', *Evaluation and Research in Education* 9(2), 75–89.

Ainscow, M., Hopkins, D., Southworth, G. and West, M. (1994) *Creating the Conditions for School Improvement*. London: David Fulton Publishers.

Bartolome, L. I. (1994) 'Beyond the methods fetish: towards a humanizing pedagogy', *Harvard Education Review* 64(2), 173–94.

Booth, T. and Ainscow, M. (2000) *The Index for Inclusion*. Bristol: Centre for Studies on Inclusive Education.

Chambers, R. (1992) *Rural Appraisal: Rapid, Relaxed and Participatory*. Brighton: Institute of Development Studies.

Hammersley, M. (1992) *What's Wrong with Ethnography?* London: Routledge.

Hopkins, D., Ainscow, M. and West, M. (1994) *School Improvement in an Era of Change*. London: Cassell.

Iano, R. P. (1986) 'The study and development of teaching: With implications for the advancement of special education', *Remedial and Special Education* 7(5), 50–61.

Kemmis, S. and McTaggart, R. (1982) *The Action Research Planner*. Victoria: Deakin University Press.

Lewin, K. (1946) 'Action research and minority problems', *Journal of Social Issues* 2, 34–6.

Poplin, M. and Weeres, J. (1992) *Voices from the Inside: A Report on Schooling from Inside the Classroom*. Claremont, CA: Institute for Education in Transformation.

Reason, P. (1988) *Human Inquiry in Action: Developments in New Paradigm Research*. London: Sage.

Reason, P. and Rowan, J. (1981) *Human Inquiry: A Sourcebook for New Paradigm Research*. Chichester: Wiley.

Robinson, V. M. J. (1998) 'Methodology and the research-practice gap', *Educational Researcher* 27, 17–26.

Skrtic, T. M. (1991) 'Students with special educational needs: Artifacts of the traditional curriculum', in M. Ainscow (ed.), *Effective Schools for All*. London: David Fulton Publishers.

Stubbs, S. (1995) 'The Lesotho National Integrated Education Programme: A Case Study of Implementation'. MEd Thesis, University of Cambridge.

Trent, S. C., Artiles, A. J. and Englert, C. S. (1998) 'From deficit thinking to social constructivism: a review of theory, research and practice in special education', *Review of Research in Education* 23, 277–307.

Winter, R. (1989) *Learning from Experience: Principles and Practice in Action Research*. London: Falmer Press.

CHAPTER 8

USING COLLABORATIVE INQUIRY

Ainscow, M., Booth, T. and Dyson, A. (2006) Inclusion and the standards agenda: negotiating policy pressures in England. *International Journal of Inclusive Education* 10(4–5), 295–308

Introduction

Informed by the experience of developing and using the Index for Inclusion, my research was increasingly using collaborative forms of action research as the methodology to stimulate the development of inclusive practices in schools. This paper presents the findings of a three-year study that illustrates what this involves. In particular, it shows how an engagement with evidence collected within schools can stimulate experimentation with new, more inclusive ways of working. Particularly powerful techniques in this respect involve the use of mutual observation, sometimes through video recordings, and evidence collected from students about teaching and learning arrangements within a school. I argue that, under certain conditions, such approaches provide *interruptions* that stimulate self-questioning, creativity and action. In so doing, they sometimes lead to a reframing of perceived problems that, in turn, draw attention to overlooked possibilities for addressing barriers to participation and learning. The English national 'standards agenda' was a major force shaping the directions taken by schools within the study. While it constrained inclusive development, it also provided a particular focus and led schools to consider issues that might otherwise have been overlooked.

Inclusion and the standards agenda: negotiating policy pressures in England

In recent years, inclusion has become a 'global agenda' (Pijl *et al.*, 1997). International organizations and national governments have committed themselves to the inclusive development of education at least at the level of rhetoric (for a recent review, see Mitchell, 2005). In England, this has taken the form of a subscription to the principles of the Salamanca Statement (UNESCO, 1994) and the promulgation of a range of guidance documents to schools (including the *Index for Inclusion* by Booth & Ainscow, 2002; Booth *et al.*, 2000), which imply not only that schools should educate increasing numbers of students with disabilities, but that they should concern themselves with increasing the participation and broad educational achievements of *all* groups of learners who have historically been marginalized. At the same time, the Government in

England, as in many other countries, has been pursuing a second—and arguably more powerful—agenda. This has focused on what has come to be called 'the standards agenda', an approach to educational reforms which seeks to 'drive up' standards of attainment, including workforce skill levels and ultimately national competitiveness in a globalized economy (Wolf, 2002; Lipman, 2004). The vigour with which this second agenda has been pursued has led some commentators to describe England as a 'laboratory' for educational reform (Finkelstein & Grubb, 2000).

Whilst in principle higher standards of attainment arc entirely compatible with inclusive school and educational system development, the standards agenda has concentrated on a narrow view of attainment as evidenced by national literacy, numeracy and science tests. Further this agenda is intimately linked to other aspects of policy: the marketization of education; a directive relationship between government and schools that potentially bypasses the participation of teachers in their own work and disengages schools from their local communities; and a regime of target setting and inspection, creating an 'accountability culture' (O'Neill, 2002) to force up standards. It is not surprising, therefore, that many studies of the English education scene have detected significant tensions as schools attempt both to become more inclusive and to respond to these features of the standards agenda (e.g. Booth *et al.*, 1997, 1998, Rouse & Florian, 1997, Bines, 1999, Thomas & Dwyfor Davies, 1999, Thomas & Loxley, 2001, Audit Commission, 2002). Since schools are held to account for the attainments of their students and are required to make themselves attractive to families who are most able to exercise choice of school for their children, low-attaining students, students who demand high levels of attention and resource and students who are seen not to conform to school and classroom behavioural norms become unattractive to many schools. This may go some way to explaining why progress towards the inclusion of students in mainstream schools from special schools continues to be painfully slow (Norwich, 2002), why schools remain ambivalent about the desirability of the inclusion agenda (Ofsted, 2004), why levels of disciplinary exclusion remain problematic (National Statistics, 2005) and why, as the standards agenda has intensified, there is evidence of a growing 'backlash' against inclusion amongst both politicians and educationalists (Cameron, 2005; Warnock, 2005).

Unpromising as this context may seem from the point of view of inclusion, it is nonetheless, we suggest, able to add in important ways to our knowledge of inclusive developments in schools. Although we now have a substantial and growing set of accounts of schools which are seen to move in the direction of greater inclusion, the literature on such schools is skewed in particular ways. A recent review of that literature (Dyson *et al.*, 2002, 2004) concluded that the majority of accounts were uncritical and superficial and, moreover, tended to report atypical schools which were seen to be 'particularly inclusive' often in terms of a narrow meaning of inclusion as concerned with students categorized as 'having special educational needs'. The existence of such schools was commonly attributed to the impact of forceful head teachers who were able to engender a powerful commitment to inclusion and/or to the unexplained existence of an inclusively oriented 'culture' within the school. Although more subtle and probing studies exist (e.g. Skidmore, 1999, 2004; Dyson & Millward, 2000; Benjamin, 2002), it remains true that we know relatively little about how unexceptional schools, struggling with the demands of seemingly unsympathetic policy environments, can develop inclusive cultures policies and practices.

Such knowledge is important if we are to move to a position where inclusive approaches are the rule rather than the exception in national education systems. The remainder of this paper, therefore, reports a study aimed at contributing to our understanding of these issues.

Developing inclusion with schools

The study, which took place from 1999 to 2003, was called 'Understanding and Developing Inclusive Practices in Schools' and was one of four national research networks funded as the first phase of the Economic and Social Research Council's Teaching and Learning Research Programme. The Network involved small teams of researchers from Manchester, Newcastle and Canterbury Christ Church Universities engaging with three local education authorities (LEAs) and groups of schools within them. The schools were invited to participate by their LEAs. Although a small number of the schools, particularly from a London Borough, saw themselves explicitly as moving towards inclusion, most did not express their orientation in these terms when they joined the project. The schools were therefore, typical of many English schools in simply wishing to 'do their best' by all of their students within the constraints of their situations.

Participating schools were invited to explore ways of developing inclusion in their own contexts in collaboration with university researchers. Rather than providing the schools with a detailed, prescriptive model of inclusion or seeking to direct their development, we suggested that inclusion might be defined in three overlapping ways: as reducing barriers to learning and participation for all students; as increasing the capacity of schools to respond to the diversity of students in their local communities in ways that treat them all as of equal value; and the putting of inclusive values into action in education and society. We saw inclusive values, as elaborated by Booth (2005), as concerned with issues of equity, participation, rights, community, compassion, respect for diversity and sustainability. These three perspectives all move away from a narrow view of inclusion as concerned only with disabled students or those categorized as 'having special educational needs'. Inclusion becomes not an aspect of education or a policy or set of policies for education but a principled way of viewing the development of education and society. This was consistent with the approach in the *Index for Inclusion* (Booth & Ainscow, 2002; Booth *et al.*, 2000). Attention was also drawn to the inclusion guidance produced by Ofsted, the national schools' inspectorate, in response to the McPherson Inquiry into the police investigation into the racist murder of a Black school student (McPherson of Cluny, 1999; Ofsted, 2000).

Within this broad definition, we invited schools to review and develop their own practices. The university teams and LEA staff acted as partners to the schools as they undertook research to identify the barriers to learning and participation experienced by their students and to find ways to reduce those barriers. We engaged with them in a process of 'critical collaborative action research' (Macpherson *et al.*, 1998). Our role was to offer schools technical and practical support in undertaking their own investigations, and to draw on our knowledge and experience of inclusion and school development to enter into dialogue about their assumptions and decision-making. Nevertheless, decisions about the direction to be taken by each school remained firmly in its own hands.

The research process varied from site to site in response to local priorities and possibilities. In most cases, the school established a small project team, including the head teacher, and identified a focus for its work. This took the form of an aspect of practice and provision that it wished to review and develop. Evidence was gathered by the schools and by the university researchers, with meetings between the two teams to exchange information and explore its implications. These processes of dialogue were extended by meetings of schools within each LEA and by four national conferences for school, LEA and university teams from across the Network.

Some cameos of school concerns

Other publications present our findings more fully than is possible here (e.g. Ainscow, 2002; Ainscow *et al.*, 2003, 2004, 2006). For the purposes of this paper, we wish to concentrate on some of the ideas we called upon to make sense of the complex ways in which schools responded to participation in the Network. However, some cameos provide a flavour of this complexity:

Cameo 1: Enhancing participation in learning. In an urban high school, university researchers participated with a group of teachers interested in developing their approaches to teaching and learning. The initial discussions of this group gave an insight into the culture of teaching and learning in the school, and into some of the barriers to learning experienced by students. The group agreed jointly to evaluate video recordings of their lessons in order to challenge assumptions about certain groups of students, and conducted interviews with students about their experience in school. The videos encouraged reflection on thinking and practice, and the sharing of ideas about how colleagues could help one another to make their lessons more participative. For example, the recording of a modern language lesson focused the group's attention on issues of pace and support for participation, whilst discussion of the strengths of a science lesson indicated the value of students generating their own questions to deepen their understanding of subject content. In each case, it was evident that the discussions contained moments of uncertainty for other teachers who were confronted with examples of practice that challenged their own assumptions. This was potentially threatening, particularly because the staff were also involved in carrying out the requirements set by a recent inspection.

Cameo 2: Shifting assumptions. In a primary school, students identified as having 'moderate learning difficulties' were taught separately from their peers for substantial parts of the school day in a 'resource base'. Teachers expressed the view that this was the only way to educate this group. In a series of meetings with teachers the university team raised questions about the implications of such practice for the way students were valued within the school. This provoked a debate about the inevitability of current practice, which coincided with some work by an advisory teacher on developing group work and problem-solving approaches in classrooms. At the same time as teachers began to integrate these approaches into their teaching, they also began to accept students categorized as 'having learning difficulties' into their classrooms and found, to their surprise, that the children could achieve far more than the teachers had supposed. By the end of the project, these students were spending the majority of their time in mainstream classes.

Cameo 3: Broadening horizons. Visits between schools were part of the developmental process built into the work of the Network. Schools from two of the LEAs, where the approach to inclusion was low-key and pragmatic, were much influenced by visits hosted by a third LEA with an explicit commitment to developing inclusive cultures, policies and practices. One of the most cautious of the visiting head teachers, initially saw the host schools' commitment to inclusion as containing more rhetoric than substance and had been sceptical of the value of Network. Nonetheless, he found his own fundamental assumptions called into question. He felt that the narrow focus of the project in his own school might have been given a greater sense of direction by being viewed within the framework of a broad set of principles. He commented, 'I wonder now whether we started at the 'wrong end'? I feel we focused very much on improving learning [practice]. Maybe we should have taken a broader view like [the host authority]'.

Cameo 4: Failing to construct a dialogue. In another of the secondary schools in the Network, with a relatively advantaged intake, teachers expressed concern about a small minority of students who did not attend regularly, or whose behaviour was seen as disruptive. Its response was to establish a Learning Support Unit (LSU) which they thought would tackle the problems presented by these students, so that teaching elsewhere could continue undisturbed. When university researchers interviewed some of these students, it became clear that they felt themselves to be alienated by the culture of the school, as evidenced in teaching approaches, relations between staff and students and what they saw as favouritism shown to students from more advantaged backgrounds. When these findings were fed back to the school team, however, the head teacher made it clear that he did not wish these issues to be pursued and that the only form of evaluation he was interested in was a quantitative analysis of reductions in absence and disciplinary exclusions from the school, both subject to government concern. He did not wish to consider the possibility that there might be limitations in dealing with disruption by seeing it as only contained within a few problematic students.

Cameo 5: Trusting in experience. One of the primary schools felt the need to respond to the emphasis on literacy in national policy and, in particular, to the concern about standards of writing. It took the consciously bold step (especially in the context of external school inspections, a prescriptive National Literacy Strategy and the public accountability of schools for 'results') of significantly reducing the amount of time devoted to the explicit teaching of literacy skills and replacing it with group based language-development activities arising out of shared experiences. As the head explained: 'We're going down the route of looking at our teaching strategies, and how children learn, and the skills they need to learn, as learners—not the curriculum bit, but the actual learning techniques and strategies they have. Because that tends to be very limited with our children. And we actually want to broaden their range of learning strategies, their thinking skills. We want to create more opportunities of first hand experience, the discussion, practising these thinking skills'.

Making sense of developments in schools

These cameos illustrate the extent to which development in each school had its unique features. However, they also point to some common patterns which underpinned these differences:

Standards and inclusion

In broad terms, what we saw in participating schools was neither the crushing of inclusion by the standards agenda, nor the rejection of the standards agenda in favour of a radical, inclusive alternative. Certainly, many teachers were concerned about the impacts on their work of the standards agenda and some were committed to view of inclusion which they saw as standing in contradiction to it. However, in most schools the two agendas remained intertwined. On the one hand, therefore, we were often aware of the ways in which the standards agenda narrowed and subverted the schools' commitment to inclusion. Invited to develop inclusive practices, for instance, many schools (like those in cameos 1, 2 and 5) focused immediately on questions of attainment, seeing such a focus as *the* way to be concerned about the achievement of students. Similarly, the school in cameo 4 saw its Learning Support Unit as *the* way of maintaining problematic students in the school. Potentially more inclusive approaches were, in these contexts, commonly passed over.

On the other hand, the focus on attainment in these schools evidently prompted teachers to examine issues in relation to the achievements and participation of hitherto marginalized groups that they had previously overlooked. Likewise, the concern with inclusion tended to shape the way the school responded to the imperative to raise standards. This was particularly evident when, towards the end of the Network's life, we asked teachers from schools in the three LEAs to consider what outcomes their work had generated for students. Although they saw themselves as producing the 'observables' of raised attainment, improved attendance and so on, they did not find that this was possible simply through officially sanctioned practice, such as the national Numeracy and Literacy Strategies. Many of the children they taught did not, they argued, learn effectively from such practices. Through the Network and its associated research and development processes, they had attempted to make sense of why this was and to explore different kinds of practice that might be more successful. They felt, they told us, that they had had to develop the responsiveness of their schools to the characteristics of these students in ways which promoted students' engagement with learning and their sense of themselves as learners. While these actions would eventually be reflected in the measures for which they were held accountable by government, such holistic developments were, they suggested, valuable 'for [their] own sake', not simply as a means to an end.

There was, therefore, a mutual colonization of the standards and inclusion agendas in schools' work. If the former in many ways constrained and subverted the latter, there were also ways in which it was itself shaped by inclusive values and offered a focus for the realization of those values in practice.

Communities of practice

In trying to make sense of the relationship between these external imperatives and the processes of change in schools, we were struck by a strong sense in each of the schools of 'the way we do things here'. We observed the possibilities for change emerging from the hours of formal as well as informal discussions and sharing of experiences over hurriedly taken lunches. One teacher, for instance, described the way she hoped to adopt and share a new set of practices:

Hopefully I'll be able to use . . . a lot of these ideas really, and see them working. And then hopefully, other people on the staff as well will be able to see them working, and I'll get to say to them, 'try doing this—it does work'. Not, 'try doing this—I've read it in a book' so to speak. Because we can all read things in a book and think, oh well, it will work there, or work there, but it won't work here. Well if we can get it to work here, that proves that it does work, people are more willing to take on board ideas I think, when they've seen evidence that it's been working.

To understand this sense of 'the way we do things here', we found it helpful to draw upon the idea of 'communities of practice', as developed by Wenger (1998). Wenger gives a particular meaning to practice in this context, in terms of those things that individuals within a community do to further a set of shared goals, drawing on available resources. This includes not only the engagement with their formal tasks but how they make it through the day, commiserating about the pressures and constraints within which they have to operate. Such communities develop group loyalties, concerns about accountability to each other and value the views and resources developed by the group more than those presented by 'outsiders'. Staff teams in our study can be seen as communities of practice, intimately bound up with their own particular norms, values, beliefs and assumptions. As Wenger put it:

> Communities of practice are not intrinsically beneficial or harmful. . . . Yet they are a force to be reckoned with, for better or for worse. As a locus of engagement in action, interpersonal relationships, shared knowledge, and negotiation of enterprises, such communities hold the key to real transformation—the kind that has real effect on people's lives. . . . The influence of other forces (e.g. the control of an institution or the authority of an individual) are no less important, but . . . they are mediated by the communities in which their meanings are negotiated in practice.
>
> (Wenger, 1998, p. 85)

This 'negotiation of meaning' is, we suggest, precisely what we saw as schools in our study made their own sense of the tensions and contradictions between the standards and inclusion agendas. It explains, amongst other things, why they did not simply submit to the imperatives of the former. It also explains how they could and did change. Communities of practice are stable only to an extent. Because they are engaged continually in the joint construction of meaning, established meanings—and hence established understandings and practices—can be called into question. New imperatives, new circumstances, new community members and new views from established members constantly enter into this exchange. We see in cameo 3, for instance, how something as apparently straightforward as a visit to an LEA where things are done differently can provoke a significant rethinking of 'the way we do things here'. On the other hand, change does not follow immediately upon each and every external intervention, whether from national policies or from the sorts of dialogues in which we were engaged with the schools. Nor is there any guarantee that change will be in an inclusive direction. The closing down of negotiation that took place in the school in cameo 4 is an example of this. The question for us, therefore, is why change occurs in some cases but not others and how and why that change can become inclusive.

Change and development

We found two sources of ideas helpful in attempting to understand this question. These were Argyris & Schön's (1978, 1996) distinction between single and double-loop learning, and Skrtic's (1991a, b, 1995) distinction between bureaucracies and adhocracies, together with his notion of the recognition of 'anomalies' as the catalyst for the transition from one to the other. Argyris and Schön describe the way that organizations 'learn', to different extents and levels. 'Single-loop learning' involves improvements to existing practice without any fundamental reconsideration of the assumptions on which that practice is based. 'Double-loop learning' involves responding to questions about the underlying aims of practice and the implicit theories which underpin it. Skrtic, who is specifically concerned with how schools respond to student diversity, also proposes a fundamental distinction in the way organizations solve problems. He argues that bureaucratic organizations deal with problems by creating different sub-units and specialisms to contain them whilst practice elsewhere in the organization remains undisturbed. However, 'adhocratic' organizations see such problems as an opportunity to rethink their existing practices in fundamental ways. Skrtic argues that bureaucratic organizations can become adhocratic if enough of their members recognize 'anomalies' in existing practice.

Both of these accounts, therefore, make a distinction between processes which allow 'the way we do things here' to be maintained and those which call for a reorientation which, in Wenger's terms, require new meanings to be negotiated. Both accounts, moreover, see the key factor which differentiates these processes as being the recognition of some 'anomaly' which disturbs and cannot be accommodated within existing frames of reference. We would argue that we witnessed the appearance of many such disturbances—the visit to the 'inclusive' LEA in cameo 3, the close examination of classroom practice in cameo 1, the intervention of the advisory teacher and the raising of questions about the role of the 'unit' in cameo 2, for instance. In each of these cases, there was sufficient disturbance of existing frames of reference for established practices to be problematized and, ultimately, changed. Insofar as those established practices were less inclusive than the new ones which replaced them, the process of disturbance offers a mechanism whereby schools can develop in more inclusive directions.

However, it is also clear that different schools respond to disturbances in different ways. The school in cameo 4, for instance, responded to the presence of students who were not accommodated within existing practices and to our challenges about the nature of those practices in a way that we saw as limiting its learning. As Skrtic predicts, it created a sub-unit to deal with its problem so that established practice could continue undisturbed. By contrast, the school in cameo 5 faced a situation common to many primary schools at the time—the pressure to follow the requirements of the National Literacy Strategy as the means to increase student attainments. While many schools responded to this situation instrumentally (Tymms, 2004; Statistics Commission, 2005), this school recognized an anomaly which problematized its existing practice and led to significant changes in that practice. The implication of these two cases would seem to be that anomalies do not simply *present* themselves, but have to be *recognized* as such.

One factor which differentiates these schools' response to anomalies is the attitude of the two headteachers—one willing to open questions up, one seeking to close them down. We might see the former as a manifestation of what Lambert et al (1995) call 'constructivist' leadership which can engage colleagues in what we have earlier characterized as shared meaning-making. We were also able to identify other factors which support the recognition of anomalies. The exploration of evidence and alternative perspectives arising from different assumptions was particularly important. These included our encouragement to schools to reflect on evidence which they had asked us to collect, as well as our attempts to construct dialogues and the part played by visits between schools and LEAs in the Network. Particularly powerful in stimulating a rethinking of practice was the work of the advisory teacher, mentioned in cameo 2, who took over teachers' classes and involved them in group-work, thinking-skills and problem-solving activities. The impact was, in the words of one teacher, 'revolutionary in school'. Another teacher explained why:

> I also think that all the alternative things, all the things that she's given me, are—any teacher could execute. But, I think they need to see you do it. You see it's all right her giving us the book of alternative forms of recording, but like a lot of teachers, if she'd just given me it and I hadn't had knowledge of what she meant, I might have thought 'oh yes very good', and pushed it in a drawer and never picked it up again. I think you actually need to see her doing it with the children.

Here again we are in the territory of communities of practice, where processes of meaning-making in a particular community and in the local context of that community are at work; 'what we see working here' is more important than what others tell us to do. However, in this case, established patterns of practice and meaning are disturbed sufficiently for distinctly new patterns to begin to emerge.

Development and inclusive development

We believe, therefore, that we can explain how and why some of the participating schools engaged in the sorts of more fundamental rethinking characterized by 'development' and why some did not. However, this still does not explain why development should be in a more inclusive direction. Why, in other words, should schools not respond to anomalies by rethinking their understandings and reconstituting their practices in less rather than more inclusive ways?

The answer to this question clearly lies partly in the attitudes and values of those who make up the community/ies of practice in the school and, in particular, of those head teachers who can exercise positional power and other forms of influence on those attitudes and values. In this respect it may be seen as encouraging that, when the rather aggressive standards-based policies are mediated by those communities of practice, the outcomes often have distinctly inclusive components. However, it seems to us that it is not necessary to rely entirely on the appearance of inclusively oriented communities of practice in schools. Instead, there is something in the business of teaching, in these schools at least, which exerts a pull—albeit one that is easily counteracted—in an inclusive direction.

It is perhaps so obvious that it is easy to overlook the fact that the sorts of disturbances which are evident in the cameos set out above and, indeed, in all of our work with participating schools, arose frequently from what we might call a 'lack of fit' between the established practices of the school and the characteristics and responses of the school's students. In each case, what concerned teachers was that some or all of their students were not responding to those practices—in particular, that they were not learning or behaving—in the way that they wished. In some cases, this was a negative realization in the sense that attainments were low (as in cameo 5) or behaviour was unacceptable to teachers (as in cameo 4). In other cases, the realization was more positive, as in cameo 1, where the teachers realized that their students had more potential for learning than they had previously acknowledged. Teaching, it would seem, involves repeated encounters with student diversity and whilst the option of constraining that diversity to fit established routines is ever-present, there is always the potential for that diversity to create disturbances within those routines.

This brings us back to the intertwining of the standards and inclusion agendas. We noted above that the focus on attainment may cause schools to identify issues that were previously overlooked. More specifically, our cameos indicate that the standards agenda directs schools to look carefully at the impact of their practices on students. Certainly, the gaze which is required is a narrow one, concerned almost exclusively with whether or not students are acquiring tightly defined skills and items of knowledge. Nonetheless, we see (for instance in cameo 1) how the question of whether students are achieving in this narrow sense can lead on to further questions of why they fail to learn and how they might learn. In other words, it opens up the possibility of a fuller engagement with the actual, diverse characteristics of those students and to this extent can be co-opted to support an inclusive orientation.

Some implications for the development of inclusion

This paper has suggested that a study located in the English context might increase one's understanding of how non-exceptional schools working in an unpromising policy environment develop—or fail to develop—inclusive practices. We have argued that, in fact, the relationship between the standards and inclusion agendas as they intersect in schools is not the sort of simple opposition that some other studies might lead us to expect. Such external agendas are mediated by the norms and values of the communities of practice within schools and they therefore become part of a dialogue whose outcomes can be more rather than less inclusive. We have further suggested that the process of meaning-making within communities of practice is dynamic. Change is always possible and we have outlined some of the circumstances under which change is more likely to become development and development is more likely to become inclusive.

Our argument has drawn upon established theoretical perspectives. However, we think that these perspectives have something to offer to those concerned with the development of inclusion in schools. We noted above how the existing literature focuses on atypical 'inclusive schools' with exceptional leaders standing out against the generality of non-inclusive approaches. We might add that other parts of the inclusion literature—including some of our own work (Booth, 1995; Booth *et al.*, 1998; Dyson & Millward, 2000)—have been engaged in what Corbett & Slee (2000) characterize as 'cultural vigilantism', in the sense of a constant scrutiny of policy and practice to identify and expose any compromise of inclusive principles. We continue to believe that both these kinds of study are important to the further development of inclusion in education. However, our work suggests that the possibilities for inclusive development are inherent in all schools and are realized in often quite unexceptional and unpromising circumstances. We make no claims, of course, that the developments in our schools were anything other than deeply ambiguous. However, their example suggests that some more widespread move in an inclusive direction is possible and that such a move might result from supporting the incremental development of schools rather than from a radical transformation of understandings and practices.

Moreover, the role of national policy emerges from our study in something of a new light. From the ground-breaking work of Fulcher (1989) onwards, there has been a powerful tradition in the inclusion literature of scepticism about the capacity of policy to create inclusive systems, either because the policy itself is ambiguous and contradictory, or because it is 'captured' by non-inclusive interests as it interacts with the system as a whole. Certainly, some of our own work can be located within this critical tradition (Booth, 1996; Booth *et al.*, 1997; Dyson & Slee, 2001; Dyson, 2005). However, what our study shows is the way in which schools can engage with unfavourable policy imperatives to produce outcomes that are by no means inevitably non-inclusive. Moreover, current English education policy seems to contain at least some elements that promote these outcomes, both in its own somewhat equivocal commitment to inclusion and in those aspects of the standards agenda which focus attention on hitherto marginalized learners. It is, therefore, possible to imagine how strengthening and extending these elements might support further inclusive developments in schools.

The ideas that more inclusive approaches can emerge out of internal school dynamics and that it is possible to intervene in these dynamics opens up new possibilities for national policy. The marketization of education is expanding in influence around the world. A radical shift in national policies, however desirable, is unlikely until, perhaps, the contradictions become even more evident between market-driven ideologies and the desire of large sections of the population for an equitable high quality education in decent neighbourhoods for all children. We suggest, therefore, that the efforts of those concerned to put inclusive values into action cannot be directed only at the radical critique of educational policies, important as such critiques will continue to be. Rather, we must also concentrate on trying to expand the inclusive aspects of current policy and support teachers to take greater control over their own development. In reframing ideas about achievements so that they are underpinned by inclusive values we can get past the unhelpful idea that notions of standards, broadly defined and re-appropriated, and inclusion are in opposition to each other. We suggest that such measured attempts to take control of a 'comprehensive' agenda for the development of participation and learning in schools continues to offer hope of moving beyond the emergence of a few exceptional schools towards the gradual building of a school system that is more genuinely and sustainably inclusive.

Acknowledgements

This research was funded by Award No. L139 25 1001 and as such is part of the Teaching and Learning Research Programme of the UK's Economic and Social Research Council. The members of the three university research teams in the Network were as follows: Canterbury: Tony Booth, Roy Smith and Carrie Weston; Manchester: Mel Ainscow, Peter Farrell, Jo Frankham and Andy Howes; and Newcastle: Alan Dyson, Alan Millward and Francis Gallannaugh. An earlier version of the paper was presented at the annual meeting of the American Educational Research Association, Chicago, IL, USA, April 2003.

References

Ainscow, M. (2002) Using research to encourage the development of inclusive practices, in: P. Farrell & M. Ainscow (Eds), *Making special education inclusive* (London, Fulton).

Ainscow, M., Booth, T. & Dyson, A. (2004) Understanding and developing inclusive practices in schools: a collaborative action research network, *International Journal of Inclusive Education*, 8(2), 125–139.

Ainscow, M., Booth, T. & Dyson, A. (2006) *Improving schools, developing inclusion* (London, Routledge) (in press).

Ainscow, M., Howes, A. J., Farrell, P. & Frankham, J. (2003) Making sense of the development of inclusive practices, *European Journal of Special Needs Education*, 18(2), 227–242.

Argyris, C. & Schön, D. A. (1978) *Organizational learning* (Reading, MA, Addison-Wesley).

Argyris, C. & Schön, D. A. (1996) *Organizational learning II: Theory, method and practice* (Reading, MA, Addison-Wesley).

Audit Commission (2002) *Special educational needs: a mainstream issue* (London, Audit Commission).

Benjamin, S. (2002) *The micropolitics of inclusive education: an ethnography* (Buckingham, Open University Press).

Bines, H. (1999) Inclusive standards? Current developments in policy for special educational needs in England and Wales, *Oxford Review of Education*, 26(1), 21–31.

Booth, T. (1995) Mapping inclusion and exclusion: concepts for all?, in: C. Clark, A. Dyson & A. Millward (Eds), *Towards inclusive schools?* (London, David Fulton).

Booth, T. (1996) A perspective on inclusion from England, *Cambridge Journal of Education*, 26(1), 87–99.

Booth, T. (2005) Keeping the future alive: putting inclusive values into action, *Forum for Promoting 3–19 Comprehensive Education*, 47(2+3), 151–158.

Booth, T. & Ainscow, M. (2002) *Index for inclusion: developing learning and participation in schools* (2nd edn) (Bristol, Centre for Studies on Inclusive Education).

Booth, T., Ainscow, M., Black-Hawkins, K., Vaughan, M. & Shaw, L. (2000) *Index for inclusion: developing learning and participation in schools* (Bristol, Centre for Studies on Inclusive Education).

Booth, T., Ainscow, M. & Dyson, A. (1997) Understanding inclusion and exclusion in the English competitive education system, *International Journal of Inclusive Education*, 1(4), 337–354.

Booth, T., Ainscow, M. & Dyson, A. (1998) England: inclusion and exclusion in a competitive system, in: T. Booth & M. Ainscow (Eds), *From them to us: an international study of inclusion in education* (London, Routledge).

Cameron, D. (2005) Speech to the Oxford Conference in Education, 2 August 2005 (David Cameron. Available online at: http://www.davidcameronmp.com/articles/viewnews.php?id=abf255ae1514859dd9a97c69dda1a35e (accessed on 3 August 2005).

Corbett, J. & Slee, R. (2000) An international conversation on inclusive education, in: F. Armstrong, D. Armstrong & L. Barton (Eds), *Inclusive education: policy contexts and comparative perspectives* (London, David Fulton).

Dyson, A. (2005) Philosophy, politics and economics? The story of inclusive education in England, in: D. Mitchell (Ed.), *Contextualising inclusive education: evaluating old and new international perspectives* (London, Routledge).

Dyson, A. & Millward, A. (2000) *Schools and special needs: issues of innovation and inclusion* (London, Paul Chapman).

Dyson, A. & Slee, R. (2001) Special needs education from Warnock to Salamanca: the triumph of liberalism, in: J. Furlong & R. Phillips (Eds), *Education, reform and the state: twenty-five years of politics, policy and practice* (London, RoutledgeFalmer).

Dyson, A., Howes, A. & Roberts, B. (2002) A systematic review of the effectiveness of school-level actions for promoting participation by all students (EPPI-Centre Review, version 1.1), in: *Research evidence in education library* (London, EPPI-Centre, Social Science Research Unit, Institute of Education).

Dyson, A., Howes, A. & Roberts, B. (2004) What do we really know about inclusive schools? A systematic review of the research evidence, in: D. Mitchell (Ed.), *Special educational needs and inclusive education: major themes in education* (London, RoutledgeFalmer).

Finkelstein, N. D. & Grubb, W. N. (2000) Making sense of education and training markets: lessons from England, *American Educational Research Journal*, 37(3), 601–631.

Fulcher, G. (1989) *Disabling policies? A comparative approach to education policy and disability* (Lewes, Falmer).

Lambert, L., Walker, D., Zimmerman, D. P., Cooper, J. E., Lambert, M. D., Gardner, M. E. & Ford Slack, P. J. (1995) *The Constructivist Leader* (New York, Teachers College Press).

Lipman, P. (2004) *High stakes education* (London, RoutledgeFalmer).

Macpherson, I., Aspland, T., Elliott, B., Proudford, C., Shaw, L. & Thurlow, G. (1998) A journey into learning partnership: a university and state system working together for curriculum change, in: B. Atweh, S. Kemmis & P. Weeks (Eds), *Action research in practice* (London, Routledge).

McPherson of Cluny, Sir W. (Chair) (1999) *The Stephen Lawrence Inquiry*. Cm 4262-I (London, Stationery Office).

Mitchell, D. (Ed.) (2005) *Contextualising inclusive education: evaluating old and new international perspectives* (London, Routledge).

National Statistics (2005) *Permanent and fixed period exclusions from schools and exclusion appeals in England, 2003/04* (London, DfES).

Norwich, B. (2002) *LEA inclusion trends in England 1997–2001, statistics on special school placements and pupils with statements in special schools* (Bristol, CSIE).

O'Neill, O. (2002) Called to account. Lecture 3, Reith Lectures 2002 (London, BBC). Available online at: http://www.bbc.co.uk/radio4/reith2002/lecture3.shtml (accessed on 20 September 2005).

Ofsted (2000) *Evaluating educational inclusion* (London, Ofsted).

Ofsted (2004) *Special educational needs and disability: towards inclusive schools* (London, Ofsted).

Pijl, S. J., Meijer, C. J. W. & Hegarty, S. (Eds) (1997) *Inclusive education: a global agenda* (London, Routledge).

Rouse, M. & Florian, L. (1997) Inclusive education in the market-place, *International Journal of Inclusive Education*, 1(4), 323–336.

Skidmore, D. (1999) Discourses of learning difficulty and the conditions of school development, *Educational Review*, 51(1), 17–28.

Skidmore, D. (2004) *Inclusion: the dynamic of school development* (Buckingham, Open University Press).

Skrtic, T. M. (1991a) *Behind special education: a critical analysis of professional culture and school organization* (Denver, CO, Love).

Skrtic, T. M. (1991b) The special education paradox: equity as the way to excellence, *Harvard Educational Review*, 61(2), 148–206.

Skrtic, T. M. (Ed.) (1995) *Disability and democracy: reconstructing (special) education for postmodernity* (New York, NY, Teachers College Press).

Statistics Commission (2005) *Measuring standards in English primary schools.* Report No. 23 (London, Statistics Commission).

Thomas, G. & Dwyfor Davies, J. (1999) England and Wales: competition and control— or stake-holding and inclusion, in: H. Daniels & P. Garner (Eds), *World yearbook of education 1999: inclusive education* (London, Kogan Page).

Thomas, G. & Loxley, A. (2001) *Deconstructing special education and constructing inclusion* (Buckingham, Open University Press).

Tymms, P. (2004) Are standards rising in English primary schools?, *British Educational Research Journal,* 30(4), 477–494.

UNESCO (1994) *Final Report: World conference on special needs education: access and quality* (Paris, UNESCO).

Warnock, M. (2005) *Special educational needs: a new look* (London, Philosophy of Education Society of Great Britain).

Wenger, E. (1998) *Communities of practice: learning, meaning and identity* (Cambridge, Cambridge University Press).

Wolf, A. (2002) *Does education matter? Myths about education and economic growth* (London, Penguin).

CHAPTER 9

FUTURE DIRECTIONS FOR SPECIAL SCHOOLS

Ainscow, M. (2006) Towards a more inclusive education system: where next for special schools? In R. Cigman (ed.), *Included or excluded? The challenge of the mainstream for some SEN children.* London: Routledge

Introduction

This paper took me back to my early experiences as a practitioner in special education, not least the efforts we had made in the 1970s and 80s to link the work of special schools with the strengthening of the mainstream. A 2005 paper by Mary Warnock – who had led an influential review of the field in the late 1970s – intensified the debate in the UK about the place of special schools within the inclusive education agenda. Should they, for example, continue to work in much the same way, attempting to provide a distinctive educational experience for groups of children seen as having similar needs? Or should they seek to develop new roles with due regard to the inclusion agenda within the mainstream? This paper addresses these questions by locating the debate in an international context and by considering examples of innovatory practice from the field. The experiences of the special schools described offer many reasons for optimism. They suggest that where those involved are prepared to think and act in new ways, they can make significant new contributions to the development of a more inclusive education system. The chapter concludes with some comments about the implications for national policy.

Mary Warnock's recent pamphlet *Special Educational Needs: A New Look*, has intensified the debate about inclusive education. In some ways this has been helpful; it has moved the issue nearer to the centre of the ongoing debate about the future of education in this country. Unfortunately, it has also had a negative impact, in the sense that it has tended to encourage some in the field to retreat into traditional stances.

Within these overall debates, questions about the future of special schools are particularly problematic. Should they continue to work in much the same way, attempting to provide a distinctive educational experience for groups of children seen as having similar needs? Or should they seek to develop new roles with due regard to the inclusion agenda within the mainstream?

In this chapter, I address these questions by locating the debate in an international context and considering examples of innovatory practice from the field. I conclude with some comments about the implications for national policy.

International developments

The 1990s saw considerable efforts in many countries to develop more equitable forms of schooling. The United Nations' strategy of 'Education for All' encouraged such initiatives, focusing specifically on the need to reach out to excluded and marginalised groups of learners, not least those with disabilities. Further impetus was encouraged by UNESCO's 'Salamanca Statement on Principles, Policy and Practice in Special Needs Education' (UNESCO, 1994), which provides a framework for thinking about how to move policy and practice forward. Arguably the most significant international document that has ever appeared in special education, the statement argues that regular schools with an inclusive orientation are: 'the most effective means of combating discriminatory attitudes, building an inclusive society and achieving education for all'. Furthermore, it suggests, such schools can: 'provide an effective education for the majority of children and improve the efficiency and ultimately the cost-effectiveness of the entire education system'.

Salamanca encourages us to look at educational difficulties in a new way. This new direction in thinking is based on the belief that changes in methodology and organisation made in response to students experiencing difficulties can, under certain conditions, benefit all children. Since the late 1980s a growing number of scholars in different countries have taken this new thinking forward (e.g. Ballard, 1997; Booth, 1995; Kugelmass, 2001; Mittler, 2000; Skrtic, 1991; Slee, 1996). They argue that progress towards more inclusive education systems requires a move away from practices based on the traditional perspectives of special education, towards approaches that focus on developing 'effective schools for all' (Ainscow, 1991).

This has been characterised as an 'organisational paradigm' (Dyson and Millward, 2000). It involves a shift away from explanations of educational failure that concentrate on the characteristics of individual children and their families, towards an analysis of the barriers to participation and learning experienced by students within school systems (Booth and Ainscow, 2002). Recently my colleagues and I have referred to this approach as 'school improvement with attitude' (Ainscow *et al.*, 2006), meaning:

- the process of increasing the participation of students in, and reducing their exclusion from, the curricula, cultures and communities of local schools;
- restructuring the cultures, policies and practices of schools so that they respond to the diversity of students in their locality;
- the presence, participation and achievement of all students vulnerable to exclusionary pressures, not only those with impairments or those who are categorised as 'having special educational needs'.

Within this formulation, inclusion is seen as a continuous process. An inclusive school is one that is on the move, rather than one that has reached a perfect state. It seems to me that this new thinking provides the special education field with new opportunities for representing the interests of those learners who become marginalised within existing educational arrangements.

Collaborative inquiry

With this in mind, I recently worked with a network of special school head teachers, who are all associated with the Specialist Schools Trust, in carrying out a research project to explore ways of moving thinking and practice forward. The project involved the use of an approach that we refer to as 'collaborative inquiry'. This advocates practitioner research, carried out in partnership with academics, as a means of developing better understanding of educational processes (Ainscow, 1999). Kurt Lewin's dictum that you cannot understand an organisation until you try to change it is, perhaps, the clearest justification for this approach (Schein, 2001).

The study led to the production of a series of 'accounts of practice'. These focus on ways in which special schools in different parts of England are attempting to work in partnership with mainstream schools in order to foster the development of inclusive practices. Reflecting on the accounts that were produced, it is noticeable that the schools were working in many different ways. In what follows I try to give a sense of the range of approaches we found. These differences reflect the variety of contexts and local policies within which the schools were operating. They also point to the overall lack of direction that currently exists within the field.

Setting up enclaves

Some special schools had developed arrangements whereby some of their students spend parts of the week located on the sites of mainstream schools. These experiences throw light on the potential benefits of this approach, as well as some of the difficulties. For example, staff in an urban special school that has students attending a number of mainstream schools described how the presence of young people with disabilities had opened up many opportunities for social learning among pupils within the mainstream. A senior teacher in a partner secondary school talked with obvious pride about how some of his pupils had learnt to accept youngsters from the special school. Mention was also made of how staff in the mainstream were developing more positive attitudes to these pupils.

For special school pupils involved in mainstream opportunities there was evidence of how they had matured as a result of being involved in a wider range of curriculum and social opportunities. It was impressive to see, for example, how they mixed freely and with self-confidence in the context of a large secondary school. Developments in language were seen as a particular benefit. Being required to make choices was also seen as a helpful source of social learning. It was noted too that the special school pupils had benefited as a result of being taught by a greater range of specialist teachers and having opportunities to use more specialist facilities and resources.

Parental support for these developments was said to be growing, as more and more pupils had opportunities to have positive experiences in mainstream contexts. In addition, the experience of being involved in mainstream activities was seen to be influencing attitudes of special school staff towards notions of inclusion.

At the same time, these experiences drew attention to some of the dilemmas and challenges that face those in special education as they seek to explore new ways of working within the 'inclusion agenda'. For example, this particular special school has outstanding facilities and resources, not least in terms of technology. Given this evident strength, why should parents see mainstream as a positive option? At the same time, in order to ensure the continuation of its current financial arrangements, the school needs to maintain its pupil numbers. So, what incentive is there to put more efforts in strengthening mainstream provision? Additionally, is it sensible to invest staff time in supporting individual pupils within mainstream schools if this reduces the quality of provision made for those within the special school context?

The head teacher referred to staffing issues, noting that a key strategic dilemma relates to the need to arrange staff time so that they can move between schools. Mention was also made of wider contextual factors that can act as barriers to further development. In particular, it was noted that the government's standards agenda was tending to leave mainstream schools with less space, time and resources in order to experiment with collaborative arrangements. In addition, rigidity of curriculum and teaching approaches, and the impact of performance league tables, were also seen as problems.

Finally, it was noted that confusion about the purposes of inclusion can act as a barrier to further development, leading some in the school to argue that greater progress would be possible if there was a clearer lead from government. At present, it was argued, so much depends on the actions of individuals in the field.

Supporting individual pupils

Some special schools had developed strategies for providing various forms of outreach support for individual pupils within mainstream schools. Again, there was evidence of potential benefits and difficulties in this type of response. Staff in one school described how they had explored a variety of strategies for working with mainstream partners and how these had developed as a result of the experimentation that had taken place. While these strategies imply a number of different aims, they all seem to be driven by a concern to use specialist resources and knowledge in new ways in order to improve learning opportunities for vulnerable children and young people.

This particular special school is in a small town and acts as a 'hub' for a range of other activities within mainstream schools across the local education authority. These include the involvement of five 'advanced skills' teachers who offer support to teachers and pupils in other schools. The school also provides training for teaching assistants in the authority.

Staff in both the special and the mainstream schools spoke with obvious pride about the impact on the achievement and self-esteem of the pupils involved. There was considerable evidence, too, of impact on the attitudes and practice of staff. Interestingly, there seemed to be general acceptance that the learning was a two-way process. Specific reference was made to the impact of the inclusion activities on value-added test scores in the primary schools, and how they had strengthened practice in the secondary school in ways that had helped with post-Ofsted action plans.

Perhaps even more significant was the evidence suggesting that the work of this particular special school, including its success in gaining specialist college and, more recently, Leading Edge status, had raised the profile of the school and created a very different view within the local community of the role of special education, thus addressing Mary Warnock's concern that special schools are held in 'low esteem'. (The aim of Leading Edge partnerships [DfES, 2003] is to raise standards of teaching and learning by teaming up schools which are considered strong all-rounders with others needing support.) The head summed this up when she commented: 'We are seen as a school that can cut the mustard.' She went on to explain: 'It helps the image of the school. We are seen as less of a dumping ground and more of a place where you will find help.'

At the same time there had been striking changes in the population of pupils now placed at the school, as the mainstream had grown in its capacity to cater for children experiencing difficulties. These population changes had also been influenced by policy moves to reduce the number of pupils placed in residential provision outside the LEA.

Reflecting on the partnership arrangements with the mainstream schools, the head teacher of the special school sensed that it may have gone as far as it can go. She commented: 'They are not moving on.' In particular, she explained, despite the progress that has been made and the level of collaboration that now exists, there is still resistance to special school pupils being placed on the registers of the partner schools. She added: 'As long as it is seen as a project it's not really inclusion.'

Apparently the main concern in the mainstream is that this could have a negative impact on the schools' overall test and examination results, as summarised in the performance league tables. Also the schools are anxious about getting too much of a reputation for their special needs work, since this might lead to more requests for admission from parents of children who need additional support.

Strengthening capacity

Throughout the country there is increasing evidence of school-to-school collaboration being used in order to support improvement efforts (Ainscow and West, 2006). In some instances, the intention is that school networks will involve a new type of special school, which will act as inclusion support centres. Such initiatives open up possibilities for special schools to strengthen capacity for inclusion within mainstream schools. Commenting on these possibilities, one head teacher noted: 'We can become the hub for a range of services, so they can't do without us.'

Any shift in responsibility would need to be accompanied by changes in funding arrangements. Specifically, funding would have to be delegated to groups of schools. This would mean that the use of the expensive and time-consuming process of writing statements to release funding from LEAs to schools would become largely redundant.

Some interesting examples of this type of arrangement are beginning to emerge. For example, a secondary special school in one urban LEA has become an area resource centre promoting the use of technology for pupils who experience difficulties in learning. This is an approach that Mary Warnock supports in her 2005 pamphlet. In another urban authority, three district partnerships of schools have been created, each of which involves one special school (now known as 'support centres'). Significant resources have been transferred to the partnerships, and teams of head teachers share responsibility for the participation and achievement of all learners in their district. Members of various support services have also been relocated on to the sites of the special schools with the intention of fostering the multi-agency work that is demanded by the government's 'Every Child Matters' policy. This context creates new possibilities for using the expertise within the special school to benefit a larger number of pupils. It also means that opportunities for special school pupils to participate in mainstream activities can occur as a matter of routine.

In theory, the various co-located special schools that are currently being built around the country should facilitate similar merging of responsibilities and sharing of resources. For example, plans are well advanced to federate one special school with a primary and secondary school in a new building, which will cater for 1,400 pupils on a site that is designed to ensure maximum possibilities for inclusive education. This exciting development can be seen as the culmination of over 15 years of effort to redefine the role of special education provision within this particular LEA. Interestingly, the head teacher of the special school has been appointed to the post of executive head of the new organisation.

A special school in a rural district has developed a strong presence within a local network of schools. The main purpose of these activities is to help the schools to develop a much greater capacity for supporting the participation and learning of children who experience difficulties. In developing this work the head teacher emphasised the need to ensure the viability of his own school within what he sees as a context of uncertainty. He explained that this creates a strategic dilemma, in that success in strengthening mainstream provision could eventually lead to the demise of the special school.

The network, which involves 25 schools, is well established and involves a range of cooperative activities. In many ways it is an excellent example of the collaborative arrangements that the government is now seeking to encourage, not least in that its management rests with the head teachers themselves. One head explained: 'It's from the bottom up, rather than the authority saying this is what you need.'

Cooperation about special needs and inclusion is a key element within the network, and the special school is very much the lead partner. Emphasis is placed on two linked strategies: staff development and consultancy in respect to individual pupils.

Staff development takes a variety of forms, all aimed at strengthening the capacity of mainstream staff to respond to pupils experiencing difficulties. For example, the school offers full-day workshops on specialised teaching strategies. These may be offered within schools for all staff, or at the special school site for visiting groups. One member of staff argued that such training activities were valued because they were led by practising teachers. He explained: 'When we go out we speak as practitioners with credibility. It's not just theory. We tend to throw in anecdotes from our own teaching that brings it to life.' It was noticeable that quite a number of the staff have recent mainstream experience. One teacher who works on training and consultancy in relation to autism commented: 'It really helps that I was a secondary science teacher. Some of my colleagues are less confident because of not having that experience.'

The special school also organises the work of the network's SENCO (special educational needs coordinator) forum. All the schools that are involved pay an annual membership fee of £175. Training events are paid for separately. This income is used to pay for supply staff, so that special teachers can be released. One teacher commented: 'I used to get embarrassed about saying schools had to pay. Now they realise that somebody has to pay for my release.'

Consultancy is also paid for by the mainstream schools and is focused on providing advice and support to staff. Here a particularly interesting initiative involves experienced teaching assistants from the special school spending time in mainstream contexts.

The approach that this network is developing, with its emphasis on capacity building, contrasts with the work of other special schools that are more focused on pupil re-integration strategies. Of course, questions have to be asked about the impact of such approaches. In this particular case, if we accept 'take up' as an indicator, the evidence is encouraging. Apparently almost every week members of staff are involved in leading workshops for mainstream groups, sometimes for whole staffs. In addition, demand continues to increase for consultancy support in relation to particular pupils. Of course, all these activities involve schools in paying for the services that are provided.

At the same time, it is evident that progress within the mainstream varies from school to school. Commenting on this, one member of staff explained: 'Some schools are more committed to inclusion. The ones that are successful with inclusion are the ones that have management that are committed to it.' It is also worth noting that very few special school pupils spend time in mainstream lessons and none have been re-integrated into the mainstream. Finance is seen as one of the barriers to such arrangements.

An interesting feature of this work is the way in which this special school has had to re-think its internal organisational arrangements in order to allow teachers and teaching assistants to be away from their in-school duties. This involves a strong emphasis on agreed policies that encourage consistency, and team work arrangements that mean that no individual is indispensable. Staff involved in mainstream activities are also well briefed about the rationale for their work.

At the same time there are still barriers that limit progress. The school is stretched to serve a diverse population that includes some very challenging individuals. The fact that it has children from various LEAs adds to the pressure and, of course, makes it difficult to set up local arrangements for the re-integration of some pupils. Like other special schools that are engaged in innovatory activities relating to inclusion, it has to ensure its own viability, not least in terms of pupil numbers. It is also positioned on the edge of the LEA, in ways that can make it feel slightly detached.

Barriers are created, too, by the sense of uncertainty about where the LEA is heading in relation to its overall policy for special needs. Concern was expressed about the authority's attitude towards the new roles that the school has developed, particularly in relation to the dissemination of expertise about how to teach children with particular disabilities. As in other LEAs, there is also concern about how the developing outreach role of the special school fits in with the way other support services are developing. Indeed, some staff at the school feel that they are working in competition with the LEA services.

So, like other special schools that are exploring new ways of working, this school offers striking challenges for management and leadership. In particular, those who take on these roles see themselves faced with what seem like endless dilemmas. For example, in talking about the support that is provided to schools in the network, the head teacher commented: 'It's very wobbly. I feel very wobbly about what we can offer at any one time.'

Drawing out the lessons

From the examples I have presented we see evidence of three overall approaches to the development of the work of special schools. These are:

- the development of enclaves within mainstreams schools, so that special school pupils can experience mainstream curriculum;
- strategies to provide direct support for individual pupils in the mainstream who are seen as being likely for possible transfer to special provision, or vulnerable to exclusion;

- the development of new roles for the special school in strengthening inclusive practices more generally within the mainstream.

The first two of these approaches are focused on individual pupils in ways that reflect the traditions of special education practice, whereas the third approach reflects what I referred to earlier as an organisational perspective. As we have seen, each has potential to improve services for vulnerable groups of pupils and each presents difficulties and strategic dilemmas. And of course there is potential for the three approaches to be linked.

Visitors to special schools such as the ones I have described are struck by the willingness of those involved to experiment. To use a phrase mentioned earlier, they are schools that are 'on the move'. In this sense they reveal many of the features of what Senge (1989) calls 'a learning organisation', that is, an 'organisation that is continually expanding its capacity to create its future'. It is also evident that all of this has emanated from the leadership provided by particular head teachers and their senior teams. Through their energy and enthusiasm they seem to have been successful in developing cultures of creativity and risk-taking, despite the uncertainties that they face in taking this work forward.

All of this has placed these particular special schools at the centre of developments regarding inclusion within their LEAs. As we have seen, these developments have been challenging and demanding of time, particularly for the head teachers themselves. Their vision for special schools is essentially transformative, and in some cases goes well beyond anything that currently exists. It implies new thinking regarding many aspects of the work of their schools, including the forms of governance and management that will be needed, and the approaches to the curriculum, pastoral care, budgets, roles and responsibilities, and strategies for teaching and learning.

Of course sometimes the new ideas under consideration have not found favour among key stakeholders. For example, some staff in partner mainstream schools have expressed anxiety about their ability to deal with children with more severe disabilities. Similarly, some staff in the special schools are anxious about their ability to cope within mainstream contexts. As a result, the process of negotiating agreements has required persistent yet sensitive leadership and, inevitably, some compromises have had to be made in order to achieve a degree of consensus on the overall rationale for the developments.

Across all the schools there was another striking aspect of leadership that needs to be noted. This was a capacity to understand local contexts in order to determine opportunities and resources for moving thinking and practice forward, and an ability to address possible barriers to progress. The success that has been achieved is not so much about importing solutions from elsewhere; rather it involves people within the local context inventing relevant and feasible strategies that fit existing circumstances.

Running through all this are challenges regarding the management of innovation. Research suggests that, by and large, schools find it difficult to cope with change (Hopkins *et al.*, 1994). In this respect they face a double problem: they cannot remain as they now are if they are to respond to new challenges; but at the same time they also need to maintain some continuity between their present and their previous practices. There is, therefore, a tension between *development* and *maintenance*. The problem is that schools tend to generate organisational structures that predispose them towards one or the other. Schools (or parts of schools) at the development extreme may be so over-confident of their innovative capacities that they take on too much too quickly, thus damaging the quality of what already exists. On the other hand, schools at the maintenance extreme may either see little purpose in change, or have a poor history of managing innovation.

During times of stability, of course, a tendency to maintenance presents little difficulty. On the other hand, periods of profound change and uncertainty heighten the tensions that are created within maintenance-oriented systems. Our own research indicates that the patterns of organisation and practice within special schools present a particularly extreme version of the maintenance–development dilemma (Ainscow *et al.*, 2003). They are, by their nature, organisations that are particularly focused on doing everything possible to overcome the difficulties of unusual populations of learners. Therefore they have a tradition of intensive relationships between adults and children that have a particular focus on individualised approaches to learning. They also tend to have close links with families. In addition, the involvement of relatively large numbers of external support specialists from the education, social service and health departments further consumes planning time. As a result, finding time to plan for change seems to be a particular problem and, indeed, external visitors to special schools often find that there are few opportunities during the day to have discussions with members of staff.

Consequently, leaders in special education have to address the unusual management contexts created by this intensive form of the maintenance–development dilemma. In particular, they must address the question: what forms of leadership practice can enable special schools to provide high-quality education within existing circumstances, while at the same time developing new roles in relation to developments in the mainstream?

Implications for national policy

What, then, does all of this suggest regarding national policy? Recent moves have been generally successful in encouraging local authorities and schools to move in a more inclusive direction. Too often, however, special schools have been omitted from these policy initiatives in a way that has left many within that sector feeling isolated and devalued. The time is now ripe for a national lead to emerge showing how the expertise and resources within special schools can be redirected in ways that will add support to the changes taking place in mainstream schools. Such a move would, I believe, open up new opportunities for special school staff to continue their historical task of providing support for the most vulnerable learners in the education system. Interestingly, as Baroness Warnock reminds us, this was one of the recommendations she and her colleagues made as a result of the government inquiry in 1978.

Government talk of a possible 'third way' approach has been helpful in stimulating further debate about these matters in the field. On the other hand, there is a danger that if this approach leads to ambiguous messages, it will prevent the clarity of thinking that could help provide an effective lever for change (Ainscow, 2005). There is therefore a need for a clear national policy statement that will encourage further experimentation of the sort that I have described. At the same time, there is also a need for government to provide a statement of its commitment to inclusion, accompanied by a clear statement of what an inclusive system might actually look like, that could then be used to guide policy development and inform monitoring procedures.

In a recent advice note to the schools minister Lord Adonis, my colleagues Alan Dyson, Peter Farrell and I argued that any such statement should emphasise the positive benefits of inclusion for parents and children, rather than inclusion as an ideological principle to be accepted as an article of faith. Specifically, it might be useful to emphasise the distinction between needs, rights and opportunities. All children have needs (e.g. for appropriate teaching), but they also have the right to participate fully in a common social institution (a local mainstream school) that offers a range of opportunities for them. The current system too often forces parents to choose between ensuring that their child's needs are met (which often implies special school placement) and ensuring that they have the same rights and opportunities as other children (which, according to the Salamanca Statement, not to mention a considerable consensus of public opinion, implies mainstream school placement). The aim therefore should be to create a system where these choices become unnecessary.

We also argued that the government should emphasise the idea that inclusion is about the development of mainstream schools, rather than the reorganisation of special schooling. The aim has to be to increase the capacity of all main-stream schools, so that, like the best schools today, they can meet the needs of all children, while offering them similar rights and opportunities. This has implications for a changed role for special schools in the medium term and the disappearance of special schools entirely in the longer term. However, it is vital to note that the disappearance of the bricks and mortar of special schools does not imply the disappearance of the skills, attitudes, values and resources which those buildings currently contain.

Finally we stressed that the education of children with 'special educational needs' should be seen as part of a wider set of issues relating to the education of all children who experience difficulties in school and, ultimately, of all children. This led us to conclude that the distinction between 'SEN' and 'non-SEN' children is a largely outmoded one, which ignores the considerable developments that have occurred in the system's ability to identify and respond to a wide range of difficulties.

Some final thoughts

The experiences of the special schools described in this chapter offer many reasons for optimism. They suggest that where those involved are prepared to think and act in new ways, they can make significant new contributions to the development of a more inclusive education system. While these experiments are still at the early stages of development, they offer leads as to how successful strategies might evolve. At the same time, it is important to stress the importance of analysing local contexts, recognising that an approach that works in one place may not be easily transposed to another location.

Those in leadership roles in special schools have a key role to play in providing leadership for such developments at the local level. They will therefore need support in learning how to develop, within their schools, organisation, cultures that encourage experimentation and collective problem-solving in response to the challenge of pupil diversity. Such cultures are necessary for an effective response to the increasingly challenging populations within the special schools. It may well be that they are also the most important gift that the special education community can offer to the movement towards more inclusive forms of education.

Acknowledgements

I would like to acknowledge the contributions of the head teachers who were my co-researchers in the project described in this chapter. Thanks must also go to my colleagues Alan Dyson, Peter Farrell and Andy Howes, who contributed to the development of the ideas that are presented, and to Vivian Heung and Kiki Messiou, who commented on an earlier draft.

References

Ainscow, M. (ed.) (1991), *Effective Schools for All*, London: Fulton

Ainscow, M. (1999), *Understanding the Development of Inclusive Schools*, London: Falmer Press

Ainscow, M. (2005), 'Developing inclusive education systems: what are the levers for change?', *Journal of Educational Change*, 6 (2), 109–24

Ainscow, M., T. Booth and A. Dyson with P. Farrell, J. Frankham, F. Gallannaugh, A. Howes and R. Smith (2006), *Improving Schools, Developing Inclusion*, London: Routledge

Ainscow, M., S. Fox and J. O'Kane (2003), *Leadership and Management in Special Schools: A Review of the Literature*, Nottingham: National College for School Leadership

Ainscow, M. and M. West (eds) (2006), *Leading Improvements in Urban Schools*, Buckingham: Open University Press

Ballard, K. (1997), 'Researching disability and inclusive education: participation, construction and interpretation', *International Journal of Inclusive Education*, 1 (3), 243–56

Booth, T. (1995), 'Mapping inclusion and exclusion: concepts for all?', in C. Clark, A. Dyson and A. Millward (eds), *Towards Inclusive Schools?*, London: Fulton

Booth, T. and M. Ainscow (2002), *The Index for Inclusion* (2nd edn), Centre for Studies on Inclusive Education

Dyson, A. and A. Millward (2000), *Schools and Special Needs: Issues of Innovation and Inclusion*, London: Paul Chapman

Hopkins, D., M. Ainscow and M. West (1994), *School Improvement in an Era of Change*, London: Cassell

Kugelmass, J. W. (2001), 'Collaboration and compromise in creating and sustaining an inclusive school', *Journal of Inclusive Education*. 5 (1), 47–65

Mittler, P. (2000), *Working towards Inclusive Education*, London: Fulton

Schein, E. H. (2001), 'Clinical inquiry/research', in P. Reason and H. Bradbury (eds), *Handbook of Action Research*, London: Sage

Senge, P. M. (1989), *The Fifth Discipline: The Art and Practice of the Learning Organisation*, London: Century

Skrtic, T. M. (1991), 'Students with special educational needs: artifacts of the traditional curriculum', in M. Ainscow (ed.), *Effective Schools for All*, London: Fulton

Slee, R. (1996), 'Inclusive schooling in Australia? Not yet', *Cambridge Journal of Education*, 26 (1), 19–32

UNESCO (1994), *Final Report: World Conference on Special Needs Education: Access and Quality*, Paris: UNESCO

Warnock, M. (2005), *Special Educational Needs: A New Look*, London: Philosophy of Education Society of Great Britain.

CHAPTER 10

LEVERS FOR CHANGE

Ainscow, M. (2005) Developing inclusive education systems: what are the levers for change? *Journal of Educational Change* 6(2), 109–124

Introduction

My work with schools had increasingly pointed to the way that the direction of their improvement efforts is influenced by wider contextual factors. Reflecting on a series of studies, in a variety of national contexts, this paper attempts to pinpoint the factors that have greatest leverage in this respect. It focuses on factors within schools that influence the development of thinking and practice, as well as wider contextual factors that may constrain such developments. It is argued that many of the barriers experienced by learners arise from existing ways of thinking. Consequently, strategies for developing inclusive practices have to challenge taken-for-granted assumptions, in order to encourage an exploration of overlooked possibilities for moving practice forward. Other important levers relate to the overall principles that guide policy priorities within an education system; the views and actions of others within the local context, including members of the wider community that the school serves; the staff of the departments that have responsibility for the administration of the school; and the criteria that are used to evaluate the performance of schools. The paper explains how this thinking was used as the basis of the 'Manchester Inclusion Standard', a review and development instrument used across most schools in the city.

The issue of inclusion is the big challenge facing school systems throughout the world. In the economically poorer countries the priority has to be with the millions of children who never see the inside of a classroom (Bellamy, 1999). Meanwhile, in wealthier countries many young people leave school with no worthwhile qualifications, whilst others are placed in various forms of special provision away from mainstream educational experiences, and some simply choose to drop out since the lessons seem irrelevant to their lives.

In some countries, inclusive education is thought of as an approach to serving children with disabilities within general education settings. Internationally, however, it is increasingly seen more broadly as a reform that supports and welcomes diversity amongst all learners (UNESCO, 2001). The argument developed in this paper adopts this broader formulation. It presumes that the aim of inclusive education is to eliminate social exclusion that is a consequence of attitudes and responses to diversity in race, social class, ethnicity, religion, gender and ability (Vitello & Mithaug, 1998). As such, it starts from the belief that education is a basic human right and the foundation for a more just society.

Ten years ago the Salamanca World Conference on Special Needs Education endorsed the idea of inclusive education (UNESCO, 1994). Arguably the most significant international document that has ever appeared in the special needs field, the Salamanca Statement argues that regular schools with an inclusive orientation are "the most effective means of combating discriminatory attitudes, building an inclusive society and achieving education for all." Furthermore, it suggests that such schools can "provide an effective education for the majority of children and improve the efficiency and ultimately the cost-effectiveness of the entire education system" (UNESCO, 1994).

During the subsequent 10 years or so, there has been considerable activity in many countries to move educational policy and practice in a more inclusive direction (Mittler, 2000). In this paper I use evidence from research carried out during that period in order to consider what needs to be done to build on the progress that has been made so far. In particular, I consider the question: *What are the "levers" that can move education systems in an inclusive direction?*

Mapping the issues

As countries have tried to move their education systems in a more inclusive direction, my colleagues and I have carried out a programme of research in order to learn from their experiences. Whilst much of this research has been carried out in the United Kingdom, it has also involved projects in countries as diverse as Brazil, China, India, Romania, Spain and Zambia (Ainscow, 2000a). These have focused on: the development of classroom practice (e.g. Ainscow, 1999, 2000b; Ainscow & Brown, 2000; Ainscow, Howes, Farrell & Frankham, 2003); school development (e.g. Ainscow, 1995; Ainscow, Barrs & Martin, 1998; Booth & Ainscow, 2002); teacher development (e.g. Ainscow, 1994, 2002); leadership practices (Kugelmass & Ainscow, 2003); and systemic change (e.g. Ainscow & Haile-Giorgis, 1999; Ainscow, Farrell & Tweddle, 2000), particularly in respect to the role of school districts (e.g. Ainscow & Howes, 2001; Ainscow & Tweddle, 2003). At the same time, through the work of the *Enabling Education Network* (EENET), we have encouraged links between groups around the world that are trying to encourage the development of inclusive education (Further details can be obtained from *www.eenet.org.uk*). Together the findings of these studies provide the foundations for the argument I present in this paper.

Much of our research has involved the use of an approach that we refer to as "collaborative inquiry". This approach advocates practitioner research, carried out in partnership with academics, as a means of developing better understanding of educational processes (Ainscow, 1999). Kurt Lewin's dictum that you cannot understand an organisation until you try to change it is, perhaps, the clearest justification for this approach (Schein, 2001). In practical terms, we believe that such understanding is best developed as a result of "outsiders", such as ourselves, working alongside practitioners, policy makers and other stakeholders as they seek practical solutions to the problems they face.

Such research leads to detailed examples of how those within particular contexts have attempted to develop inclusive policies and practices. It also provides frameworks and propositions that can be used by those within other contexts to analyse their own working situations. One such framework provides a useful map for the argument I develop in this paper (see Figure 10.1). It is

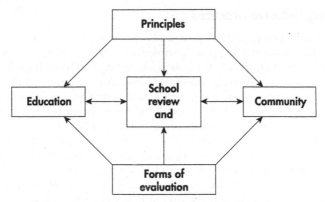

Figure 10.1 Levers for change.

intended to help us focus on factors that bear on inclusive developments within an education system. More specifically, it focuses our attention on possible levers that can help to move the system forward.

Senge (1989) sees "levers" as actions that can be taken in order to change the behaviour of an organisation and those individuals within it. He goes on to argue that those who wish to encourage change within an organisation must be smart in determining where the high leverage lies. Too often, he suggests, approaches used to bring about large-scale changes in organisations are "low leverage". That is to say, they tend to change the way things look but not the way they work. Possible examples of low leverage activity in the education field include: policy documents, conferences and in-service courses. Whilst such initiatives may make a contribution, they tend not to lead to significant changes in thinking and practice (Fullan, 1991). Our aim, therefore, must be to identify what may turn out to be more subtle, less obvious and higher leverage efforts to bring about change in schools.

The framework places schools at the centre of the analysis. This reinforces the point that moves toward inclusion should focus on increasing the capacity of local neighbourhood mainstream schools to support the participation and learning of an increasingly diverse range of learners. This is the paradigm shift implied by the Salamanca Statement. It argues that moves towards inclusion are about the development of schools, rather simply involving attempts to integrate vulnerable groups of students into existing arrangements. It is, therefore, essentially about those within schools developing practices that can "reach out to all learners" (Ainscow, 1999).

At the same time, the framework draws attention to a range of contextual influences that bear on the way schools carry out their work. As I will explain, these influences may provide support and encouragement to those in schools who are wishing to move in an inclusive direction. However, it also draws our attention to how the same factors can act as barriers to progress.

These influences relate to: the principles that guide policy priorities within an education system; the views and actions of others within the local context, including members of the wider community that the schools serve and the staff of the departments that have responsibility for the administration of the school system; and the criteria that are used to evaluate the performance of schools.

In what follows I examine these wider influences in more detail. Before doing so, however, I will summarise what our research suggests about the way inclusive developments can be encouraged at the school level.

Developing inclusive practices

We have recently completed a 3-year study that has attempted to throw further light on what needs to happen in order to develop inclusive practices in schools (Ainscow et al., 2003; Ainscow et al., in press). The study, which defined inclusive practices as involving attempts to overcome barriers to the participation and learning of students, involved teams from three universities working with groups of schools as they attempted to move practice forward. It led us to conclude that the development of inclusive practice is not, in the main, about adopting new technologies of the sort described in much of the existing literature (e.g. Florian Rose & Tilstone, 1998; Sebba & Sachdev, 1997; Stainback & Stainback, 1990; Thousand & Villa, 1991; Wang, 1991). Rather, it involves social learning processes within a given workplace that influence people's actions and, indeed, the thinking that informs these actions. This led us to interrogate our evidence in order to seek a deeper understanding of what these processes involve. To assist in this analysis we used as our guide the idea of "communities of practice", as developed by Wenger (1998), focusing specifically on the way he sees learning as "a characteristic of practice".

Although the words "community" and "practice" evoke common images, Wenger has particular definitions of these terms, giving the phrase "community of practice" a distinctive meaning. A practice, for example, need not be framed as the work and skill of a particular practitioner. Rather, a practice consists of those things that individuals in a community do, drawing on available resources, to further a set of shared goals. This goes beyond how practitioners complete their tasks, to include, for example, how they make it through the day, commiserating about the pressures and constraints within which they have to operate.

Wenger provides a framework that can be used to analyse learning in social contexts. At the centre of this framework is the concept of a "community of practice", a social group engaged in the sustained pursuit of a shared enterprise. Practices are ways of negotiating meaning through social action. In Wenger's view, meanings arise from two complementary processes, "participation" and "reification". He notes:

> Practices evolve as shared histories of learning. History in this sense is neither merely a personal or collective experience, nor just a set of enduring artefacts and institutions, but a combination of participation and reification over time (p. 87).

In this formulation, *participation* is seen as the shared experiences and negotiations that result from social interaction within a purposive community. Participation is thus inherently local, since shared experiences and negotiation processes will differ from one setting to the next, regardless of their interconnections. So, for example, within schools in our study we saw how hours of meetings, shared experiences and informal discussions over hurriedly taken lunches, also involved the development of particular meanings of frequently used phrases such as "raising standards" and "inclusion". These shared meanings help to define a teacher's experience of being a teacher. In the same way, we can assume that groups of colleagues doing similar work in another school have their own shared histories that give meaning to being a teacher in that particular context.

According to Wenger, *reification* is the process by which communities of practice produce concrete representations of their practices, such as tools, symbols, rules and documents (and even concepts and theories). So, for example, documents such as the school development plan or behaviour policy are reifications of the practice of teachers. They include representations of the activities in which teachers engage, and some illustrations of the conditions and problems that a teacher might encounter in practice. At the same time, it is important to remember that such documents often provide overly rationalised portrayals of ideal practice in which the challenges and uncertainties of unfolding action are smoothed over in the telling (Brown & Duguid, 1991).

Wenger argues that learning within a given community can often be best explained within the intertwining of reification and participation. He suggests that these are complementary processes, in that each has the capacity to repair the ambiguity of meaning the other can engender. So, for example, a particular strategy may be developed as part of a school's planning activities and summarised in a set of guidance for action, providing a codified reification of intended practice. However, the meaning and practical implications of the strategy only becomes clear as it is tried in the field and discussed between colleagues. In this way, participation results in social learning that could not be produced solely by reification alone. At the same time, the reified products, such as policy documents, serve as a kind of memory of practice, cementing in place the new learning. Such an analysis provides a way of describing the means by which practices develop within a school.

At this stage in the argument it is important to stress that I am not suggesting that communities of practice are in themselves a panacea for the development of inclusive practices. Rather, the concept helps us to attend to and make sense of the significance of social process of learning as powerful mediators of meaning. Wenger (1998) notes:

"Communities of practice are not intrinsically beneficial or harmful. . . . Yet they are a force to be reckoned with, for better or for worse. As a locus of engagement in action, interpersonal relationships, shared knowledge, and negotiation of enterprises, such communities hold the key to real transformation – the kind that has real effect on people's lives . . . The influence of other forces (e.g., the control of an institution or the authority of an individual) are no less important, but . . . they are mediated by the communities in which their meanings are negotiated in practice" (p. 85).

The methodology for developing inclusive practices must, therefore, take account of these social processes of learning that go on within particular contexts. It requires a group of stakeholders within a particular context to look for a common agenda to guide their discussions of practice and, at much the same time, a series of struggles to establish ways of working that enable them to collect and find meaning in different types of information. The notion of the community of practice is a significant reminder of how this meaning is made.

Similarly important is the development of a common language with which colleagues can talk to one another and indeed to themselves about detailed aspects of their practice (Huberman, 1993; Little & McLaughlin, 1993). It seems, moreover, that without such a language teachers find it very difficult to experiment with new possibilities. It has been noted, for example, that when researchers report to teachers what has been observed during their lessons the teachers will often express surprise (Ainscow, 1999). It seems that much of what teachers do during the intensive encounters that occur in a typical lesson is carried out at an automatic, intuitive level, involving the use of tacit knowledge. Furthermore there is little time to stop and think. This is perhaps why having the opportunity to see colleagues at work is so crucial to the success of attempts to develop practice. It is through such shared experiences that colleagues can help one another to articulate what they currently do and define what they might like to do (Hiebert, Gallimore & Stigler, 2002). It is also the means whereby taken-for-granted assumptions about particular groups of students can be subjected to mutual critique.

Our research has drawn attention to certain ways of engaging with evidence that seem to be helpful in encouraging such dialogue. Our observation is that these can help to create space for reappraisal and rethinking by interrupting existing discourses, and by focusing attention on overlooked possibilities for moving practice forward. These approaches involve:

- Surveys of staff, student and parent views,
- Mutual observation of classroom practices, followed by structured discussion of what happened,
- Group discussion of a video recording of one colleague teaching,
- Discussion of statistical evidence regarding test results, attendance registers or exclusion records,
- Data from interviews with students,
- Staff development exercises based on case study material or interview data, and
- School to school cooperation, including mutual visits to help collect evidence.

Under certain conditions all of these approaches can provide *interruptions* that help to "make the familiar unfamiliar" in ways that stimulate self-questioning, creativity and action. Here, as Riehl (2000) suggests, the role of the school principal in providing leadership for such processes is crucial. So, for example, Lambert and her colleagues seem to be talking about a similar approach in their discussion of what they call "the constructivist leader". They stress the importance of leaders gathering, generating and interpreting information within a school in order to create an "inquiring stance". They argue that such information causes "disequilibrium" in thinking and, as a result, provides a challenge to existing assumptions about teaching and learning (Lambert et al., 1995).

We have found that these kinds of actions, involving an engagement with various forms of evidence, may create space and encourage discussion. However, they are not in themselves straightforward mechanisms for the development of more inclusive practices. The space that is created may be filled according to conflicting agendas. In this way, deeply held beliefs within a school may prevent the experimentation that is necessary in order to foster the development of more inclusive ways of working. So, for example, at the end of a lesson in a secondary school during which there was a very low level of participation amongst the class, the teacher explained what had happened with reference to the fact that most of the students in the class were listed on the school's special educational needs register.

Such explanations make us acutely aware that the relationship between the recognition of anomalies in school practices and the presence of students presenting difficulties as the occasions for such recognition is deeply ambiguous. It is very easy for educational difficulties to be pathologised as difficulties inherent *within* students, even when those same difficulties are used productively to interrogate some aspects of school practice. This is true not only of students with disabilities and those defined as "having special educational needs", but also of those whose socioeconomic status, race, language and gender renders them problematic to particular teachers in particular schools. Consequently, it is necessary, I suggest, to develop the capacity of those within schools to reveal and challenge deeply entrenched deficit views of "difference", which define certain types of students as "lacking something" (Trent, Artiles & Englert, 1998).

Specifically, it is necessary to be vigilant in scrutinising how deficit assumptions may be influencing perceptions of certain students. As Bartolome (1994) explains, teaching methods are neither devised nor implemented in a vacuum. Design, selection and use of particular teaching approaches and strategies arise from perceptions about learning and learners. In this respect even the most pedagogically advanced methods are likely to be ineffective in the hands of those who implicitly or explicitly subscribe to a belief system that regards some students, at best, as disadvantaged and in need of fixing, or, worse, as deficient and, therefore, beyond fixing.

The wider context

So far I have focused on factors within schools that can act as "levers for change". However, our experience suggests that developments within individual schools are more likely to lead to sustainable development if they are part of a process of systemic change. In other words, inclusive school development has to be seen in relation to wider factors that may help or hinder progress.

Through our collaborative action research with local education authorities (LEAs) in England and school systems in other countries, we have tried to map factors at the district level that have the potential to either facilitate or inhibit the promotion of inclusive practices in schools. These are all variables which education departments either control directly, or over which they can at least exert considerable influence. We intend that this work will eventually lead to the development of a framework instrument that will provide a basis for self-review processes (Ainscow and Tweddle, 2003). Some of these factors seem to be potentially more potent. However, our research suggests that two factors, particularly when they are closely linked, seem to be superordinate to all others. These are: *clarity of definition*, and *the forms of evidence* that are used to measure educational performance.

In my own country there is still considerable confusion about what "inclusion" means (Ainscow et al., 2000). To some extent, this lack of clarity might be tracked back to central Government policy statements. For example, the use of the term "social inclusion" has been associated mainly with improving attendance and reducing the incidence of exclusions from schools. At the same time, the idea of "inclusive education" has appeared in most national guidance in connection with the rights of individual children and young people categorised as having special educational needs to be educated in mainstream schools, whenever possible. Most recently, Ofsted, the inspection agency, has introduced the term "educational inclusion", noting that "effective schools are inclusive schools." The subtle differences between these concepts adds to the sense of uncertainty as to what is intended and, of course, it is now well established that educational reform is particularly difficult in contexts where there is a lack of common understanding amongst stakeholders (e.g. Fullan, 1991).

This being the case, in our own work we have supported a number of English LEAs as they have attempted to develop a definition of inclusion that can be used to guide policy development. Predictably, the exact detail of each LEA's definition is unique, because of the need to take account of local circumstances, cultures and history. Nevertheless, four key elements have tended to feature strongly, and these are commended to those in any education system who are intending to review their own working definition. The four elements are as follows:

- Inclusion is a process. That is to say, inclusion has to be seen as a never-ending search to find better ways of responding to diversity. It is about learning how to live with difference and learning how to learn from difference. In this way differences come to be seen more positively as stimuli for fostering learning, amongst children and adults.
- Inclusion is concerned with the identification and removal of barriers. Consequently, it involves collecting, collating and evaluating information from a wide variety of sources in order to plan for improvements in policy and practice. It is about using evidence of various kinds to stimulate creativity and problem solving.
- Inclusion is about the presence, participation and achievement of all students. Here "presence" is concerned with where children are educated, and how reliably and punctually they attend; "participation" relates to the quality of their experiences whilst they are there and, therefore, must incorporate the views of the learners themselves; and "achievement" is about the outcomes of learning across the curriculum, not merely test or examination results.
- Inclusion involves a particular emphasis on those groups of learners who may be at risk of marginalisation, exclusion or underachievement. This indicates the moral responsibility to ensure that those groups that are statistically most at risk are carefully monitored, and that, where necessary, steps are taken to ensure their presence, participation and achievement in the education system.

Our experience has been that a well-orchestrated debate about these elements can lead to a wider understanding of the principle of inclusion within a community. We are also finding that such a debate, though by its nature slow and, possibly, never ending, can have leverage in respect to fostering the conditions within which schools can feel encouraged to move in a more inclusive direction. Such a debate must involve all stakeholders within the local community, including political and religious leaders, and the media. It must also involve those within the local education district office.

Our search for levers has also led us to acknowledge the importance of evidence. In essence, it leads us to conclude that, within education systems, "what gets measured gets done." England is an interesting case in this respect, leading some American researchers to describe it as "a laboratory where the effects of market-like mechanisms are more clearly visible" (Finklestein & Grubb, 2000, p. 602). So, for example, English LEAs are required to collect far more statistical data than ever before. This is widely recognised as a double-edged sword precisely because it is such a potent lever for change. On the one hand, data are required in order to monitor the progress of children, evaluate the impact of interventions, review the effectiveness of policies and processes, plan new initiatives, and so on. In these senses, data can, justifiably, be seen as the life-blood of continuous improvement. On the other hand, if effectiveness is evaluated on the basis of narrow, even inappropriate, performance indicators, then the impact can be deeply damaging. Whilst appearing to promote the causes of accountability and transparency, the use of data can, in practice: conceal more than it reveals; invite misinterpretation; and, worst of all, have a perverse effect on the behaviour of professionals. This has led the current "audit culture" to be described as a "tyranny of transparency" (Strathern, 2000).

This is arguably the most troubling aspect of our own research. It has revealed, how, within a context that values narrowly conceived criteria for determining success, such moves can act as a barrier to the development of a more inclusive education system (Ainscow, Howes & Tweddle, 2004; Ainscow et al., in press). All of this suggests that great care needs to be exercised in deciding what evidence is collected and, indeed, how it is used.

English LEAs are required by Government to collect particular data. Given national policies, they cannot opt out of collecting such data on the grounds that their publication might be misinterpreted, or that they may influence practice in an unhelpful way. On the other hand, LEAs are free to collect additional evidence that can then be used to evaluate the effectiveness of their own policy and practice in respect to progress towards greater inclusion. The challenge for LEAs is, therefore, to harness the potential of evidence as a lever for change, whilst avoiding the problems described earlier.

Our own work suggests that the starting point for making decisions about the evidence to collect should be with an agreed definition of inclusion. In other words, we must "measure what we value", rather than is often the case, "valuing what we can measure". In line with the suggestions made earlier, then, we argue that the evidence collected at the district level needs to relate to the "presence, participation and achievement" of all students, with an emphasis placed on those groups of learners regarded to be "at risk of marginalisation, exclusion or underachievement".

In one English LEA, for example, we are currently collaborating with officers and school principals on the development and dissemination of its "Inclusion Standard", an instrument for evaluating the progress of schools on "their journey to becoming more inclusive" (Moore, Jackson, Fox & Ainscow, 2004). The standard is different from most existing inclusion awards in that it focuses directly on student outcomes, rather than on organisational processes, and uses the views of students as a major source of evidence. So, for example, it does not require a review of the quality of leadership in a school. Rather, it focuses on the presence, participation and achievements of students, on the assumption that this is what good leadership sets out to secure. Similarly, the standard does not examine whether or not students are given the opportunity to take part in school activities. Rather, it sets out to assess whether students, particularly those at risk of marginalisation or exclusion, actually take part and benefit as a result. In these ways, the aims are: to increase understanding within schools of inclusion as an ongoing process; to foster the development of inclusive practices; and to use the student voice as a stimulus for school and staff development. The intention of the LEA involved is that the standard will become an integral part of schools' self-review and development processes.

Looking to the future

As we have seen, the development of inclusive policies and practices within rapidly changing education systems is a complex business. This paper is, therefore, an attempt to make a contribution to a better understanding of these complex issues in the field. As such, it is intended that the ideas discussed here will stimulate thinking and debate in ways that will enable further progress to be made in taking forward the inclusion agenda.

As my colleagues and I continue working with the education systems in which we are currently involved, both in the United Kingdom and in other parts of the world, we have two inter-linked aspirations, both of which are inherent in our approach to collaborative research. First, we hope that our partners will derive direct and practical benefits from their involvement, and that, as a result, children, young people and their families will receive more effective educational services. Secondly, we hope to make further progress in understanding and articulating some of the complex issues involved in this work. We also intend that the analysis that has been developed will provide the basis of self-review frameworks, such as the "Index for Inclusion" (Booth & Ainscow, 2002), for the development of inclusive policies, practices and cultures within schools and school systems.

As we take this work forward it is important to keep in mind the arguments presented in this paper. In particular, we have to remember that much of what goes on within organisations, such as LEAs and schools, is largely taken-for-granted and, therefore, rarely discussed. In other words, practices are manifestations of organisational cultures (Angelides & Ainscow, 2000; Schein, 1985). This leads us to assume that many of the barriers experienced by learners arise from existing ways of thinking. Consequently, strategies for developing inclusive practices have to involve interruptions to thinking, in order to encourage "insiders" to explore overlooked possibilities for moving practice forward. Our research so far indicates that a focus on the issues of definition and the related use of evidence has the potential to create such interruptions.

Acknowledgements

1. I would like to acknowledge the contributions of my colleagues Tony Booth, Alan Dyson, Peter Farrell, Andy Howes, Dave Tweddle, Windyz Ferreira, Sam Fox, Susie Miles and Mel West to the ideas presented in this paper. 2. Some of the research reported in this paper was funded by Award L139 25 1001 and as such is part of the Teaching and Learning Research Programme of the UK's Economic and Social Research Council. 3. Earlier versions of this paper were presented at the International Congress on Inclusive Education held at the Hong Kong Institute of Education in December 2003, and at the IV International Congress on Psychology and Education, Almeria, Spain, March 2004.

References

Ainscow, M. (1994). *Special Needs in the Classroom: A Teacher Education Guide.* London: Jessica Kingsley/Paris: UNESCO.

Ainscow, M. (1995). Special needs through school improvement: School improvement through special needs. In C. Clark, A. Dyson & A. Millward (eds.), *Towards Inclusive Schools?*. London: Fulton.

Ainscow, M. (1999). *Understanding the Development of Inclusive Schools*. London: Falmer.

Ainscow, M. (2000a). Reaching out to all learners: Some lessons from international experience. *School Effectiveness and School Improvement* 11(1), 1–9.

Ainscow, M. (2000b). The next step for special education. *British Journal of Special Education* 27(2), 76–80.

Ainscow, M. (2002). Using research to encourage the development of inclusive practices. In P. Farrell & M. Ainscow (eds.), *Making Special Education Inclusive*. London: Fulton.

Ainscow, M., Barrs, D. & Martin, J. (1998). Taking school improvement into the classroom. *Improving Schools* 1(3), 43–48.

Ainscow, M., Booth, T., Dyson, A., Farrell, P., Frankham, J., Gallannaugh, F., Howes, A. & Smith, R. (in press). *Improving Schools, Developing Inclusion*. London: RoutledgeFalmer.

Ainscow, M. & Brown, D. (2000). Guidance on improving teaching. Retrieved December 23, 2004 from http://lewisham.gov.uk.

Ainscow, M., Farrell, P. & Tweddle, D. (2000). Developing policies for inclusive education: A study of the role of local education authorities. *International Journal of Inclusive Education* 4(3), 211–229.

Ainscow, M. & Haile-Giorgis, M. (1999). Educational arrangements for children categorised as having special needs in Central and Eastern Europe. *European Journal of Special Needs Education* 14(2), 103–121.

Ainscow, M. & Howes, A. (2001). *LEAs and school improvement: What is it that makes the difference?* Paper presented at the British Education Research Association Conference, Leeds, England.

Ainscow, M., Howes, A., Farrell, P. & Frankham, J. (2003). Making sense of the development of inclusive practices. *European Journal of Special Needs Education* 18(2), 227–242.

Ainscow, M., Howes, A. & Tweddle, D. (2004). Making sense of the impact of recent education policies: a study of practice. In M. Emmerich (ed.), *Public services under New Labour*. Manchester, UK: University of Manchester, The Institute for Political and Economical Governance.

Ainscow, M. & Tweddle, D. (2003). Understanding the changing role of English local education authorities in promoting inclusion. In J. Allan (ed.), *Inclusion, Participation and Democracy: What is the Purpose?*. Dordrecht: Kluwer Academic Publishers.

Angelides, P. & Ainscow, M. (2000). Making sense of the role of culture in school improvement. *School Effectiveness and School Improvement* 11(2), 145–164.

Bartolome, L.I. (1994). Beyond the methods fetish: Towards a humanising pedagogy. *Harvard Education Review* 54(2), 173–194.

Bellamy, C. (1999). *The state of the world's children*: Education: UNICEF.

Brown, J.S. & Duguid, P. (1991). Organisational learning and communities of practice: Towards a unified view of working, learning and innovation. *Organisational Science* 2(1), 40–57.

Finklestein, N.D. & Grubb, W.N. (2000). Making sense of education and training markets: Lessons from England. *American Educational Research Journal* 37(3), 601–631.

Florian, L., Rose, R. & Tilstone, C. (eds.), (1998) *Planning Inclusive Practice*. London: Routledge.

Fullan, M. (1991). *The new meaning of educational change*. London, UK: Cassell.

Hiebert, J. Gallimore, R. & Stigler, J.W. (2002). A knowledge base for the teaching profession: What would it look like and how can we get one?. *Educational Researcher* 31(5), 3–15.

Huberman, M. (1993). The model of the independent artisan in teachers' professional relationships. In J.W. Little & M.W. McLaughlin (eds.), *Teachers' Work: Individuals, Colleagues and Contexts*. New York: Teachers College Press.

Kugelmass, J. & Ainscow, M. (2003). *Leadership for inclusion: A comparison of international practices*. Paper presented at the meeting of the American Educational Research Association, Chicago, April 2003.

Lambert, L. (1995). *The Constructivist Leader*. New York: Teachers College Press.

Little, J.W. & McLaughlin, M.W. (eds.), (1993) *Teachers' Work: Individuals, Colleagues and Contexts*. New York: Teachers College Press.

Mittler, P. (2000). *Working Towards Inclusive Education*. London: Fulton.

Moore, M. Jackson, M., Fox, S. & Ainscow, M. (2004). The Manchester Inclusion Standard. *Manchester City Council*.

Riehl, C.J. (2000). The principal's role in creating inclusive schools for diverse students: A review of normative, empirical, and critical literature on the practice of educational administration. *Review of Educational Research* 70(1), 55–81.

Sebba, J. & Sachdev, D. (1997). *What Works in Inclusive Education?*. Ilford: Barnardo's.

Schein, E. (1985). *Organisational Culture and Leadership*. San Francisco: Jossey-Bass.

Schein, E.H. (2001). Clinical inquiry/research. In P. Reason & H. Bradbury (eds.), *Handbook of Action Research*. London: Sage.

Senge, P.M. (1989). *The Fifth Discipline: The Art and Practice of the Learning Organisation*. London: Century.

Strathern M. (2000). The tyranny of transparency. *British Educational Research Journal* 26(3), 309–321.

Stainback, W. & Stainback, S. (eds.), (1990) *Support Networks for Inclusive Schooling*. Baltimore: Brookes.

Thousand, J.S. & Villa, R.A. (1991). Accommodating for greater student variance. In M. Ainscow (ed.), *Effective schools for all*. London: Fulton.

Trent, S.C. Artiles, A.J. & Englert, C.S. (1998). From deficit thinking to social constructivism: A review of theory, research and practice in special education. *Review of Research in Education* 23, 277–307.

UNESCO. (1994). *Final Report: World Conference on Special Needs Education: Access and Quality*. Paris: UNESCO.

UNESCO. (2001). *The Open File on Inclusive Education*. Paris: UNESCO.

Wang, M.C. (1991). Adaptive education; an alternative approach to providing for student diversity. In M. Ainscow (ed.), *Effective schools for all*. London: Fulton.

Vitello, S.J. & Mithaug, D.E. (eds.), (1998). *Inclusive Schooling: National and International Perspectives*. Mahwah, NJ: Lawrence Erlbaum.

Wenger, E. (1998). *Communities of Practice: Learning, Meaning and Identity*. Cambridge: Cambridge University Press.

CHAPTER 11

LEADERSHIP AND COLLABORATION

Ainscow, M. and West, M. (eds.) (2006) *Improving urban schools: leadership and collaboration*. Maidenhead: Open University Press (Chapter 12: Drawing the lessons)

Introduction

The publication of this book reflected my growing interest in system-level change as a necessary strategy for fostering equity in education. It argues that the findings of the research reported in the book point to important new possibilities for improving the quality of education in urban contexts. Given that there is untapped potential within the system, it is proposed that the aim must be to develop leadership practices that encourage collaboration within and between schools, so that individual knowledge, experience and creativity can be shared for the benefit of all. It is also argued that such collaborations have to reach out to the wider community. The chapter goes on to examine the implications of these arguments for policy development, and considers their significance at the national, district and institutional levels. This analysis proved to be important in relation to developments reported in the readings that follow.

The accounts presented in this book provide interesting insights into some of the pressures on and developments within urban educational contexts in England during a period of extraordinary change. Our analysis of these accounts leads us to conclude that significant advances in urban schooling are unlikely to be achieved unless those who remain on the margins of the system are transformed into full participants. However, as we have seen, external efforts to raise standards in poorly performing schools often create barriers to the development of a more inclusive approach.

The government has argued that the raising of 'standards' must also promote equity: that a powerful emphasis on raising attainment need not simply benefit children who are already performing at a high level. Implemented properly, and supported by the various inclusion initiatives, the standards agenda is, it is argued, of even greater potential benefit to previously low-attaining children in poorly-performing schools: it is about excellence for the many, not just the few.

Yet the national strategies, whatever their benefits, have tended to reduce the flexibility with which schools can respond to the diverse characteristics of their students. As the accounts of what happens inside schools that are deemed to be 'failing' demonstrate, this has been a particular problem for those urban schools that are seen to be performing poorly, since the short-term pressure to deliver satisfactory 'metrics' can postpone the development of strategies necessary for longer term improvement. And, as is evident from the study of schools that have made sustained progress, despite the drag-anchor of being identified as 'below floor targets', headteachers are acutely aware of such pressures.

While the need to escape such designations can be useful in galvanising early efforts, since the designation itself becomes a common enemy upon which energies can be focused, they may also be limiting and inhibit ambition – amongst students and teachers alike. At the same time, the development during the 1990s of an educational market-place, coupled with the recent emphasis on policies fostering greater diversity between schools, seems in some areas to have created a quasi-selective system in which the poorest children, by and large, attend the lowest-performing schools. Consequently, the lowest-performing and, many would argue, the least advantaged schools, fall progressively further and further behind their high-performing counterparts (Edwards & Tomlinson, 2002). In terms of these effects, through selective advantaging and disadvantaging of schools, it can be argued that those very policies that have generally led to increased standards, have also increased, rather than decreased, disparities in education quality and opportunity between advantaged and less privileged groups. Giroux and Schmidt (2004) explain how similar reform policies in the United States have turned some schools into 'test-prep centres'. As a result, such schools tend to be increasingly ruthless in their disregard of those students who pose a threat to their 'success', as determined by standardised, but narrow, assessment procedures.

Nevertheless, our analysis of the experiences described in this book also offers some reasons for optimism, not least in that it suggests that the system has considerable untapped potential to improve itself. As we have seen, there are skills, knowledge and, most importantly, creativity within schools, and within their local communities, that can be mobilised to improve educational provision. We have seen examples of how school staff groups can come together to strengthen and increase the impact of one another's efforts; we have seen the impact of headteachers pooling their knowledge and experience for the benefit of a particular school, or for a group of schools; we have seen the potential for cooperation between schools and their local authority, and with the wider community; and, running throughout all the chapters, we have also seen the potential of partnerships between school staff and researchers.

All of this demonstrates what can be achieved when those who have a stake in urban education engage in authentic collaborative activity. Of course, collaboration has itself been a regular feature of national policy in recent years, best illustrated by Excellence in Cities and the Leadership Incentive Grant, both initiatives specifically targeted on schools in challenging urban environments. Nevertheless, and despite this press for greater collaboration within and between schools, there has been a tendency to view urban schools through a deficit lens, focusing on what they lack rather than the resources that they can draw on. As a result, it has often been assumed that externally driven strategies are the only feasible means of achieving improvement. While our own recent work with LIG collaboratives (Ainscow and West, 2005) leaves us in no doubt about the importance of additional resources as a stimulus to school to school collaboration, we are also aware of the potency of local ownership and local ideas. Our experiences suggest that national improvement strategies have, too often, fallen into the trap of overlooking the evidence that local interpretation and adaptation can shape and strengthen the way proposals are implemented.

Indeed, it seems to us that this helps to explain why these initiatives have had rather mixed effects. Dyson's description of 'Northtown' schools provides an excellent illustration of both how the local element can and must contribute, and how national policies can discourage such contributions.

Of course, the pressures arising from inspection and from the publishing of Ofsted reports and test and examination results have certainly focused minds. In some instances, this has also inspired a degree of rethinking and experimentation. But, as some of the Chapters make clear, it has sometimes encouraged staff to take a rather insular approach – after all, what one school 'contributes' to the success of another does not appear in any league table. At the same time, the political imperative to achieve rapid results, particularly the desire to identify strategies that 'work' and then to 'up-scale' these through centrally determined prescriptions, has created barriers to progress. Further, the tendency to designate some schools as failing, or causing concern, can place restrictions on the willingness of those involved to take risks. Again, there is a pertinent example here – 'Shepherd School', opted to exclude the local community and establish, instead, some sort of educational oasis, where national policies (and the values implicit in these) were imposed even more strongly to eliminate the (presumably malign) influences of the local environment. It avoided the risks of opening up the school to the community, and instead pursued strategies that required changes in the community, rather than changes in the way we think about the business of schools, in order to achieve sustainable success.

However, we remain optimistic that schools can find ways to work together and with their communities that will enable some of the disadvantages of location and catchment to be overcome. The remainder of this chapter sets out what we feel is needed if this is to happen. It is organised around what we see as the major themes arising from the accounts we have gathered together here. These are: the need to think more deeply about what collaboration means; the importance of leadership within collaboration and the pressures collaboration places on school leaders; strategies and practices that can promote collaborative activity; and the importance of identifying and using the skills and imagination of existing staff, since there is no alternative teaching force 'out there' that, if we could only attract them, will come in and transform our more challenging schools. Finally, we focus on what emerges from these studies as a key issue – knowing how to get things moving.

Understanding collaboration

The development of collaboration as a strategy for school improvement is far from straightforward within the English context, where competition and choice continue to be driving forces within national education policy. This is why powerful levers are needed that will challenge existing assumptions and, at the same time, move thinking and practice forward. However, we feel that there is also a need to explicate what it is collaboration brings that adds value to school improvement efforts.

Our own understanding of the potential of collaborative working practices has been shaped, in part, by the projects reported in this book. It has also been influenced by the ideas of Wenger (1998), Senge (1990) and Hargreaves (2003). Wenger, in putting forward his notion of 'communities of practice', describes the transfer and creation of knowledge within the workplace. Essentially, the members of a work community pass on their knowledge and ideas to one another through processes of 'negotiation' in which common meanings are established. 'New' knowledge acquired in this way can then be tested out in practice – though inevitably it will be modified as it is subjected to new experiences and contexts. As it moves around within the community, passing from practitioner to practitioner, knowledge is continually modified and refined. In this way, it becomes possible for knowledge to be re-cycled around the community and returned to the originator – though transformed through the process. Thus, the virtuous circle is completed, with knowledge and understanding increased through each iteration.

Senge, in his writings on learning organisations, suggests that knowledge within organisations takes two forms – the explicit and the tacit. Explicit knowledge (which will embrace established wisdom), is relatively easy to transfer, but is likely to be generalised rather than specific. On the other hand, tacit knowledge is caught rather than deliberately passed on, but can only be caught if the right circumstances exist. Consequently, what can be achieved through explicit and tacit exchanges is limited – learning organisations need to find ways to generate tacit-to-explicit and explicit-to-tacit transfers. Again, our conception of collaborative practice is that it provides just such an opportunity, as individuals work together on common goals, sharing and using one another's knowledge and, through the processes of sharing, reflection and re-cycling, create new knowledge.

David Hargreaves also notes the tacit nature of much of teachers' knowledge, when explaining why it has proved so difficult to transfer good practice from one teacher to another. This leads him to conclude that what he describes as 'social capital' is needed within the teaching communities. Social capital here represents shared values and assumptions that, because they are commonly 'owned' by community members, are available for all members of the community to draw on when transferring knowledge and understandings. For him, building social capital involves the development of networks based on mutual trust, within which good practice can spread in natural ways.

Bearing these ideas in mind, we suggest that collaboration within and between schools is a practice that can both transfer existing knowledge and, more importantly, generate context specific 'new' knowledge. Further, we feel that the studies reported in this book give strong indications of how such processes can be initiated and managed. At the same time, these experiences also point to certain conditions that are necessary in order to make collaboration effective. In summary, these are as follows:

- The presence of incentives that encourage key stakeholders to explore the possibility that collaboration will be in their own interests;
- The development of a sense of collective responsibility for bringing about improvements in all the partner organisations;
- Headteachers and other senior staff in schools who are willing and able to drive collaboration forward;
- The identification of common improvement priorities that are seen to be relevant to a wide range of stakeholders;
- External help from credible consultants/advisers (from the local authority or elsewhere) who also have the disposition and confidence to learn alongside their school-based partners; and
- A willingness and desire amongst local authority staff to support and engage with the collaborative process, exploring and developing new roles and relationships.

In our view, the absence of such conditions will mean that attempts to encourage teachers and schools to work together are likely to result in little more than time-consuming meetings, which sooner or later will be seen as ineffective and discontinued. This conclusion is, in itself, important for future national initiatives that seek to invest resources in the notion of schools working together in partnerships or networks. Strategies for developing these conditions – or fostering their development at the local level – will be an important determinant of the success such initiatives can expect. This analysis also suggests that the Government's current emphasis on the spread of 'independent specialist schools' and academies needs to be handled sensitively, if it is not to further disadvantage schools and groups of learners that are already struggling against the odds.

Leadership for collaboration

We now turn to another theme emerging from our analysis of these studies – leadership. However, we would like to emphasise that whilst it is true that, by and large, schools do not improve without effective leadership from the inside, it is also the case that the wider context influences the progress of such improvement efforts, for good or ill. This is the power of what is characterised in Chapter 7 as 'inter-dependence'. It leads us to argue that, while in order to secure sustained improvement, schools do have to become more autonomous and self-improving, at the same time, our attention should not be drawn away from the ways that neighbouring schools can add value to one another's efforts.

The research summarised in this book has led us to formulate a typology of the sorts of relationships that can exist within a network of schools. Where the individual school locates itself within the typology is a critical factor in determining whether or not collaborative arrangements bring benefits, and the attitude of the headteacher appears to be a crucial determinant of positioning. The typology, which draws on the ideas of Michael Fielding (2002), postulates four levels of collaborative endeavour, as follows:

Association – This is the traditional pattern, where there are some links between schools through occasional LEA meetings and in-service events. By and large, however, it does not involve sharing of knowledge or resources.

Cooperation – This is where closer links develop through participation in meetings and activities that provide opportunities to contribute experiences. As a result there may be some incidental sharing of knowledge and resources, and thus some transfer of existing knowledge.

Collaboration – This involves schools working together to address particular problems or challenges. By their nature, such activities require the sharing of knowledge and resources, but often these initiatives are focused on specific objectives and are not sustained. However, there are limited opportunities for knowledge creation, though re-cycling is less common, as such collaboration most often assumes 'stronger' and 'weaker' partners.

Collegiality – This involves a wider and longer-term relationship, between schools and teachers, in which there is recognition of interdependence and, to a degree, the sharing of responsibility for one another's progress. It leads to the bringing together of existing knowledge and resources within an agreed set of values, and potentially the creation of new knowledge for all. In this way, collegiality provides a network within which social capital can be built up.

Such a typology suggests that the aim must be to foster moves towards the more powerful, inter-dependent, collaborative relationships that can strengthen the capacity of all partner schools to deliver forms of education that can respond effectively to student diversity. In this regard, the distinction made by Fielding between 'collaboration' and 'collegiality' is particularly helpful. He characterises 'collaboration' as being driven by a set of common concerns, narrowly functional, and focused strongly on looked-for gains. In such contexts, the partners in a collaborative activity are regarded as a resource, or a source of information, rather than as members of a 'community of practice'. Fielding goes on to suggest that collaboration is, therefore, a plural form of individualism in which participants are typically intolerant of time spent on anything other than the task in hand. He argues that, once the task has been completed or priorities have changed, the drive behind collaboration is weakened and such collaborative working arrangements will become more tenuous, and may disappear altogether. 'Collegiality', on the other hand, is characterised as being a much more robust relationship. It is reciprocal and overridingly communal, and is rooted in shared ideals and aspirations and mutually valued social ends. Collegiality is, therefore, by definition, less reliant upon the pursuit of narrowly defined objectives or gains, but is based on a deeper commitment to exchange and development.

We have found that, in practice, instances of schools working together usually do not extend to collegial activity. Of course, it may be that collaboration is the forerunner to collegiality, and what we are seeing is groups of schools feeling their way towards more sustained and sustainable partnerships. Nor are the benefits of collaboration to be dismissed; the studies reported here show that, in many instances, stakeholders have experienced the practical benefits of collaborating, albeit in contexts where the outcomes tended to be narrowly defined. There is also evidence that, in at least some cases – the schools working together across a local authority for example, or the headteachers combining their efforts for the benefit of a single school – the success achieved through collaborative arrangements is leading to the development of a common language and to shared aspirations that might, in the longer term, provide a basis for collegial, urban communities.

Within school communities, more now needs to be done to strengthen collaborative activities and understandings, so that these develop towards a genuine sense of collegiality. Our view is that this will be achieved, in part, by encouraging headteachers to take on collective responsibility for the performance of all schools within a group or network. Specifically, the aim must be to develop more collegial relationships, based on a common commitment to improvement across schools, and to principles of equity and social justice. Provided heads genuinely feel that they are in control of the priorities that emerge from such a process, we would be optimistic that this could be achieved. In our discussions with heads, we find few who do not believe that the principle of collaboration with other schools is a good one, though many find the need to maximise the performance of their own schools (as measured by test results) in the short term militates against the development of sustained collaborative relationships. It appears that the sharp, individual accountability framework that kick-started improvement efforts in the early 1990s may now, especially in the most deprived and difficult educational contexts, pose an obstacle to the development of that sense of collective accountability for the wider school and student populations which best serves the needs of vulnerable pupils.

As we have explained, over recent years English schools have had to respond to a constant stream of innovations aimed at raising standards. In common with many other social organisations undergoing significant transformation efforts, in schools that are under pressure to improve the search is on for what Fullan (1991) describes as 'order and correctness'. He suggests that teachers searching for 'order' in times of complex social and organisational change will, inevitably, experience ambiguity regarding the direction and purposes of the change. Indeed, the search for 'order' is itself an attempt to determine what actions to take when faced with ambiguous situations – as where headteachers of 'failing' schools face the twin demands of providing clear direction for the staff, while simultaneously developing their capacity to play a much greater role in decision-making. Where a number of heads find themselves in similarly difficult situations, it seems that collaboration across schools can be an important source of reassurance in times of uncertainty.

It is also the case that those who can help to create a sense of common purpose in such contexts are more likely to be able to bring about change. This may, in part at least, throw some light on what has occurred in the more successful collaborative arrangements we have described. Unusual and challenging factors, emanating as they do from both outside and inside schools, have created a sense of ambiguity. The collaborative arrangements introduced by some groups of headteachers have helped one another to cope with this. Further, as a result of their combined efforts, these headteachers are gradually identifying common principles around which their staffs can be drawn together, generating a new impetus for change across the whole school group.

Research suggests that such ambiguities in organisations increase the extent to which action is guided by values and ideology (see, for example, Weick, 1991). Consequently, the values of 'powerful people' (i.e. those who can reduce ambiguity) greatly influence how the organisation works and what it can become. Thus, those who can resolve ambiguity for themselves and for others can implant a new set of values into an organisation. This has the potential to create a new set of relevancies and competencies, and, in so doing, is itself a source of innovation. In this way, ambiguity sets the scene for organisations to learn more about themselves and their environments, allowing them to emerge from their struggles and uncertainties into different and better adapted structures.

It seems, therefore, that the perspectives and skills of headteachers and other senior staff are central to an understanding of what needs to happen in order that the potential power of collaboration can be mobilised. Their visions for their schools, their beliefs about how they can foster the learning of all of their students, and their commitment to the power of inter-dependent learning, appear to be key influences. All of this means, of course, that replication of these processes in other schools or groups of schools will be difficult, particularly if those in charge are unwilling or unable to make fundamental changes in established beliefs and working patterns. This being the case, there is a very strong case for providing school leaders with professional development opportunities specifically focused on collaborative practice, which will support them in taking this work forward. The action learning approach, adopted by the headteachers whose activities are described in Chapter 9, provides a powerful strategy for such development activities.

Of course, the emphasis on school level leadership within a change model grounded in the notion that a combination of robust national policies and strong school management is the surest way to increase attainment, has very significant implications for the roles of local authority staff. It means that they will have to adjust their priorities and ways of working in response to the development of collaborative arrangements that are led from within schools. And, at a time when they too are under increasing pressure to deliver improvements in results across their stocks of schools, this can lead to misunderstandings and tensions between senior staff in schools and their local authority partners.

Despite such difficulties, we cannot conceive of a way for collaboration to continue as a central element of effective school improvement strategies, without some form of local co-ordination. As we have seen, the contributions of local authority advisers can be significant in the development of collaborative arrangements. Specifically, local authority staff can support and challenge schools in relation to the agreed goals of collaborative activities, whilst head-teachers share responsibility for the overall management of improvement efforts within their schools.

We feel that this distinction sharpens understanding of the sorts of roles that local authority staffs need to take on: *not* managing and leading change, but rather working in partnership with senior people in schools to strengthen collaborative ways of working. In such contexts they can ensure that specific challenges which derive from their knowledge of the bigger picture across the authority are addressed, and also contribute to the clarity of purpose and practical working arrangements, as well as playing an important role in the monitoring and evaluation of progress. At the same time, they can help to broker the sharing of resources and expertise. However, the changes in attitude and practice that this implies will be challenging to the existing thinking of many experienced local authority staff. Consequently, they too need professional development opportunities that will assist them in rethinking their ways of working with and supporting schools.

In our view, national policy-makers would be naive to overlook the influence of what happens at the local authority level, particularly in urban districts. As we have seen, local history, inter-connections between schools and established relationships are always important local factors, helping to shape what happens, even when they are overlooked. Consequently, levers need to be found, of the sort provided by the Leadership Incentive Grant, which will be powerful in encouraging the development of inter-dependence amongst groups of schools within districts. In this way, further progress can be made towards a national education system that is geared to raising standards for all students, in all schools, through the systematic orchestration and, sometimes, the redistribution of available resources and expertise.

When considering the leadership of collaborative arrangements between schools, there is also a need to reach out to others who have an interest in the education of children and young people. In particular, it is important to ensure that parents/carers, elected members, governors, and local community agencies and organisations are aware of, and feel confident about, the new emphasis within school improvement, and the value of authentic collaboration. In this respect, the move towards the integration of support staff from different agencies within district structures (that is occurring in some parts of the country) is a very helpful development. Given the recent Children Act, such moves are, of course, essential. Indeed, the structural changes that are being introduced in response to the Every Child Matters policy provide a potentially helpful interruption to the established flow of services within urban areas. The aim must be to use the space that this creates to rethink and, indeed, regroup. However, so far the indications are not altogether promising, with representatives of the various interest groups tending to retreat within established professional boundaries as often as they seek to form new professional alliances.

Fostering school-to-school collaboration

As we have seen, there is evidence that school-to-school collaboration can add considerable value to the efforts of urban schools as they seek to develop their practices. However, this does not represent an easy option for the schools themselves, particularly in a context within which competition and choice continue to be the main drivers. There is also the problem of sustainability to consider. The examples we have presented have, for the most part, emerged as a result of schools being offered short-term incentives linked to the demonstration of collaborative planning and activity.

In February 2005 the Secretary of State for Education, Ruth Kelly, was quoted as saying:

> 'In the future I think cooperation will become not only the norm, it will probably be the only way of delivering a decent all-round education for all pupils . . . . . We have to get schools to operate as part of a network to deliver a fully comprehensive education.'

But, within an education system that places emphases on both competition and choice, why should schools choose to work together? Even where substantial incentives to collaborate are available, achieving authentic collaboration has proved a challenge, requiring, as we have argued elsewhere, the surrendering of some degree of independent control in return for collective influence (Ainscow, West, Howes & Stanford, 2005). However, we have also noted that, in some instances, arrangements that were initially stimulated through external incentives have been adopted by the partner schools, who have begun to use their own resources to sustain collaborative arrangements that have clearly benefited all.

We are similarly encouraged by the experiences reported in the various studies presented here. We find in these accounts ample evidence that school-to-school collaboration does have an enormous potential for fostering system-wide improvement, particularly in challenging urban contexts. They show how collaboration between schools can often provide an effective means of solving immediate problems, such as staffing shortages; how it can have a positive impact in periods of crisis, such as during the closure of a school; and, how, in the longer run, schools working together can contribute to the raising of expectations and attainment in schools that have had a record of low achievement. There is also some evidence here that collaboration can help to reduce the polarisation of schools according to their position in 'league tables', to the particular benefit of those students who seem marginalised at the edges of the system and whose performance and attitudes cause increasing concern. This does, of course, add support to the argument presented by Ruth Kelly.

There is evidence, too, that when schools seek to develop more collaborative ways of working, this can have an impact on how teachers perceive themselves and their work. Specifically, comparisons of practice can lead teachers to view underachieving students in a new light. Rather than simply presenting problems that are assumed to be insurmountable, such students may be perceived as providing feedback on existing classroom arrangements. In this way they may be seen as sources of understanding as to how these arrangements might be developed in ways that could be of benefit to all members of the class.

Of course, the approaches to collaboration reported in these studies vary considerably in scope and ambition, and in terms of their impact on practice and learning outcomes. Their impact ranges from the direct and short term, to the indirect and longer term. Some strategies are essentially short-term 'fixes', aimed at immediate issues of concern (such as getting out of special measures), but with little or no potential for longer term impact. Others are intended to bring about much more fundamental changes (for example, changes in the school's culture or image), which may take several years to achieve, or before any difference is noted. Many strategies fall somewhere in between (for example, coordinated local strategy for inclusion; setting up an action-learning set for headteachers), offering some combination of short-term impact and longer term development.

Looking at the accounts, it seems that activities that have a direct and immediate impact on achievement tended to be *relatively* easy to implement. Other strategies involve processes that are intended to increase the capacity of schools and their staffs to develop more effective teaching and learning arrangements in response to identified needs. By their nature, these take a little longer to implement, not least because they require the negotiation of common priorities and shared values. They also require an investment of human resources in order to create a framework for management and coordination, as we saw in the account of the four schools that worked together to improve conditions in one of their number. This reminds us that trust takes time to develop.

Examples such as this underline that in moving collaboration forward, from a strategy for addressing various forms of delinquency, to one that embraces and plans for the development of all schools and students within a network, the issue of shared leadership is a central driver. As we have argued, it requires the development of leadership practices that involve many stakeholders, collectively sharing responsibility for improving the achievement of learners in all of the schools within a collaborative. Often this necessitates significant changes in beliefs and attitude, and new relationships, as well as improvements in practice. The goal, however, must be to ensure that collaboration is between school communities, and not restricted to headteachers, not least because arrangements that rely on one person are unlikely to survive the departure of those individuals who brokered them.

Using available expertise

A key to improvement in urban schools is, then, to make use of the pressure for change stemming from national policies, whilst mobilising available human resources at the local level around a common sense of purpose. This is most likely to be achieved when local leadership makes connections between national policies and local priorities. It also means that there is a need to create locally the organisational conditions and climate within which stakeholders will feel encouraged to work together creatively to invent new and more effective responses to old problems – especially those of learners who are not making satisfactory progress. This requires the development of leadership that will encourage action and shared responsibility at all levels of the system. And with regard to children's learning experiences, the classroom level is crucial, since it is clear that teachers *are* decision-makers and, therefore, policy-makers (Fulcher, 1989). Changing policy and practice at that level is particularly difficult, however, in that it most often requires changes in thinking and beliefs.

As we have seen, at the heart of the processes in schools where changes in practice do occur, is the development of a common vocabulary in which colleagues can talk to one another about and, indeed, reflect themselves on, the detail of their practice. Without such a vocabulary, teachers find it very difficult to describe in detail what they do presently and how this might be altered. Consequently, a language of classroom practice seems a prerequisite to the exploration of new possibilities. It seems that much of what teachers do during the multiple and intensive encounters that occur daily in the classroom, is carried out at an automatic, intuitive level. Furthermore, there is little time to stop and think. This is why the opportunity to see colleagues at work in the classroom is so crucial to the success of attempts to develop practice. It is through such shared experiences that colleagues can help one another to describe what they currently do and articulate what they might like to do (Hiebert, Gallimore, & Stigler, 2002). In essence, together, they can create a language of practice. This also offers a means whereby taken-for-granted assumptions about particular groups of students can be revisited, challenged, and subjected to mutual critique.

As we saw, engaging with evidence can be especially helpful in encouraging such dialogue between practitioners. Specifically, it can help to create space for reappraisal and rethinking, by interrupting existing discourses, and by focusing attention on overlooked possibilities for moving practice forward. However, the introduction of inquiry-based approaches that seek to build on existing expertise within schools is particularly difficult in challenging urban contexts. The tensions between the efforts such approaches require and the intensive pressure to achieve rapid improvements in test and examination results, may discourage staff from committing themselves to what are, by their nature, improvement strategies which take time to have an impact. This is why leadership at the school level is so crucial; it must make space for such developments, despite the pressures from external scrutiny.

Moving forward

In recent years we have been privileged to work with a group of headteachers who were brought together because they had been successful in bringing about significant improvement in schools in difficult urban contexts. One project we worked on with this group involved the design of strategies that could help others to follow a similar journey of improvement in their own schools. As part of this work, we developed a framework that heads could use to identify areas of successful practice in the school, while at the same time pinpointing less effective areas where ways of working needed to be changed (Ainscow, West & Stanford, 2003).

The heads involved in this work recalled that there had been a sense of helplessness in some of their schools that had to be overcome before progress was possible. It seems that the first, important achievement of these headteachers was to move their school communities on, beyond this feeling of 'helplessness', to the belief that things could and must change. Such a belief involves developing teachers' capacity to imagine what might be achieved, and increasing their sense of accountability for bringing this about. In a number of cases, it involved tackling habits, most often relating to behaviour or attendance, that had settled into norms within the school. Such habits had come to be regarded as part of the landscape, rather than things that could and should be changed. Sometimes, the change needed was within the community – parents who were happy with the school as it was, rather than seeking improvements; families that looked to the school to improve attainment, but did not link this to their own support for the school.

What became evident was that the first step, creating the initial momentum and the self-belief among staff and students alike that goes with it, was seen as the most difficult to take. Though the initial achievement may have been modest in relation to what the school eventually achieved, these headteachers felt that progress became easier as the school's capacity and self-confidence increased over time. It was *knowing how to make a start* that mattered.

We concluded that the starting point must, most often, be with an analysis of *the quality of student experience* that is provided within a school. This can be thought of in terms of three interconnected dimensions:

- *Presence*, i.e. how reliably and punctually students attend school and lessons
- *Participation*, i.e. the quality of their experiences whilst they are there (therefore, incorporating the views of the students themselves)
- *Achievement*, i.e. the outcomes of learning, as measured by test and examination results.

At the same time, it is important to think of the way the school's resources are mobilised in relation to student experience, by analysing three sets of 'arrangements' – those relating to the classroom, to management and to the wider context. *Classroom arrangements* are concerned with the quality of interactions between staff and students, and focus specifically on the teaching repertoires used, relationships, and the support provided for learners. *Management arrangements* are about the way that staff and resources are deployed, and embraces leadership and staff development strategies. *Contextual arrangements* refer to the school's engagement with relevant stakeholders, both local (in the environment) and professional (in the system), and its links with community and external support agencies.

Drawing on research findings from school improvement and effectiveness studies, it is possible to identify factors that influence the quality of these arrangements. The presence (or absence) of these factors is likely to determine the strength of leverage that is brought to bear on student experience. Furthermore, there are factors that students can themselves contribute to the quality of their own experience.

Since it will be the way these arrangements combine with one another, and with student determined variables, that influences the quality of learning, it seems sensible to analyse for the presence or absence of these factors. Indeed, by analysing classroom, school and contextual arrangements, it is possible to see how leverage might be increased. Then, by monitoring student experience, both the impact of these levers and the influence of student related variables can be assessed.

Continuing with the search for powerful levers, then, we believe that it will be helpful to those at the local level who are encouraging schools to collaborate if national policy initiatives continue to emphasise the principle of collaboration as being a fundamental element of efforts to raise standards across the education system; and, remembering that 'what gets measured gets done', regulatory frameworks must pay due attention to this same principle. In our view this is the way '*to get schools to operate as part of a network to deliver a fully comprehensive education*'.

Clearly, then, there are implications here for the way the government develops and implements national policy. It needs to reflect on how the general increase in standards achieved over the past ten years can be spread more effectively to those areas of social and economic deprivation where the most difficult school environments are found. It needs to think carefully about how a policy framework that facilitates improvement efforts in already successful schools may hinder similar efforts in schools facing more challenging circumstances. It needs to acknowledge (because, surely, it must already understand) that strategies which have been successful for the majority of schools have nevertheless created additional problems for the minority. Unfortunately, there is little evidence as yet that a more carefully calibrated strategy is forthcoming.

Our analysis of these studies suggests that certain types of national action can indeed be powerful in providing incentives for change and in encouraging a sense of common purpose within and between school communities. Here the role of evidence in relation to regulation seems to be a significant lever for change. Government needs to concentrate its attention on this factor and the recent changes in the Ofsted school inspection framework are encouraging in this respect. At the same time, it needs to recognise that matters of the detail of policy implementation are not amenable to central regulation. Rather, these have to be dealt with by those who are close to and, therefore, in a better position to understand local contexts. They should be trusted to act in the best interests of the children and young people they serve, and encouraged to work together, pooling their knowledge and experience, for the benefit of students and teachers alike.

Concluding remarks

We prefaced this book with a working definition of what we understand by the term urban education, pointing out that, while this is a relatively new term in some countries, it is one that is already established in other parts of the world. It is to this international phenomenon of difficult schools in disadvantaged areas and communities that we turn finally.

In the last few years we have been involved in school improvement projects in cities as diverse as Beijing, Bucharest, Hong Kong, Lisbon and Sao Paulo. We also have close links with fellow researchers in Australia, Canada and the USA who are engaged in similar activities. These international experiences convince us that the ideas we have explored and the conclusions we have reached in this book have relevance beyond the shores of our own country.

Throughout the world, policy-makers and practitioners are faced with the challenge of underachievement amongst children and young people in urban contexts. And, in responding to these challenges, there is increasing evidence that collaboration within schools and between schools is seen as being the best way forward. It seems, then, that it is not only in England that there is reason to believe that *within* urban schools and their communities there is far greater potential for school improvement than is currently being utilised. Unfortunately, however, whilst national reform efforts have heightened the sense of urgency in relation to the challenge of urban education, they have also tended to create barriers to the sharing and creation of knowledge.

There is, therefore, a need for a major shift in overall policy direction. As we have argued in this chapter, this must involve an emphasis on forms of leadership that will foster collaboration and creativity at the local level. In this respect, the idea of school-to-school collaboration seems to be one that has found its moment. The evidence we have presented in this book suggests that, under certain conditions, partnerships between schools can generate powerful levers for change.

References

Ainscow, M., West, M., Howes, A. and Stanford, J. (2005) Why should secondary schools collaborate? An advice paper for the DfES on ways of fostering school-to-school co-operation. University of Manchester: Leadership Development Unit

Ainscow, M., West, M. and Stanford, J. (2003) Making a New Start: A practical guide for headteachers on how to analyse schools causing concern in order to determine priorities for action. University of Manchester: Leadership Development Unit

Fielding, M. (1999) Radical collegiality: affirming teaching as an inclusive professional practice. *Australian Educational Researcher* 26 (2), 1–34

Fulcher, G. (1989) Disabling Policies? A Comparative Approach to Education Policy and Disability. London: Falmer

Fullan, M. (2001). *Leading in a culture of change.* San Francisco: Jossey-Bass

Giroux, H.A. and Schmidt, M. (2004) Closing the achievement gap: a metaphor for children left behind. *Journal of Educational Change* 5, 213–228

Hargreaves, D.H. (2003) Leadership for transformation within the London Challenge. Annual lecture at the London Leadership Centre, 19 May 2003

Hiebert, J., Gallimore, R. and Stigler, J.W. (2002) A knowledge base for the teaching profession: what would it look like and how can we get one? *Educational Researcher* 31(5), 3–15

Senge, (1990) *The Fifth Discipline: The Art and Practice of the Learning Organisation.* Century

Wenger, E. (1998) *Communities of Practice: Learning, Meaning and Identity.* Cambridge University Press

Weick, K.E. (1985) Sources of order in underorganised systems: Themes in recent organisational theory. In Y.S. Lincoln (Ed.), Organisational Theory and Inquiry. Beverly Hills: Sage

CHAPTER 12

EDUCATION FOR ALL

Ainscow, M. and Miles, S. (2008) Making education for all inclusive: where next?
Prospects 37(1), 15–34

Introduction

The argument presented in this paper provided the conceptual framework for the 48th session of the International Conference on Education, held in 2008, and attended by Ministers of Education and officials from 153 countries. It suggests that a common sense of purpose around inclusive education, together with a consistent use of language, is essential if the United Nations' Education for All (EFA) policy is to be effective. It suggests that this does not require the introduction of new techniques. Rather, it involves: collaboration within and between schools, closer links between schools and communities, networking across contexts, and the collection and use of contextually relevant evidence. The paper provides an explanation of the confusion that exists regarding the meaning of the term 'inclusive education'. Adopting the idea that this should be seen as a 'principled approach to education', it draws on research evidence relating to teaching and learning, school development, leadership and the development of education systems. This research is mostly from economically developed contexts, but it is also drawn from the experience of the UNESCO teacher education project, which was conducted in over 80 countries, and case study material gathered by the Enabling Education Network (EENET), which supports practitioners in documenting their experience of working towards more inclusive education, primarily in developing countries.

Introduction

The articles in this special edition of *Prospects* focus on what is arguably the biggest challenge facing school systems throughout the world: that of providing an effective education for all children and young people. In economically poorer countries this is mainly about the estimated 72 million children who are not in primary school (UNESCO 2008). Ensuring that all children complete primary education is an essential step towards reducing poverty and human deprivation in what Hulme (2007) refers to as the world's biggest promise in the form of the Millennium Development Goals (MDGs). Meanwhile, in wealthier countries—despite the resources available—many young people leave school with no worthwhile qualifications, others are placed in various forms of special provision away from mainstream educational experiences, and some simply choose to drop out since the lessons seem irrelevant to their lives.

Faced with these challenges, there is evidence of an increased interest in the idea of *inclusive education*. However, the field remains confused about the actions that need to be taken to move policy and practice forward. In some countries, inclusive education is still thought of as an approach to serving children with disabilities within general education settings. Internationally, however, it is increasingly seen more broadly as a reform that supports and welcomes diversity among all learners (UNESCO 2001). It presumes that the aim of inclusive education is to eliminate social exclusion that is a consequence of attitudes and responses to diversity in race, social class, ethnicity, religion, gender and ability (Vitello and Mithaug 1998). As such, it starts from the belief that education is a basic human right and the foundation of a more just society.

Fourteen years ago, the Salamanca World Conference on Special Needs Education endorsed the idea of inclusive education (UNESCO 1994). Arguably the most significant international document that has ever appeared in the field of special education, the Salamanca Statement argued that regular schools with an inclusive orientation are "the most effective means of combating discriminatory attitudes, building an inclusive society and achieving education for all". Furthermore, it suggested that such schools can "provide an effective education for the majority of children and improve the efficiency and ultimately the cost-effectiveness of the entire education system" (UNESCO 1994, para 3).

It is worth noting that the Salamanca event followed soon after the groundbreaking Jomtien Conference of 1990, which committed almost all the countries in the world to achieve the goal of EFA. This was particularly significant because it acknowledged that large numbers of vulnerable and marginalized groups of learners were excluded from education systems worldwide. However, despite the apparent unequivocal nature of the Jomtien declaration, the decision to hold the Salamanca conference would seem to imply that the phrase "education for all" actually meant "almost all", accepting the historical assumption that a small percentage of children have to be seen as "outsiders", whose education must be catered for by a separate, parallel system, usually known as special education.

Given that the implication of the Salamanca Statement, as we read it, is the bringing together of the two separate systems in order to ensure that education for all really does mean "all", in this paper we consider why progress towards a unified strategy for educational improvement has been so disappointing in many countries. This leads us to recommend a way forward, one that sets out to ensure that EFA is genuinely inclusive. We go on to draw on research evidence to consider the practical implications of such a formulation, focusing on the implications for teaching and learning, school development, leadership and the development of education systems. Whilst much of this research is from economically developed contexts, we also draw on the experience of a UNESCO teacher-education project that involved developments in over 80 countries (Ainscow 1999) and the work of the Enabling Education Network (EENET), supporting practitioners in countries of the South to document their experience of working towards more inclusive forms of education in the context of limited material resources.

Defining inclusion

The confusion that exists internationally within the field arises, in part at least, from the fact that the idea of inclusive education can be defined in a variety of ways (Ainscow et al. 2000). It is also important to remember that there is no one perspective on inclusion within a single country, or even within a school (Booth 1996; Booth and Ainscow 1998; Dyson and Millward 2000).

A recent analysis of international research (Ainscow et al. 2006b) suggests a typology of five ways of ways of thinking about inclusion. These are: (a) inclusion concerned with disability and "special educational needs"; (b) inclusion as a response to disciplinary exclusions; (c) inclusion as being about all groups vulnerable to exclusion; (d) inclusion as the promotion of a school for all; and (e) inclusion as Education for All. Before we explain the formulation that we recommend in this paper, we shall summarize what is implied by each of the five perspectives.

Perspective 1: disability and "special educational needs"

There is a common assumption that inclusion is primarily about educating disabled students and others categorized as "having special educational needs" in mainstream schools. The usefulness of such an approach has been questioned, since it focuses on a "disabled" or "special needs" part of the students, ignoring other ways in which participation may be impeded or enhanced. The *Index for inclusion*, a self-review instrument for schools that has been used in many countries in recent years (Booth and Ainscow 2002), dispensed with the notion of "special educational needs" to account for educational difficulties, replacing it with notions of "barriers to learning and participation" and "resources to support learning and participation". In this context, support was seen as all activities that increase the capacity of schools to respond to diversity.

There is a danger, however, that, in rejecting a view of inclusion tied to special educational needs and disability, attention is deflected from the continued segregation of students categorized in this way. Inclusion can involve the assertion of the rights of disabled young people to a local mainstream education, a view vociferously propounded by some disabled people. A rights perspective invalidates such arguments. Thus, compulsory segregation is seen to contribute to the oppression of disabled people, just as other practices marginalize groups on the basis of race, gender or sexual orientation (Corbett 2001).

At the same time, there is concern about the significant effect of categorizing students within education systems. The practice of segregation within special schools involves a relatively small number of students (for example, approximately 1.3% in England), yet it exerts a disproportionate influence within the education system. It seems to perpetuate a view that some students "need" to be segregated *because* of their deficiency or defect. Yet those who argue that placement in special schools is a neutral response to "need" consider that some children are best served in such settings. Indeed, nowadays the term "inclusive education" is sometimes used in England to describe practices within special schools (Spurgeon 2007). The special educational needs view of educational difficulty undoubtedly remains the dominant perspective in most countries (Mittler 2000). Special education absorbs difficulties that arise in education for a wide variety of reasons within the frame of individual defect.

Perspective 2: disciplinary exclusions

Although inclusion is most commonly seen as being associated with children categorized as "having special educational needs", in many countries it is also closely connected to "bad behaviour". The mere mention of the word "inclusion" in some schools can make teachers fearful of being asked to take on disproportionate numbers of students whose behaviour is considered to be "difficult" and who may have been excluded (or expelled) from other schools.

It has been argued that disciplinary exclusion cannot be understood without being seen in the context of preceding events, the nature of relationships and the approaches to teaching and learning in a school (Booth 1996). Even at the level of simple measurement, the figures for formal disciplinary exclusion mean little when separated from numbers for informal disciplinary exclusion. For example, sending children home for an afternoon, truancy and the categorization of students as having emotional and behavioural difficulties can all be seen as informal disciplinary exclusions. The informal exclusion of school-age girls who become pregnant, and who may be discouraged from continuing their schooling, continues to distort the gender composition of the official exclusion figures in some countries.

Perspective 3: groups vulnerable to exclusion

There is an increasing trend for inclusion in education to be viewed more broadly in terms of overcoming discrimination and disadvantage in relation to any groups of students who are vulnerable to exclusionary pressures (Mittler 2000). In some countries this broader perspective is associated with the terms "social inclusion" and "social exclusion". When used in an educational context, *social inclusion* tends to refer to barriers faced by groups whose access to schools is under threat, such as girls who become pregnant or have babies while at school, looked-after children (those in the care of public authorities) and gypsies/travellers. Commonly, though, the language of social inclusion and exclusion is often used more narrowly to refer to children who are (or are in danger of being) excluded from schools and classrooms because of their "behaviour".

This broader use of the language of inclusion and exclusion is somewhat fluid. There may well be common processes that link the different forms of exclusion experienced by disabled children, children who are excluded from school for disciplinary reasons, and people living in economically poor communities. The nature of such exclusionary processes and their origins in social structures require further research.

Perspective 4: the promotion of a school for all

A different strand of thinking about inclusion is related to the development of the common school for all—or comprehensive school. In the United Kingdom, for example, the term "comprehensive school" is used in the context of secondary education and was established as a reaction to a system that had previously allocated children to different types of school on the basis of their attainment at the age of 11, and which reinforced social class-based inequalities.

The comprehensive school movement in England is similar to the *Folkeskole* tradition in Denmark, the "common school" tradition in the USA, and the unified compulsory education system in Portugal. It involves creating a single type of "school for all" which serves a socially diverse community. In Norway, however, the idea of "the school for all" was as much about creating an independent singular Norwegian identity as it was to do with the participation of people within diverse communities. Although this strong emphasis on education for local communities facilitated the disbanding of segregated special institutions, it was not followed by an equally strong movement to reform the common school to embrace and value difference. There was an emphasis on assimilating those perceived to be different into a homogeneous normality rather than transformation through diversity.

Perspective 5: education for all

This fifth way of thinking about inclusive education tends to be almost exclusively associated with countries of the South, especially those where education is neither free nor compulsory. International efforts to promote EFA intensified following the first "World Conference on Education for All" held in Jomtien, Thailand, with its slogan of "EFA by the year 2000" (UNESCO 1990). The significance of Jomtien was its acknowledgement of the exclusion of large numbers of vulnerable and marginalized groups of learners from education systems worldwide. It also presented a vision of education as a much broader concept than schooling, beginning with early childhood, emphasizing women's literacy and recognizing the importance of basic literacy skills as part of lifelong learning. This was a landmark conference in the development of thinking about inclusive education, even though this concept was not widely used at that time.

Although the initial vision of EFA was broad and ambitious, the rhetoric of "all" has so far failed to reach the poorest and most disadvantaged children, including those with disabilities (Miles and Singal, forthcoming). With international attention focused on achieving the MDGs, EFA has become increasingly focused on ensuring access to, and completion of, 5 years of universal primary education for all children by 2015. Yet a broader notion of all and a greater appreciation of difference in the education system could hold the key to improving the quality of the education delivered in those 5 years (Ainscow 1999).

Moving towards inclusion

Given these different, though potentially complementary, views of inclusive education, progress remains disappointing in many countries. For example, in her analysis of 17 EFA plans from the South and South-East Asia region, Ahuja (2005) notes that the idea of inclusive education was not even mentioned. In fact, special schools and residential hostels were often put forward as a strategy for meeting the needs of a wide range of disadvantaged students, and non-formal education was seen as a solution to the educational needs of marginalized groups. This is a worrying trend, especially given the negative effects of institutionalization on vulnerable groups of children (United Nations 2005). Similarly, in a study of countries engaged in the Fast Track Initiative (FTI) of EFA, World Vision UK (2007, p. 1) found that "a number of FTI-endorsed countries, particularly those which are approaching universal primary education, do now have national education sector plans which address the inclusion of disabled children. [. . .] However, in a number of countries, policies and provision for disabled children remain cursory or have not been implemented". The report notes that in five of the FTI-endorsed countries there was no mention at all of disabled children.

It is also important to note that, even in the developed world, not all educationalists have embraced the inclusive philosophy and some are resistant to the idea (Brantlinger 1997; Freire and César 2002; Fuchs and Fuchs 1994). Indeed, some disability-focused organizations argue for separate, "specialist" services. Most notably, many organizations of deaf people argue that separate educational provision is the only way to guarantee their right to education through the medium of sign language and access to deaf culture (Freire and César 2003). Yet in the Ugandan context, for example, Kristensen et al. (2006) found special school contexts to be lacking in specialist knowledge and equipment. Meanwhile, the development of small specialist units located within the standard school environment is seen by many as a way of providing specialist knowledge, equipment and support to particular groups of children whose needs are difficult to accommodate in mainstream classrooms.

Consequently, as we consider the way forward, it is important to recognize that the field of inclusive education is riddled with uncertainties, disputes and contradictions. Yet, throughout the world, attempts are being made to provide more effective educational responses for all children, whatever their characteristics and, encouraged by the Salamanca Statement, the overall trend is towards making these responses within the context of general educational provision (see the special edition of the *European journal of psychology of education*, December 2006). As a consequence, this is leading to a reconsideration of the future roles and purposes of practitioners throughout the education system, including those who work in special education. This, of course, also has major implications for the direction of national policies and the development of practice in the field.

With this in mind, we want to argue that progress in relation to both the EFA agenda and inclusive education requires greater clarity about what becoming more inclusive involves. For us, it is a *principled approach to education*, which involves:

- The process of increasing the participation of students in, and reducing their exclusion from, the curricula, cultures and communities of local schools;
- Restructuring the cultures, policies and practices in schools so that they respond to the diversity of students in their locality;
- The presence, participation and achievement of all students vulnerable to exclusionary pressures, not only those with impairments or those who are categorized as "having special educational needs".

Certain features of this way of conceptualizing inclusive education are, in our view, of particular importance: (a) inclusion is concerned with *all* children and young people in schools; (b) it is focused on presence, participation *and* achievement; (c) inclusion and exclusion are linked together, such that inclusion involves the active combating of exclusion; and (d) inclusion is seen as a never-ending process. Thus, an inclusive school is one that is on the move, rather than one that has reached a perfect state. Inclusion, therefore, is a process requiring on-going vigilance.

We are conscious of some limitations in this way of thinking. In particular, we are aware that it identifies education with schooling, whereas we view a school as only one of the sites of education within communities. In this sense, we see the role of schools as supporting the education of communities, not monopolizing it. We would also wish to emphasize the significance of the participation of staff, parents/carers and other community members. It seems to us that we shall not get very far in supporting the participation and learning of all students if we reject their identities and family backgrounds, or if we choose not to encourage the participation of staff in schools in decisions about teaching and learning activities. We also believe that it is essential to connect inclusion/ exclusion in education more broadly with inclusionary and exclusionary pressures within society.

Putting these ideas together leads us to our broad support for national approaches to education based on comprehensive community pre-school, school and post-school education, and to see educational entitlement as a worldwide commitment. We are thus committed to the *inclusive development of education for all*.

Such a formulation is consistent with what some scholars have defined as the "organizational paradigm" of inclusive education (Dyson and Millward 2000). This requires new thinking that challenges deeply ingrained assumptions among many educators across the world. Specifically, it requires a move away from explanations of educational failure that concentrate on the characteristics of individual children and their families, towards an analysis of the barriers to participation and learning experienced by students within education systems (Booth and Ainscow 2002). Here, the notion of barriers draws our attention, for example, to ways in which lack of resources or expertise, inappropriate curricula or teaching methods, and attitudes can limit the presence, participation and achievement of some learners. Indeed, it has been argued that those students who experience such barriers can be regarded as "hidden voices" who, under certain conditions, can encourage the improvement of schools in ways that would benefit all of their students (Ainscow 1999).

This approach, which we see as a new direction of travel—an *inclusive turn*—is more likely to be successful in contexts where there is a culture of collaboration that encourages and supports problem-solving (Carrington 1999; Kugelmass 2001; Skrtic 1991). It involves those within a particular context working together to address barriers to education experienced by some learners.

What, then, does taking an inclusive turn mean for moving policy and practice forward? What needs to be done to develop schools that can "reach out" effectively to all children and young people, whatever their circumstances and personal characteristics? What does research suggest about how teachers and schools might develop more inclusive practices?

In addressing these issues we focus specifically on the nature of inclusive practices. In so doing we examine the ways in which curricula are interpreted through the approaches to teaching used in particular contexts. We go on to examine the ways in which inclusive practices develop, and how factors at different levels of the system bear on such developments. This leads us to argue that teachers are the key to the development of more inclusive forms of education. Their beliefs, attitudes and actions are what create the contexts in which children and young people are required to learn. This being the case, the task must be to develop education systems within which teachers feel supported as well as challenged in relation to their responsibility to keep exploring more effective ways of facilitating the learning of all students. All of this has major implications for school organization and leadership, and overall educational policy.

Inclusive teaching

It has been argued that the approaches developed as part of what is now often referred to as special needs education have, despite good intentions, continued to create barriers to progress as schools have been encouraged to adopt them (Ainscow 1998; Slee 1996). Recently, researchers who have reviewed the empirical basis of specialized methods for particular categories of students concluded that there is little support for a separate special needs pedagogy (Davis et al. 2004; Lewis and Norwich 2005). Put simply, effective teaching is effective teaching for all students.

At the same time, it has been argued that the preoccupation with individualized responses that have been a feature of special education continues to deflect attention away from the creation of forms of teaching that can reach out to all learners within a class and the establishment of school conditions that will encourage such developments (Ainscow 1997). This may help to explain why integration efforts that depend on the import of practices from special education tend to foster the development of new, more subtle forms of segregation, albeit within mainstream settings. Thus, for example, some countries in recent years have witnessed the introduction of teaching assistants who work alongside class teachers in order to facilitate the presence of those students categorized as having special needs. It has been found that, when such support is withdrawn, teachers often feel they can no longer cope. Meanwhile, the requirement for individualized education plans has encouraged some school leaders to feel that many more children will require such responses, thus creating budget problems within education systems (Ainscow et al. 2000; Fulcher 1989). At the same time, in some countries the category "special educational needs" has become a repository for various groups who suffer discrimination in society, such as those from minority backgrounds (Trent et al. 1998). In this way special education can be a way of hiding discrimination against some groups of students behind an apparently benign label, thus justifying their poor attainments and, therefore, their need for separate educational arrangements.

The recognition that inclusive schools will not be achieved by transplanting special education thinking and practice into mainstream contexts points to other possibilities. Many of these relate to the need to move from the individualized planning frame, referred to above, to a perspective that seeks to *personalize* learning through an engagement with the whole class (Ainscow 1999). In this sense, many ideas about effective teaching are relevant. However, what is particular to an inclusive pedagogy is the way teachers conceptualize notions of difference.

As Bartolome (1994) explains, teaching methods are neither devised nor implemented in a vacuum. The design, selection and use of particular teaching approaches and strategies arise from perceptions about learning and learners. In this respect, she argues, even the most pedagogically advanced methods are likely to be ineffective in the hands of those who implicitly or explicitly subscribe to a belief system that regards some students, at best, as disadvantaged and in need of fixing or, worse, as deficient and therefore beyond fixing.

In thinking about what inclusive practice involves we also have to be sensitive to the complex nature of teaching. Reflecting on their observations of classroom practices internationally, Stigler and Hiebert (1999) suggest that teaching should not be seen as a loose mixture of individual features "thrown together" by individual practitioners. Rather, they suggest, the practice of a teacher "works like a machine", with the different elements interconnected. This means that individual features of practice only make sense in relation to the whole. Commenting on this formulation, Hargreaves (2003) suggests that teaching practices take the form of "scripts" that are deeply embedded within teachers, reflecting their life experiences and taken-for-granted assumptions. Consequently, changing one or two features of practice is unlikely to lead to significant improvements in teaching quality, since such superficial changes will leave most elements of the original script undisturbed.

Studying practice

In the United Kingdom two recent studies have looked closely at how practices that respond effectively to learner diversity develop. Perhaps significantly, both projects involved researchers working collaboratively with practitioners.

The first study, *Learning without limits*, examined ways of teaching that are free of determinist beliefs about ability (Hart 2003; Hart et al. 2004). In order to study the way they operated, the researchers worked closely with a group of teachers who had rejected ideas of fixed ability. They started from the belief that constraints are placed on children's learning by ability-focused practices that lead young children to define themselves in comparison to their peers.

The researchers argue that the notion of ability as inborn intelligence has come to be seen as "a natural way of talking about children" that summarizes their perceived differences. They go on to suggest that, in England, national policies reflect this assumption, making it essential for teachers to compare, categorize and group their pupils by ability in order to provide appropriate and challenging teaching for all. Thus, for example, school inspectors are expected to check that teaching is differentiated among "more able", "average" and "less able" pupils. In this context, what is meant by ability is not made explicit, leaving scope for teachers to interpret what is being recommended in ways that suit their own beliefs and views. However, it is noted that the policy emphasis on target-setting and value-added measures of progress leaves little scope for teachers who reject the fixed view of measurable ability to hold on to their principles.

Through a close examination of the practices and thinking of their teacher partners, the researchers set themselves the task of identifying "more just and empowering" ways of making sense of learner diversity. In summary, they argue, this would involve teachers treating patterns of achievement and response in a "spirit of transformability", seeking to discover what is possible to enhance the capacity of each child in their class to learn and to create the conditions in which their learning can flourish more fully and effectively.

The researchers explain that the teachers in their study based their practices on a strong conviction that things can change and be changed for the better, recognizing that whatever a child's present attainments and characteristics, given the right conditions, everybody's capacity for learning can be enhanced. Approaching their work with this mind-set, the teachers involved in the study were seen to analyze gaps between their aspirations for children and what was actually happening.

The second study, *Understanding and developing inclusive practices in schools*, also pointed to the importance of inquiry as a stimulus for changing practices. The study involved 25 schools in exploring ways of developing inclusion in their own contexts, in collaboration with university researchers (Ainscow et al. 2003, 2004, 2006). Significantly, this process took place in the context of the British Government's extensive efforts to improve standards in public education, as measured by test and examination scores. This has involved the creation of an educational "market-place", coupled with an emphasis on policies fostering greater diversity between types of school. The result is a quasi-selective system in which the poorest children, by and large, attend the poorest-performing schools: similar policy trends are evident in a number of other developed countries. However, despite this apparently unfavourable national policy context, what was noted in the schools that participated in the study was neither the crushing of inclusion by the so-called standards agenda, nor the rejection of the standards agenda in favour of a radical, inclusive alternative. Certainly, many teachers were concerned about the impacts of the standards agenda on their work and some were committed to views of inclusion which they saw as standing in contradiction to it. However, in most of the schools the two agendas remained intertwined. Indeed, the focus on attainment appeared to prompt some teachers to examine issues in relation to the achievements and participation of marginalized groups that they had previously overlooked. Likewise, the concern with inclusion tended to shape the way the school responded to the imperative to raise standards.

In trying to make sense of the relationship between external imperatives and the processes of change in schools, the study drew on the ideas of Wenger (1998) to reveal how external agendas were mediated by the norms and values of the "communities of practice" within schools and how they become part of a dialogue, the outcomes of which can be more rather than less inclusive. In this way, the role of national policy emerges from the study in a rather new light. This suggests that schools may be able to engage with what might appear to be unfavourable policy imperatives to produce outcomes that are by no means inevitably non-inclusive.

Moving practice forward

Together, the findings of these two studies lead to reasons for optimism. They indicate that more inclusive approaches can emerge from a study of the existing practice of teachers set within the internal social dynamics of schools. They also suggest that it is possible to intervene in these dynamics in order to open up new possibilities for moving policy and practice forward.

Research suggests that developments of practice are unlikely to occur without some exposure to what teaching actually looks like when it is being done differently, and exposure to someone who can help teachers understand the difference between what they are doing and what they aspire to do (Elmore et al. 1996). It also suggests that this has to be addressed at the individual level before it can be solved at the organizational level. Indeed, there is evidence that increasing collaboration without some more specific attention to change at the individual level can simply result in teachers coming together to reinforce existing practices rather than confronting the difficulties they face in different ways (Lipman 1997).

At the heart of the processes in schools where changes in practice do occur is the development of a common language with which colleagues can talk to one another and, indeed, to themselves about detailed aspects of their practice (Huberman 1993). Without such a language teachers find it very difficult to experiment with new possibilities. Much of what teachers do during the intensive encounters that occur is done at an automatic, intuitive level.

Furthermore, there is little time to stop and think. This is why having the opportunity to see colleagues at work is so crucial to the success of attempts to develop practice. It is through shared experiences that colleagues can help one another to articulate what they currently do and define what they might like to do (Hiebert et al. 2002). It is also the means whereby space is created within which taken-for-granted assumptions about particular groups of learners can be subjected to mutual critique.

This raises questions about how best to introduce such ways of working. Here, a promising approach is that of "lesson study", a systematic procedure for the development of teaching that is well established in Japan and some other Asian countries (Hiebert et al. 2002; Lo et al. 2005; Stigler and Hiebert 1999). The goal of lesson study is to improve the effectiveness of the experiences that the teachers provide for all their students. The core activity is collaboration on a shared area of focus that is generated through discussion. The content of this focus is the planned lesson, which is then used as the basis for gathering data on the quality of experience that students receive. These lessons are called "study lessons" and are used to examine the teachers' practices and the responsiveness of the students to the planned activities. Members of the group work together to design the lesson plan, which is then implemented by each teacher. Observations and post-lesson conferences are arranged to facilitate the improvement of the research lesson between each trial.

Lesson study can be conducted in many ways. It may, for example, involve a small subgroup of volunteer staff, or be carried out through departmental or special interest groupings. It can also happen "across schools", and is then part of a wider, managed network of teachers working together. The collection of evidence is a key factor in the lesson study approach. This usually involves the use of video recordings. Emphasis is also placed on listening to the views of students in a way that tends to introduce a critical edge to the discussions that take place.

Our own research has also shown how the use of evidence to study teaching can help to foster the development of more inclusive teaching (Ainscow et al. 2003). Specifically, it can help create space for reappraisal and rethinking by interrupting existing discourses, and by focusing attention on overlooked possibilities for moving practice forward. Particularly powerful techniques in this respect involve the use of mutual observation, sometimes through video recordings (Ainscow 1999, 2003), and evidence collected from students about teaching and learning arrangements within a school (Ainscow and Kaplan 2006; Messiou 2006; Miles and Kaplan 2005). Under certain conditions such approaches provide *interruptions* that help to make the familiar unfamiliar in ways that stimulate self-questioning, creativity and action. In so doing they can sometimes lead to a reframing of perceived problems that, in turn, draws the teacher's attention to overlooked possibilities for addressing barriers to participation and learning.

Here our argument is informed by the work of Robinson (1998), who suggests that practices are activities that solve problems in particular situations. This means that to explain a practice is to reveal the problem for which it serves as a solution. So, in working closely with practitioners, we have found that we can draw inferences about how school staff has formulated a problem and the assumptions that are involved in the decisions made. We have also observed how initial formulations are sometimes rethought as a result of an engagement with various forms of evidence.

However, this is not in itself a straightforward mechanism for the development of more inclusive practices. A space that is created may be filled according to conflicting agendas. Studies have documented examples of how deeply-held beliefs within schools may prevent the experimentation that is necessary to foster the development of more inclusive ways of working (Ainscow and Kaplan 2006; Howes and Ainscow 2006). This reminds us that it is easy for educational difficulties to be pathologized as difficulties inherent within students. This is true not only of students with disabilities and those defined as "having special educational needs", but also of those whose socio-economic status, race, language and gender renders them problematic to particular teachers in particular schools. Consequently, it is necessary to explore ways of developing the capacity of those within schools to reveal and challenge deeply entrenched deficit views of "difference", which define certain types of students as "lacking something" (Trent et al. 1998). This involves vigilance in scrutinizing how deficit assumptions may be influencing perceptions of certain students.

This, in turn, points to the importance of cultural factors. Schein (1985) suggests that cultures are about the deeper levels of basic assumptions and beliefs that are shared by members of an organization, operating unconsciously to define how they view themselves and their working contexts. The extent to which these values include the acceptance and celebration of difference, and a commitment to offering educational opportunities to all students, coupled with the extent to which they are shared across a school staff, relate to the extent to which students are enabled to participate (Kugelmass 2001).

Hargreaves (1995) argues that cultures can be seen as having a reality-defining function, enabling those within an institution to make sense of themselves, their actions and their environment. A current reality-defining function of culture, he suggests, is often a problem-solving function inherited from the past. In this way, today's cultural form created to solve an emergent problem often becomes tomorrow's taken-for-granted recipe for dealing with matters shorn of their novelty.

Changing the norms that exist within a school is difficult to achieve, particularly within a context that is faced with so many competing pressures and where practitioners tend to work alone in addressing the problems they face (Fullan 1991). On the other hand, the presence of children who are not suited to the existing "menu" of the school can provide some encouragement to explore a more collaborative culture within which teachers support one another in experimenting with new teaching responses. In this way, problem-solving activities gradually become the reality-defining, taken-for-granted functions that are the culture of a school that is more geared to fostering inclusive ways of working. At the same time, this can make an important contribution to the development of schools that will be effective for all children (Ainscow 1999).

The implication of all of this is that becoming more inclusive is a matter of thinking and talking, reviewing and refining practice, and attempting to develop a more inclusive culture. Such a conceptualization means that we cannot divorce inclusion from the contexts within which it is developing, nor the social relations that might sustain or limit that development (Dyson 2006). It is in the complex interplay between individuals, and between groups and individuals, that shared beliefs and values exist and change, and it is impossible to separate those beliefs from the relationships in which they are embodied.

Inclusive cultures

There is a body of critical literature highlighting the problems and complexities that emerge when schools attempt to develop towards greater inclusion (Dyson and Millward 2000). These literatures point to the internal complexities of schools as organizations, and the constraints and contradictions that are generated by the policy environments in which they exist. As such, they usefully problematize the assumptions underlying the more mechanistic approaches to improvement, but stop short of saying how inclusion might actually be developed.

A more promising family of approaches to development starts from the assumption that increasing inclusion is less a set of fixed practices or policies than a continuous process of deconstructing and reconstructing (Skrtic 1991; Thomas and Loxley 2001); what Corbett and Slee (2000) have called the "cultural vigilantism" of exposing exclusion in all its changing forms and seeking instead to "foster an inclusive educational culture".

Where writers have addressed these matters, they tend to place particular emphasis on the characteristics of schools as organizations that stimulate and support processes of interrogation. The American scholar Tom Skrtic argues that schools with what he calls "adhocratic" configurations are most likely to respond to student diversity in positive and creative ways (Skrtic 1991). Such schools emphasize the pooling of different forms of professional expertise in collaborative processes. Children who cannot easily be educated within the school's established routines are not seen as "having" problems, but as challenging teachers to re-examine their practices to make them more responsive and flexible. Similarly, our own work has led us to outline "organizational conditions"—distributed leadership, high levels of staff and student involvement, joint planning, a commitment to enquiry and so on—that promote collaboration and problem-solving amongst staff, and which therefore produce more inclusive responses to diversity (Ainscow 1999).

These themes are further supported by a review of international literature that examines the effectiveness of school actions in promoting inclusion (Dyson et al. 2002). The review concludes that there is a limited, but by no means negligible, body of empirical evidence about the relationship between school action and the participation of all students in the cultures, curricula and communities of their schools. In summary, it suggests that:

- Some schools are characterized by an "inclusive culture". Within such schools, there is some degree of consensus among adults around values of respect for difference and a commitment to offering all pupils access to learning opportunities. This consensus may not be total and may not necessarily remove all tensions or contradictions in practice. On the other hand, there is likely to be a high level of staff collaboration and joint problem-solving, and similar values and commitments may extend into the student body, and into parent and other community stakeholders in the school.
- The extent to which such "inclusive cultures" lead directly and unproblematically to enhanced student participation is not clear. Some aspects of these cultures, however, can be seen as participatory by definition. For instance, respect for diversity from teachers may itself be understood as a form of participation by children within a school community. Moreover, schools with such cultures are also likely to be characterized by forms of organization (such as specialist provision being made in the ordinary

classroom, rather than by withdrawal) and practice (such as constructivist approaches to teaching and learning) which could be regarded as participatory by definition.

- Schools with "inclusive cultures" are also likely to be characterized by the presence of leaders who are committed to inclusive values and to a leadership style that encourages a range of individuals to participate in leadership functions. Such schools are also likely to have good links with parents and with their communities.
- The local and national policy environment can act to support or to undermine the realization of schools' inclusive values.

On the basis of this evidence, the Dyson review team makes a number of recommendations for policy and practice. The team suggests that attempts to develop inclusive schools should pay attention to the development of "inclusive cultures" and, particularly, to the building of some degree of consensus around inclusive values within school communities. This leads them to argue that principals and other school leaders should be selected and trained in the light of their commitment to inclusive values and their capacity to lead in a participatory manner. Finally, they conclude that the external policy environment should be compatible with inclusive developments if it is to support rather than to undermine schools' efforts.

According to the review, there are general principles of school organization and classroom practice that should be followed, notably: (a) the removal of structural barriers between different groups of students and staff; (b) the dismantling of separate programmes, services and specialisms; and (c) the development of pedagogical approaches (such as constructivist approaches and co-operative learning) that enable students to learn together rather than separately. It is also argued that schools should build close relations with parents and communities based on developing a shared commitment to inclusive values.

The implications for practice of such an orientation are illustrated in the *Index for inclusion* (Booth and Ainscow 2002)—referred to earlier—which enables schools to draw on the knowledge and views of staff, students, parents/carers and governors about barriers to learning and participation that exist within the existing "cultures, policies and practices" of schools in order to identify priorities for change. In connecting inclusion with the detail of policy and practice, the *Index* encourages those who use it to build their own view of inclusion, related to their experience and values, as they work out which policies and practices they wish to promote or discourage. The *Index* can support staff in schools in refining their planning processes so that they involve wider collaboration and participation, and introduce coherence to development (see Rustemier and Booth 2005).

Such approaches are congruent with the view that inclusion is essentially about attempts to embody particular values in particular contexts (Ainscow et al. 2004). Unlike mechanistic views of school improvement, they acknowledge that decisions about how to improve schools always involve moral and political reasoning, as well as technical considerations. Moreover, they offer specific processes through which inclusive developments might be promoted. Discussions of inclusion and exclusion can help, therefore, to make explicit the values that underlie what, how and why changes should be made in schools. Inclusive cultures, underpinned by particular organizational conditions, may make those discussions more likely to occur and more productive when they do occur.

Leadership for inclusion

It seems, then, that inclusive practices are likely to require challenges to the thinking of those within a particular organization and, inevitably, this raises questions about leadership. A recent literature review concludes that learner diversity and inclusion are increasingly seen as key challenges for educational leaders (West et al. 2003). For example, Leithwood et al. (1999) suggest that with continuing diversity, schools will need to thrive on uncertainty, have a greater capacity for collective problem-solving, and be able to respond to a wider range of learners. Sergiovanni (1992) also points to the challenge of student diversity and argues that current approaches to school leadership may well be getting in the way of improvement efforts.

Lambert et al. (1995) argue for what they see as a constructivist view of leadership. This is defined as the reciprocal processes that enable participants in an educational community to construct common meanings that lead toward a common purpose about schooling. They use this perspective to argue that leadership involves an interactive process entered into by both learners and teachers. Consequently, there is a need for shared leadership, with the principal seen as a leader of leaders. Hierarchical structures have to be replaced by shared responsibility in a community that becomes characterized by agreed values and hopes, such that many of the control functions associated with school leadership become less important or even counter-productive.

The most helpful theoretical and empirical context, however, is provided by Riehl (2000), who, following an extensive review of the literature, develops "a comprehensive approach to school administration and diversity". She concludes that school leaders need to attend to three broad types of task: (a) fostering new meanings about diversity; (b) promoting inclusive practices within schools; and (c) building connections between schools and communities. She goes on to consider how these tasks can be accomplished, exploring how the concept of practice, especially discursive practice, can contribute to a fuller understanding of the work of school principals. This analysis leads the author to offer a positive view of the potential for school principals to engage in inclusive, transformative developments. She concludes: "When wedded to a relentless commitment to equity, voice, and social justice, administrators' efforts in the tasks of sensemaking, promoting inclusive cultures and practices in schools, and building positive relationships outside of the school may indeed foster a new form of practice" (p. 71).

The role of networking

What emerges from the evidence summarized so far is how social learning processes, stimulated by inquiry within particular contexts, can foster a greater capacity for responding to learner diversity. Achieving a deeper, more sustainable impact on the culture of schools is much more difficult, though. This necessitates longer-term, persistent strategies for capacity-building at the school level (Harris and Chrispeels 2006). It also requires new thinking and, indeed, new relationships at the systems level. In other words, efforts to foster inclusive school development are more likely to be effective when they are part of a wider strategy (Ainscow 2005).

This has led to an increasing emphasis on the idea of sharing expertise and resources between schools, and linking educational development with wider community development. Such an approach is consistent with what Stoker (2003) calls "public value management", with its emphasis on network governance. Stoker argues that the origins of this approach can be traced to criticisms of the current emphasis on strategies drawn from private sector experience. He goes on to suggest that the formulation of what constitutes public value can only be achieved through deliberation involving the key stakeholders and actions that depend on mixing, in a reflexive way, a range of intervention options. Consequently, "networks of deliberation and delivery" are seen as key strategies. In the education service this implies the negotiation of new, interdependent relationships between schools, administrations and communities (Hargreaves 2003).

There is some evidence that school-to-school collaboration can strengthen the capacity of individual organizations to respond to learner diversity (Ainscow and Howes 2007; Howes and Ainscow 2006). However, this does not represent an easy option for the schools themselves, particularly in policy contexts within which competition and choice continue to be the main policy drivers. Recent studies, for the most part, have focused on situations where schools have been given short-term financial incentives linked to the demonstration of collaborative planning and activity (Ainscow and West 2006; Ainscow et al. 2006a; Chapman 2005; Chapman and Allen 2006). These studies suggest that collaboration between schools can help to reduce the polarization of schools, to the particular benefit of those students who find themselves at the edges of the system and whose performance and attitudes cause concern. There is evidence, too, that when schools seek to develop more collaborative ways of working, this can have an impact on how teachers perceive themselves and their work. Specifically, comparisons of practices can lead teachers to view underachieving students in a new light. Rather than simply presenting problems that are assumed to be insurmountable, such students may be perceived as providing feedback on existing classroom arrangements. In this way, they may be seen as sources of understanding as to how these arrangements might be developed in ways that could be of benefit to all members of the class.

Networking can be extended much more widely to encourage the sharing of experiences and ideas regarding ways of developing inclusive practices across national borders (Miles and Ahuja 2007). It was with this possibility in mind that the Enabling Education Network (EENET) was established in 1997, with the technical and financial support of a group of concerned international organizations, including UNESCO. The purpose of EENET is to contribute to the development of effective, relevant, appropriate sustainable education policy and practice internationally, and to support and promote the inclusion of marginalized groups in education worldwide (Miles 2002). Inclusive initiatives are supported by sharing relevant information and experience internationally, but primarily between southern countries, since much educational practice in the North is not relevant to Southern contexts (Stubbs and Ainscow 1996). One of the motivating factors behind the establishment of EENET was the firm conviction, based on the work of Save the Children (UK) and UNESCO, that lessons drawn from experience gained with the implementation of inclusive education in countries of the South had a great deal to teach practitioners in Northern contexts.

EENET's annual publication, *Enabling education*, is disseminated to almost 2,000 individuals and organizations in over 150 countries, and its website has been accessed by people in over 190 countries. Due to the inequities of access to digital technology, EENET prioritises the dissemination of materials in "hard copy" form. Although many network users have access to computers and can send e-mails, few have affordable access to the Internet to search for information. Increasingly, CD-ROMs containing key documents are compiled for EENET readers, as this saves the relatively high cost involved in downloading big e-mail attachments or documents from the Internet in countries where telephone charges and printing costs are exorbitant. The most popular documents are available in Spanish, French, Portuguese, Arabic and Russian, but EENET faces difficulties in accessing documents written in non-English-speaking countries of the South. Experience in English-speaking countries tends to be disseminated more widely than experiences from other parts of the world.

EENET shares information about inclusive education, written and generated by and for a wide range of stakeholders, including children, parents and consumer groups, as well as teachers, policy-makers, academics and teacher-trainers. Some of these documents have been produced through processes of collaborative inquiry, similar to those described earlier in this paper. Although the network is located at the University of Manchester, it has adopted a non-academic style to ensure wide accessibility. Documents posted on the website are not necessarily representative of inclusive education practice, nor are they peer-reviewed. Practitioners are simply encouraged to share their experience, their ideas and their training materials. Nevertheless, the EENET website is regarded by many as an important emerging database and a unique international resource on inclusive, enabling education. Most of the evidence for this has so far been anecdotal. However, a detailed analysis of all correspondence received was carried out recently and the final report contains many examples of the way EENET information is used, by whom and in which countries (Lewis 2003).

Concluding remarks

As we look to the future it is important not to underestimate the challenges facing education systems as they try to make EFA inclusive. For example, Lewin (2007) explains that in Sub-Saharan Africa more than 25 million children of primary age and 75 million of secondary age are excluded from education. Within this overall agenda, ensuring that the most marginalized groups of children, in the poorest countries, gain access to and participate in an education of good quality remains a major challenge. It is currently estimated that one-third of the world's out-of-school population are disabled, and that only 2% of disabled children attend school (UNESCO 2007). Article 24 in the new United Nations Convention on the Rights of Persons with Disabilities requires all signatories to ensure that all disabled children "can access an inclusive, quality, free primary and secondary education on an equal basis with others in the communities in which they live" (United Nations 2006, Art. 24, 2b). Although not a homogenous group, disabled children tend to be identified internationally as being excluded from education in countries of the South in disproportionately large numbers (Mittler 2005). Yet definitions and perceptions of disability and special needs are culturally and contextually determined and statistics inevitably vary between contexts. Stubbs (1995) argues that a focus on demographic data and statistics obscures contextual problems associated with negative attitudes, policies and institutions which exclude children.

This reminds us that education involves complex social processes. Furthermore, education systems are not developed in isolation. Rather, such development has to be understood in relation to particular geographical, political and economic factors, as well as culturally and contextually specific values and beliefs. This applies whether we are talking about the resource-rich countries of the North, or economically disadvantaged countries of the South.

Whilst we do not wish to romanticize resource-poor environments, we believe that there are lessons to be learned from the experience of educational practitioners in Southern countries who face seemingly insurmountable resource barriers in their day-to-day work. These lessons are essentially about the sorts of social processes we have outlined in this paper. Often they involve stakeholders working together to address barriers to participation and learning, rather than the use of resource-intensive, specialized technological solutions.

With this in mind, in this paper we have argued that strategies for EFA must become more inclusive. We have also argued that it is essential to be clear about what this involves in order to bring all stakeholders together around a common sense of purpose and use of language. As we have explained, none of this requires the introduction of particular techniques; rather, it involves processes of social learning within particular contexts. Collaboration within and between schools, closer links between schools and communities, networking across contexts, and the use of evidence as a means of stimulating experimentation are all seen as key strategies for moving such processes in a more inclusive direction. As Copland (2003) suggests, inquiry can be the "engine" to enable the distribution of leadership that is needed in order to foster participation, and the "glue" that can bind people together around a common purpose.

We have also argued that all of this has major implications for leadership practice at different levels within schools and education systems. In particular, it calls for co-ordinated and sustained efforts by teachers and educational administrators around the idea that improving outcomes for all students is unlikely to be achieved unless there are changes in the behaviours of adults. Consequently, the starting point must be with teachers—in effect, enlarging their capacity to imagine what might be achieved, and increasing their sense of accountability for bringing this about. This may also involve tackling taken-for-granted assumptions, most often relating to expectations about certain groups of students, their capabilities and behaviours.

Our argument, then, is based on the assumption that schools and their communities *know more than they used to* and that the logical starting point for development is a detailed analysis of existing arrangements. This allows good practices to be identified and shared, whilst at the same time drawing attention to ways of working that may be creating barriers to the participation and learning of some children and young people. However, as we have stressed, the focus must not only be on practice. It must also address and sometimes challenge the thinking behind existing ways of working.

Acknowledgements

We must acknowledge the contributions of many of our colleagues to the ideas presented in this paper, particularly Tony Booth, Alan Dyson, Andy Howes and Mel West.

References

Ahuja, A. (2005). *EFA National Action Plans review study: Key findings*. Bangkok: UNESCO.

Ainscow, M. (1997). Towards inclusive schooling. *British Journal of Special Education,* 24(1), 3–6.

Ainscow, M. (1998). Developing links between special needs and school improvement. *Support for Learning, 13*(2), 70–75.

Ainscow, M. (1999). *Understanding the development of inclusive schools.* London: Falmer.

Ainscow, M. (2003). Using teacher development to foster inclusive classroom practices. In T. Booth, K. Nes, & M. Stromstad (Eds.), *Developing inclusive teacher education.* London: Routledge.

Ainscow, M. (2005). Developing inclusive education systems: What are the levers for change? *Journal of Educational Change, 6*(2), 109–124.

Ainscow, M., Booth, T., & Dyson, A. (2004). Understanding and developing inclusive practices in schools: A collaborative action research network. *International Journal of Inclusive Education, 8*(2), 125–140.

Ainscow, M., Farrell, P., & Tweddle, D. (2000). Developing policies for inclusive education: A study of the role of local education authorities. *International Journal of Inclusive Education, 4*(3), 211–229.

Ainscow, M., & Howes, A. (2007). Working together to improve urban secondary schools: A study of practice in one city. *School Leadership and Management, 27*(3), 285–300.

Ainscow, M., & Kaplan, I. (2006). Using evidence to encourage inclusive school development: Possibilities and challenges. *Australasian Journal of Special Education, 29*(2), 106–116.

Ainscow, M., Muijs, D., & West, M. (2006a). Collaboration as a strategy for improving schools in challenging circumstances. *Improving Schools, 9*(3), 192–202.

Ainscow, M., & West, M. (Eds.). (2006). *Improving urban schools: Leadership and collaboration.* Buckingham: Open University Press.

Ainscow, M., et al. (2003). Making sense of the development of inclusive practices. *European Journal of Special Needs Education, 18*(2), 227–242.

Ainscow, M., et al. (2006b). *Improving schools, developing inclusion.* London: Routledge.

Bartolome, L. I. (1994). Beyond the methods fetish: Towards a humanising pedagogy. *Harvard Education Review, 54*(2), 173–194.

Booth, T. (1996). A perspective on inclusion from England. *Cambridge Review of Education, 26*(1), 87–99.

Booth, T., & Ainscow, M. (Eds.). (1998). *From them to us: An international study of inclusion in education.* London: Routledge.

Booth, T., & Ainscow, M. (2002). *The index for inclusion* (2nd ed.). Bristol: Centre for Studies on Inclusive Education.

Brantlinger, E. (1997). Using ideology: Cases of non-recognition of the politics of research and practice in special education. *Review of Educational Research, 67*(4), 425–459.

Carrington, S. (1999). Inclusion needs a different school culture. *International Journal of Inclusive Education, 3*(3), 257–268.

Chapman, C. (2005). *External intervention and school improvement.* London: Continuum.

Chapman, C., & Allen, T. (2006). *Partnerships for improvement: The specialist schools achievement programme.* London: SST.

Copland, M. A. (2003). Leadership of inquiry: Building and sustaining capacity for school improvement. *Educational Evaluation and Policy Analysis, 25*(4), 375–395.

Corbett, J. (2001). *Supporting inclusive education: A connective pedagogy.* London: Routledge.

Corbett, J., & Slee, R. (2000). An international conversation on inclusive education. In F. Armstrong, D. Armstrong, & L. Barton (Eds.), *Inclusive education: Policy, contexts and comparative perspectives.* London: David Fulton.

Davis, P., et al. (2004). *Teaching strategies and approaches for pupils with special educational needs: A scoping study.* London: DfES (Research Report 516).

Dyson, A. (2006). Beyond the school gates: Context, disadvantage and 'urban schools'. In M. Ainscow & M. West (Eds.), *Improving urban schools: Leadership and collaboration*. Buckingham: Open University Press.

Dyson, A., Howes, A., & Roberts, B. (2002). *A systematic review of the effectiveness of school-level actions for promoting participation by all students*. London: Inclusive Education Review Group for the EPPI Centre, Institute of Education. http://eppi.ioe. ac.uk/EPPIWeb/home.aspx?page=/reel/review_groups/inclusion/review_one.htm. Accessed 30 Jan 2008.

Dyson, A., & Millward, A. (2000). *Schools and special needs: Issues of innovation and inclusion*. London: Paul Chapman.

Elmore, P. L., Peterson, P. L., & McCarthy, S. J. (1996). *Restructuring in the classroom: Teaching, learning and school organisation*. San Francisco: Jossey-Bass.

Freire, S., & César, M. (2002). Evolution of the Portuguese education system: A deaf child's life in a regular school—is it possible to have hope? *Educational and Child Psychology, 19*(2), 76–96.

Freire, S., & César, M. (2003). Inclusive ideals/inclusive practices: How far is dream from reality? Five comparative case studies. *European Journal of Special Needs Education, 18*(3), 341–354.

Fuchs, D., & Fuchs, L. S. (1994). Inclusive schools movement and the radicalisation of special education reform. *Exceptional Children, 60*(4), 294–309.

Fulcher, G. (1989). *Disabling policies? A comparative approach to education policy and disability*. London: Falmer.

Fullan, M. (1991). *The new meaning of educational change*. London: Cassell.

Hargreaves, D. H. (1995). School culture, school effectiveness and school improvement. *School Effectiveness and School Improvement, 5*(1), 115–123.

Hargreaves, D. H. (2003). *Education epidemic: Transforming secondary schools through innovation networks*. London: Demos.

Harris, A., & Chrispeels, J. H. (Eds.). (2006). *Improving schools and education systems*. London: Routledge.

Hart, S. (2003). Learning without limits. In M. Nind, K. Sheehy, & K. Simmons (Eds.), *Inclusive education: Learners and learning contexts*. London: Fulton.

Hart, S., et al. (2004). *Learning without limits*. Maidenhead: Open University.

Hiebert, J., Gallimore, R., & Stigler, J. W. (2002). A knowledge base for the teaching profession: What would it look like and how can we get one? *Educational Researcher, 31*(5), 3–15.

Howes, A., & Ainscow, M. (2006). Collaboration with a city-wide purpose: Making paths for sustainable educational improvement. In M. Ainscow & M. West (Eds.), *Improving urban school: Leadership and collaboration*. Buckingham: Open University Press.

Huberman, M. (1993). The model of the independent artisan in teachers' professional relationships. In J. W. Little & M. W. McLaughlin (Eds.), *Teachers' work: Individuals, colleagues and contexts*. New York: Teachers College Press.

Hulme, D. (2007). *The making of the Millennium Development Goals: Human development meets results-based management in an imperfect world*. Manchester: Brooks World Poverty Institute (Working Paper 16).

Kristensen, K., et al. (2006). Opportunities for inclusion? The education of learners with special educational needs and disabilities in special schools in Uganda. *British Journal of Special Education, 33*(3), 139–147.

Kugelmass, J. (2001). Collaboration and compromise in creating and sustaining an inclusive school. *International Journal of Inclusive Education, 5*(1), 47–65.

Lambert, L., et al. (1995). *The constructivist leader*. New York: Teachers College Press.

Leithwood, K., Jantzi, D., & Steinbach, R. (1999). *Changing leadership for changing times*. Buckingham: Open University Press.

Lewin, K. M. (2007). Diversity in convergence: Access to education for all. *Compare, 37*(5), 577–600 (Presidential Address, BAICE, September 2006).

Lewis, A., & Norwich, B. (Eds.). (2005). *Special teaching for special children: A pedagogy for inclusion?* Maidenhead: Open University Press.

Lewis, I. (2003). *Seven years of conversations: An analysis of EENET's correspondence records, 1997–2004*. Manchester: EENET. Retrieved 19 Feb 2008 from http://eenet. org.uk/about/seven_years.pdf.

Lipman, P. (1997). Restructuring in context: A case study of teacher participation and the dynamics of ideology, race and power. *American Educational Research Journal, 34*(1), 3–37.

Lo, M. L., Yan, P. W., & Pakey, C. P. M. (Eds.). (2005). *For each and everyone: Catering for individual differences through learning studies*. Hong Kong: Hong Kong University Press.

Messiou, K. (2006). Understanding marginalisation in education: The voice of children. *European Journal of Psychology of Education, 21*(3), 305–318.

Miles, S. (2002). Learning about inclusive education: The role of EENET in promoting international dialogue. In P. Farrell & M. Ainscow (Eds.), *Making special education inclusive*. London: Fulton.

Miles, S., & Ahuja, A. (2007). Learning from difference: Sharing international experiences of developments in inclusive education. In L. Florian (Ed.), *The Sage handbook of special education* (pp. 131–145). London: Sage.

Miles, S., & Kaplan, I. (2005). Using images to promote reflection: An action research study in Zambia and Tanzania. *Journal of Research in Special Educational Needs, 5*(2), 77–83.

Miles, S., & Singal, N. The education for all and inclusive education debate: Conflict, contradiction or opportunity? *International Journal of Inclusive Education* (forthcoming).

Mittler, P. (2000). *Working towards inclusive education: Social contexts*. London: David Fulton.

Mittler, P. (2005). The global context of inclusive education: The role of the United Nations. In D. Mitchell (Ed.), *Contextualising inclusive education* (pp. 22–36). London: Routledge/Falmer.

Riehl, C. J. (2000). The principal's role in creating inclusive schools for diverse students: A review of normative, empirical, and critical literature on the practice of educational administration. *Review of Educational Research, 70*(1), 55–81.

Robinson, V. M. J. (1998). Methodology and the research-practice gap. *Educational Researcher, 27*(1), 17–26.

Rustemier, S., & Booth, T. (2005). *Learning about the index in use: A study of the use of the index for inclusion in schools and LEAs in England*. Bristol: Centre for Studies on Inclusive Education.

Schein, E. (1985). *Organisational culture and leadership*. San Francisco: Jossey-Bass.

Sergiovanni, T. J. (1992). *Moral leadership: Getting to the heart of school improvement*. San Francisco: Jossey-Bass.

Skrtic, T. (1991). *Behind special education: A critical analysis of professional culture and school organization*. Denver: Love.

Slee, R. (1996). Inclusive schooling in Australia? Not yet. *Cambridge Journal of Education, 26*(1), 19–32.

Spurgeon, W. (2007). Diversity and choice for children with complex needs. In R. Cigman (Ed.), *Included or excluded? The challenge of the mainstream for some SEN children*. London: Routledge.

Stigler, J. W., & Hiebert, J. (1999). *The teaching gap*. New York: The Free Press.

Stoker, G. (2003). *Public value management: A new resolution of the democracy/ efficiency trade off*. http://ipeg.org.uk/publications.htm.

Stubbs, S. (1995). *The Lesotho National Integrated Education Programme: A case study on implementation*. Cambridge: Faculty of Education, University of Cambridge. Unpublished M.Ed. Thesis. Retrieved on 24 Nov 2005 from http://eenet.org.uk/ action/sthesis/contents.shtml.

Stubbs, S., & Ainscow, M. (1996). *EENET proposal to establish an information sharing network aimed at supporting and promoting the inclusion of marginalised groups in education, 6 September 1996*. Manchester: School of Education, University of Manchester.

Thomas, G., & Loxley, A. (2001). *Deconstructing special education and constructing inclusion*. Maidenhead: Open University Press.

Trent, S. C., Artiles, A. J., & Englert, C. S. (1998). From deficit thinking to social constructivism: A review of theory, research and practice in special education. *Review of Research in Education, 23*, 277–307.

United Nations. (2005). *Violence against disabled children*. New York: United Nations.

United Nations. (2006). *UN convention on the rights of persons with disabilities*. New York: United Nations.

United Nations Educational, Scientific and Cultural Organization. (1990). *World declaration on education for all*. Paris: UNESCO.

United Nations Educational, Scientific and Cultural Organization. (1994). *Final report: World conference on special needs education: Access and quality*. Paris: UNESCO.

United Nations Educational, Scientific and Cultural Organization. (2001). *The open file on inclusive education*. Paris: UNESCO.

United Nations Educational, Scientific and Cultural Organization. (2007). *EFA global monitoring report: EFA strong foundations: Early childhood care and education*. Paris: UNESCO.

United Nations Educational, Scientific and Cultural Organization. (2008). *The EFA global monitoring report. Education for all by 2015. Will we make it?* Paris: UNESCO.

Vitello, S. J., & Mithaug, D. E. (Eds.). (1998). *Inclusive schooling: National and international perspectives*. Mahwah: Lawrence Erlbaum.

Wenger, E. (1998). *Communities of practice: Learning, meaning and identity*. Cambridge: Cambridge University Press.

West, M., Ainscow, M., & Notman, H. (2003). *What leaders read: Key texts from education and beyond*. Nottingham: National College for School Leadership.

World Vision UK. (2007). *Education's missing millions. Including disabled children in education through EFA FTI processes and national sector plans*. Milton Keynes: World Vision UK.

CHAPTER 13

THE POWER OF NETWORKING

Ainscow, M. (2010) Achieving excellence and equity: reflections on the development of practices in one local district over 10 years. *School Effectiveness and School Improvement* 21(1), 75–91

Introduction

Increasingly my work had become focused on ways of using networks to support movement within individual schools. The paper illustrates what this involves. It reports on a longitudinal programme of research pointing to the potential of processes of networking between schools as a possible way forward. At the same time, it also reveals how the implementation of such collaborative approaches presents difficulties, particularly within a policy context that emphasises competition between schools as the main driver for reform. The paper goes on to explore the roles that local authorities need to take in order to promote equitable developments. The paper concludes that progress in mobilising the potential of networking requires: new thinking within schools, not least in terms of leadership practice and the use of evidence as a stimulus for experimentation; new relationships between schools and their district-level administrations; and national policies that will encourage such changes to occur.

The policy context

Since the Labour government came to office in 1997, the main focus of education in England has been on what has come to be called "the standards agenda", an approach to educational reform which seeks to "drive up" standards of attainment, including workforce skill levels and ultimately national competitiveness in a globalised economy (Lipman, 2004; Wolf, 2002). The vigour with which this agenda has been pursued has led some American commentators to describe England as a "laboratory" for educational reform (Finkelstein & Grubb, 2000).

The government has argued that the raising of standards *is* about equity: that a powerful emphasis on raising attainment will not simply benefit children who are already performing at a high level but is of even greater benefit to previously low-attaining children in poorly performing schools (Blunkett, 1999). In practice, however, the standards agenda has concentrated on a narrow view of attainment in a way that has tended to discourage the participation and learning of some groups of learners. It has also been linked to other aspects of policy that can have perverse effects, such as the marketisation of education, a directive relationship between government and schools that potentially bypasses the participation of teachers in their own work and disengages schools from their local communities, and a regime of target setting and inspection, creating an "accountability culture" to force up standards (O'Neill, 2002). Meanwhile, schools have been expected to play their part in tackling "social exclusion" (Blair, 1997; Social Exclusion Unit, 2001) by ensuring that everyone – and not just the highest attainers or those from the most advantaged backgrounds – is equipped to compete in an ever-more-demanding labour market.

It is not surprising, therefore, that the English education system has been the scene of significant tensions. Since schools are held to account for the attainments of their students and are required to make themselves attractive to families who are most able to exercise choice of school for their children, low-attaining students, students who demand high levels of attention and resource, and those who are seen not to conform to school and classroom behavioural norms are unattractive to many schools. Giroux and Schmidt (2004) explain how similar reforms in the USA have turned some schools into "test-prep centres". As a result, they tend to be increasingly ruthless in their disregard of those students who pose a threat to success, as determined by measured forms of assessment.

Nevertheless, policies for excellence and equity are not seen as standing in contradiction to one another but as constituting "two sides of the same coin" (Brehony & Deem, 2003). Rather than making fundamental choices between these two agendas, therefore, the concern of policy-makers is to find specific strategies which will enable both to be pursued simultaneously.

Making sense of practice

This complex English policy context has provided researchers with opportunities to study what has possibly been the most intensive attempt so far to bring about system-wide improvements in relation to notions of excellence and equity. Much of the recent work of my colleagues and me has been focused on this agenda (see Ainscow & West, 2006). It has mainly involved the use of *Development and Research* (D&R), an approach that we have been developing in recent years. It involves practitioners working in partnership with academics in order to develop better understandings of educational processes (Ainscow, Dyson, Goldrick, & Kerr, 2009). Lewin's dictum that you cannot understand an organisation until you try to change it is, perhaps, the clearest justification for this approach (Schein, 2001).

In practical terms, we believe that such understandings are best developed as a result of "outsiders", such as ourselves, in working alongside teachers, headteachers, local authority staff, and other stakeholders as they attempt to move practice forward by seeking practical solutions to the complex problems posed by policy implementation. We argue that this approach can be used to overcome the traditional gap between research and practice.

As we have refined our understanding of the idea of D&R, we have come to see it as a process of knowledge generation, occurring when researcher and practitioner perspectives come together in particular sites. The overall aim is to produce new knowledge about ways in which broad values, such as equity, might better be realised in future practice. Whilst this conceptualisation draws on notions of *action research* – particularly, critical collaborative action research – and of *research and development*, it does not equate precisely with either. Unlike action research, it is not focused simply on particular sites but seeks to generate transferable knowledge. Unlike research and development, it does not assume that the contribution of researchers to this process is prior to that of practitioners. In other words, researchers do not design practices that are then implemented by practitioners.

This leads us to see researchers not as pre-hoc designers but as ad-hoc supporters and post-hoc model builders. Our role is to support practitioners in developing the best possible propositions about what will promote improvements in a given situation. This involves bringing to bear knowledge gained from prior research, but, given the uniqueness of particular situations and the general nature of values, this cannot amount to a "design". Moreover, what emerges from practitioners' attempts to act on these propositions is not a finely tuned and context-independent set of practices which can be transferred wholesale to other sites. Rather, the practices developed in one site, together with their underpinning rationale, become an elaborated set of propositions to be put forward in other sites. We call these elaborated propositions "models", and the whole process we refer to as one of development and research in order to emphasise the different relationship between the two terms from that implied by "research and development".

In what follows, I summarise and reflect on a series of three linked studies that involved a D&R approach, all carried out in partnership with colleagues in "Tramton", one of the most deprived local authorities in England. This programme of activities took place during a period when this local authority came to be recognised nationally for its success in promoting school improvement. In 1997, Tramton was described by the Office for Standards in Education (Ofsted), the national inspection agency, as having "a formidable legacy of underperformance". Subsequently, it has made great strides in developing the performance of its schools in relation to its motto, "Aiming High, Including All".

As my colleagues and I worked alongside practitioners, trying to make sense of what happened in Tramton, we found ourselves using the idea of *communities of practice* as a theoretical framework for examining the ways in which those involved attempted to collaborate in addressing common areas of concern. The idea of communities of practice emerged out of traditions of sociocultural and situative theories of learning (Lave & Wenger, 1991). Like others, we have found it a helpful means of examining what happens when groups of people work together on educational change efforts (e.g., Mitra, 2008). A limitation of its use, however, is its lack of attention to the role of power in such contexts (Brown & Duguid, 2000), a factor that emerges as I retrace developments in Tramton.

Our involvement in Tramton can be seen in relation to three overlapping phases of development, as follows:

- Phase 1 (1997–2001) – raising standards;
- Phase 2 (2000–2004) – fostering inclusion;
- Phase 3 (2004–2007) – networking across the authority.

I will consider each of these phases in turn, summarising and reflecting on the evidence we collected. Furthers details about each of the studies are already available in earlier publications.

Phase 1 (1997–2001) – raising standards

Local education authorities (LEAs) in England are accountable to their electorates and to the Secretary of State for maintained schools in their areas.

However, in recent years national reforms have gradually eroded the power of LEAs. The stated aim has been to delegate greater responsibility to the level of schools in the belief that this will help to foster improvements in standards.

As we worked along LEA staff in Tramton between 1997 and 2001, shadowing, observing, and interviewing those involved, we saw how they responded to this changing policy context by developing new relationships with schools.[1] During that period, there was increasing evidence that the authority's strategy was paying off (Ainscow & Howes, 2001). Test and examination results rose across all phases of the service, with improvement rates in primary sector tests among the highest nationally. And, whilst over the period the LEA had up to 15 schools either requiring special measures or having serious weaknesses as a result of inspections carried out by Ofsted, by early 2001 the figures were down to just 2 with serious weaknesses. In addition, some schools that had previously been in crisis subsequently received positive inspection reports. As a result, in its inspection report on the LEA, Ofsted stated, "This is a remarkable, unique record that is not paralleled elsewhere in the country."

School Improvement Officers

Our research focused specifically on the work of the team of school consultants, known as School Improvement Officers (SIOs), that was the authority's support arm (Ainscow, Howes, & Tweddle, 2006). The evidence we collected through shadowing their visits to schools and interviewing other stakeholders left us in no doubt that they were remarkably creative in inventing ways of working that stimulated and supported change within schools. However, we remained unconvinced that simply lifting these approaches in order to reproduce them in a different context would have the powerful impact that they clearly had within the particular LEA. The problem with such an approach is that it overlooks the social processes of learning that enabled the strategies to have their powerful impact. Consequently, we reflected further on our evidence in order to seek a deeper understanding of what was involved in these "social processes of learning".

Wenger (1998) provides a framework that can be used to analyse learning in social contexts. At the centre of this framework is the concept of a *community of practice*, a social group engaged in the sustained pursuit of a shared enterprise. This suggests that practices are ways of negotiating meaning through social action. Wenger argues that learning within a given community can often be best explained within the intertwining of reification and participation. He suggests that these are complementary processes, in that each has the capacity to repair the ambiguity of meaning the other can engender. So, for example, we observed how particular strategies would be developed as part of SIO planning activities and summarised in a set of guidance for action, providing a codified reification of intended practice. However, the meaning and practical implications of these strategies only became clear as they were tried in the field and discussed between colleagues. In this way, participation resulted in social learning that could not be produced solely by reification alone. At the same time, the reified products, such as the policy documents that emerged, served as a kind of memory of practice, cementing in place the new learning.

We can, then, use the notion of communities of practice to offer an explanation of what happened in Tramton. It does seem that the key to the LEA's success lay in its success in encouraging networking at different levels within the service. In particular, the links encouraged between headteachers seemed to encourage the creation of many different communities of practice that helped to break down the sense of intellectual and, indeed, emotional isolation that had characterised their previous working lives. Then, through a complex set of strategies and processes, the LEA facilitated participation and reification procedures that helped such learning communities to grow. Such an analysis seems to provide a way of describing the processes that were at the heart of the authority's success. So, to what extent was this consistent with what the Government had in mind for the future of LEAs?

New roles

An analysis of the new ways in which the Government intended LEAs to operate was presented in the form of a Code of Practice (Department for Education and Employment [DfEE], 2001). In particular, LEAs were expected to monitor the performance of their schools, in order to support and challenge them. The Code suggested that monitoring of schools should be based on routinely available information, particularly test data, Ofsted inspection reports, and information from school self-review. Indeed, it concluded that an authority which makes effective use of the full range of information which is routinely available to it will rarely need to visit schools solely for the purpose of gathering further information.

Certainly, the SIOs in our study saw themselves as supporting and, where necessary, challenging school-led improvement strategies. However, all of this was set within a wider context of relationships and procedures that meant that they had developed a deep knowledge of what went on in the schools. In this way, they were able to engage senior school staff in detailed discussion of improvement strategies, bringing to bear their detailed knowledge of particular people (staff and pupils), contexts, policies, and practices.

The government's Code of Practice placed enormous emphasis on the LEA's duty to identify and support schools causing concern. It stressed that the prime focus should be to ensure that an effective headteacher and senior management team are in place, working with an effective governing body in pursuit of a good and deliverable action plan. Our observations indicated that it was through their increasingly close knowledge of the schools that SIOs were able to pick up signs that things were not altogether well. In some instances, schools were then placed on the LEA's list of schools causing concern. As a result, it was possible to mobilise additional human resources in order to enable a school to address a growing difficulty.

It is difficult to see how such interventions could be achieved simply through the use of "routinely available information" of the sort outlined within the Code of Practice. SIOs felt that they knew their schools and that it was this knowledge which made their interventions authentic. Our interview data indicated that, by and large, headteachers were in agreement.

The challenge of including all

Phillips and Harper-Jones (2003) claim that Labour's education policy has been characterised by four themes: "a determination to raise educational standards; a quest to undertake the modernisation of educational systems, structures and practices; a commitment to choice and diversity within education; and a preoccupation with . . . the culture of performativity" (p. 125). However, what possibly differentiated this Labour government from its predecessor was a "fifth theme", which Phillips and Harper-Jones rather gloss over. That is, a broad commitment to equity in and through education, variously badged as "inclusion" or "social inclusion".

This was arguably the most troubling aspect of what happened in Tramton during the period up to 2001. It revealed how, within a context that valued aggregated test and examination scores and the outcomes of inspection as the sole criteria for determining success, such moves act as a barrier to the development of a more equitable education system.

Towards the end of our study, we interviewed an external consultant who had assisted the LEA in its preparations for its Ofsted inspection, looking specifically at its approach to vulnerable groups of learners. He suggested that salaries within the LEA were evidence of what he saw as "a pecking order" of officers, influencing the way priorities were signalled within the service. SIOs, he said, were the best paid people in the department. He went on to describe the difficulties faced by lower status staff, such as educational psychologists or advisory teachers, going into a school to help make some inclusive arrangement for an individual child experiencing difficulties and seen to be pulling in the opposite direction to the SIO.

The consultant told of how, with an Ofsted inspection looming, some SIOs had encouraged various types of informal pupil exclusion, so that classes would become easier to manage. The SIO brief, as he understood it, was to get schools out of special measures very quickly or to prevent them from going into special measures in the first place. We found evidence of similar experiences, all of which led us to conclude that the apparently successful efforts of this particular LEA to respond to the government's demands for improved standards had, in practice, created barriers to the participation of certain groups of pupils. In other words, people in the authority were "aiming high" by "excluding some". This led us to argue that, within the Tramton school system, there was expertise available that could be used to strengthen equity across the service. However, we also concluded that external pressures were creating barriers that prevented the moving around of this expertise.

During 2000, we were able to stimulate discussion amongst LEA staff as to how they might place more emphasis on making the LEA's school improvement strategy more equitable. In so doing, we argued that the LEA would need a powerful strategy for change in order for it to be successful in addressing this complex set of issues. Such a strategy, we suggested, required the development of effective strategies for making better use of available expertise. All of this helped to create the opportunity for the next phase of our involvement in Tramton.

Phase 2 (2000–2004) – fostering inclusion

The second phase of development focused on the local authority's continuing desire to "aim high" and "include all". It involved a network of nine schools (primary and secondary) that set out to develop more inclusive ways of working and was part of a larger study funded by the Economic and Social Research Council's Teaching and Learning Research Programme[2] (see Ainscow, Booth, & Dyson, 2004; Ainscow, Booth, Dyson, et al., 2006; Ainscow, Howes, Farrell, & Frankham, 2003).

Participating schools were invited to explore ways of developing inclusion in their own contexts. SIOs supported the schools as they undertook research to identify the barriers to learning and participation experienced by their students and to find ways to reduce those barriers. The research process varied from site to site in response to local priorities and possibilities. Evidence was gathered by the schools and by university researchers, using observations and interviews.

Becoming inclusive

What we noted, as the developments occurred, was neither the crushing of the schools' efforts to become more inclusive by the government's policies for raising standards nor the rejection of the standards agenda in favour of a radical, inclusive alternative (Ainscow, Booth, & Dyson, 2006). In most of the schools, the two agendas remained intertwined. Indeed, the focus on attainment appeared to prompt some teachers to examine issues in relation to the achievements and participation of hitherto marginalised groups that they had previously overlooked. Likewise, the concern with inclusion tended to shape the way the school responded to the imperative to raise standards.

In trying to make sense of the relationship between external imperatives and the processes of change in these schools, we once again drew on Wenger's (1998) ideas to reveal how external agendas were mediated by the norms and values of the communities of practice within the schools and how they become part of a dialogue whose outcomes can be more rather than less inclusive. In this way, the role of national policy emerged from the study in something of a new light. This suggests that schools may be able to engage with what might appear to be unfavourable policy imperatives to produce outcomes that are by no means inevitably non-inclusive.

Our close monitoring of what happened revealed how social learning processes within schools influenced people's action and, indeed, the thinking that informed their actions (Ainscow et al., 2003). Often, this was stimulated by various forms of evidence that created a sense of interruption to existing ways of thinking and working. Particularly powerful techniques in this respect involved the use of mutual observation, sometimes through video recordings (Ainscow, 1999), and evidence collected from students about teaching and learning arrangements within a school (Ainscow & Kaplan, 2006; Messiou, 2006; Miles & Kaplan, 2005). Under certain conditions, such approaches provided *interruptions* that stimulated self-questioning, creativity, and action. In so doing, they sometimes led to a reframing of perceived problems that, in turn, drew attention to overlooked possibilities for addressing barriers to participation and learning.

However, none of this provided a straightforward mechanism for the development of more inclusive practices. We found that any space for reflection that was created as a result of engaging with evidence may be filled according to conflicting agendas. Indeed, we documented detailed examples of how deeply held beliefs within schools prevented the experimentation that is necessary in order to foster the development of more inclusive ways of working (Ainscow & Kaplan, 2006; Howes & Ainscow, 2006). This reminds us that it is easy for educational difficulties to be pathologised as difficulties inherent within students. This is why leadership is such a key factor in challenging such assumptions.

We concluded that a methodology for developing inclusive practices must take account of the social processes of learning that go on within particular contexts. From our experience, this requires a group of stakeholders within a particular context to look for a common agenda to guide their discussions of practice and, at much the same time, a series of struggles to establish ways of working that enable them to collect and find meaning in different types of information.

Thinking and talking

The implication of all of this is that becoming more inclusive is a matter of thinking and talking, reviewing and refining practice, and making attempts to develop a more inclusive culture. Within the network, a key strategy for encouraging this possibility was the development of a programme of school-to-school visits. Many of the staff involved found these occasions both enjoyable and fruitful. We were interested in why this was so, and we wanted to explore its potential as a way of sustaining the work of the network.

The visits were not, however, always successful. This seemed to be particularly so when the host teachers interpreted the visits solely as opportunities for the visitors to learn. On these occasions, the hosts positioned themselves as teachers rather than learners. Typically, the visit then consisted of a demonstration or performance of various teaching strategies that had been judged to be successful. On these occasions, those receiving the visit might merely rehearse what they already knew and respond to questions beyond the procedural as if they were challenges rather than openings for debate.

On the other hand, successful visits were usually characterised by a sense of mutual learning amongst hosts and visitors. It was noticeable, too, that the focus for these visits often took some time to identify and clarify. Indeed, the preliminary negotiations that took place were in themselves a key aspect of the process. So, for example, during one such visit, the visitors were each invited to observe two children. A simple observation framework focused on children's interactions with peers and teachers. Those to be observed were chosen by the class teacher on the basis that they were the children he knew least about in his class. In addition to observations, the visiting teachers were asked to interview the children. Again, a loose structure was devised, but the main emphasis was on the visiting teachers following up things that they had seen during observations.

Afterwards, one of the visiting teachers said that the day had been "absolutely fascinating". He added, "There is no way in your own school you could do this." The host headteacher commented more specifically on the interviews that the visitors had carried out with pupils: "It's so different to what they're like in the school . . . pupils say things to outsiders that they just wouldn't say to us." This seemed to be born out by some of the imagery used by pupils about their teachers in interviews that day. For example, one commented, "He's like a piranha looking round the class. He knows when I'm not listening." Another pupil remarked, "He could be a really good teacher if he could explain, but he gets too frustrated." The joking response by the classteacher to such statements was: "I want to go home! I've had enough now!"

The personal nature of these observations and the teacher's willingness to listen to this feedback with colleagues from his own and another school present, illustrate the extent of the challenge that was sometimes involved in this sort of collaboration. Indeed, our experience was that such visits were not "cosy", nor did they always result in a rosy glow. The key factor seemed to be that of mutual challenge, and this is, we believe, more likely under the sorts of conditions I have outlined.

In deriving lessons from this example, it is important to emphasise the variety of reasons why participants were able to frame the event as one from which everyone might learn. This was connected to the fact that the evidence that was generated, and the ways in which it was responded to, opened up further questions. The participants also had the time necessary, not just for the event itself but for formulating the agenda for the visit and for quite lengthy discussion afterwards. Further, they had a wider forum – the LEA network meetings – in which they felt comfortable enough to talk about quite "risky" findings. In this forum, they knew they had established the sorts of relationships where others were more likely to congratulate them on their work and be intrigued by what had happened rather than to pass judgments. The atmosphere and nature of the network meetings, by this point, were significantly different from earlier meetings. They were much more open ended, there was much more unstructured conversation, and there was a sense that people felt they were "amongst friends". This allowed different sorts of exchanges to take place, whereby the participants felt able to "think aloud", trying to make sense of what had happened as a consequence of their involvement in the network.

In summary, then, the work of the Tramton inclusion network, over 3 years, demonstrated the power of using evidence to stimulate collaboration between practitioners within a school and with colleagues in partner schools. These experiences suggest that successful collaboration involves a complex social process within which colleagues with very different experiences, beliefs, and assumptions learn how to learn from these differences. The problem was, however, that the network only involved nine schools and, as a result, remained a somewhat fragile initiative within the local authority.

Phase 3 (2004–2007) – networking across the authority

Building on the lessons of these earlier experiences, the Tramton local authority went on to develop an ambitious strategy for involving all schools in processes of networking. This involved the creation of a network involving all of the authority's secondary schools and eight networks that included all 58 of its primary schools. In what follows, the focus is on our analysis of what happened in the primary sector.

Establishing networks

The assumption was that strengthening processes of networking would help to spread good practice and share resources in ways that could create greater equity across the system. This echoed the findings of the Phase 2 network and, indeed, our research elsewhere (Ainscow, Muijs, & West, 2006; Ainscow & Howes, 2007; Ainscow & West, 2006). However, the setting up of the new primary networks proved to be a complex business that led to a degree of tension between local authority staff and some headteachers.

Whilst there are a few schools in the authority that serve "middle class" communities, the majority cater for children from economically poorer backgrounds. Usually, schools serve either mostly Asian heritage or mostly White populations, with just a few having a more mixed intake. Self-selection by heads themselves was the starting point for some of the groupings.

Other arrangements also occurred, and for a few schools the reason they were in a particular network was that, simply put, they were the ones that were left behind.

Because of these various factors, the eight networks were noticeably different in make up. Some were geographically very close, serving schools with similar neighbourhoods; others were much more diverse and included schools from different parts of the authority. There are many faith schools in the area, and some of the networks had a preponderance of church schools, while others had none. There was also fluidity between the networks, with schools leaving one to join another. In addition, there was some manipulation on the part of local authority officers, where, because of particular circumstances or concerns, a school was allocated to a network.

Collecting evidence

Our involvement began in the summer of 2005 and was seen as a process of evaluation.[3] Data were collected using a mix of methods: regular meetings with SIOs; observations of meetings and staff development events; analysis of various policy documents; a questionnaire survey of representatives of each of the eight networks; and interviews with key individuals in schools, the local authority, and the various support agencies. Towards the end of the 2-year period, in the summer of 2007, process and outcome data were analysed and compared with a view to determining conclusions as to the effectiveness of the initiative. These findings were validated with stakeholders groups and then used to encourage processes of reflection amongst senior staff in schools and the LEA.

We found that the degree of involvement within schools and networks varied considerably. The evidence indicated that it was headteachers, in the main, who had the power to make a network successful. Where they were committed to putting time aside to attend meetings and to enable staff to be fully involved, the network developed. So, for example, the heads in one network met once a fortnight, leading a SIO to comment, "Heads aren't going to commit to this level of time unless it is worthwhile." Other groups of heads met monthly or half-termly, and many were also in regular email contact. For some, it seems, this became one of the most important aspects of their professional lives. A SIO commented, "If the death of the isolation of headteachers is achieved, it will be a very significant development, creating the capacity for change and development."

Apart from senior staff, members of staff designated as "lead learners" were often the group most involved. Usually, they were at the forefront of curriculum developments, meeting with colleagues from other schools regularly, and leading developments in their own school. Such opportunities to try things out and report findings back to the working group appeared to provide a very powerful form of professional development. One young teacher commented, "It's one of the best things that has happened to me." An experienced teacher described how four of her lead learner colleagues, at her invitation, came to observe a numeracy lesson; they focused on four children the teacher was concerned about, carrying out a detailed observation and interviewing the children after the lesson. Their feedback was enormously helpful, said the teacher, and led to significant changes in practice; for example, one child told the observer that he could not do things quickly enough in his head and would like to write things down – the teacher therefore provided all children with whiteboards from then on.

Areas of focus

For most networks, the core purpose was that of teaching and learning. However, two networks were asked by the local authority to explore ways of integrating the role of different external children's support agencies, including those from the health and social services. For some, this complexity muddied the waters. "We lost our way", said one head, "but now we have gone back and agreed that our aim is raising standards."

Through the power they gained together, some networks began to renegotiate their relationship with the local authority. As a result, heads began to decide when and how they wanted to do things; for example, one group organised their own training for the government's new primary strategy, informing the local authority what they wanted from them, rather than waiting to be invited to the training the authority was planning.

Many headteachers found the networks so powerful that they said that they intended to continue working in this way even if there was no additional funding made available.

Drawing out the lessons

Reflecting further on the evidence we collected over 2 years points to some potentially important lessons. What occurred has to be understood as eight separate cases, each set within the wider context of the case of the local authority. All of this, in turn, has to be understood against the backcloth of the on-going changes in national policy. Inevitably, therefore, the processes and outcomes varied between the different networks.

In the most promising examples, we saw evidence of considerable progress towards school-to-school partnerships that had a significant impact on policy and practice. Here it is tempting to look for patterns in order to make generalisations as to what actions are needed to develop an effective network. However, any such conclusions must be seen as being tentative, to say the least. In terms of geography and the patterns of involvement, for example, we saw cases where a district-based approach with relatively homogeneous groups of schools had certain advantages. On the other hand, elsewhere we heard a strong case made for cross-district arrangements that bring together schools serving different contexts and pupil populations in a way that seemed to encourage learning from difference.

In some cases, historical factors played a part. As I have explained, some groupings built on successful experiences in relation to earlier projects. In some cases, too, established friendship groups amongst heads formed the basis for the creation of a network. There are, however, dangers in such arrangements as far as equity is concerned, not least when some schools are excluded.

Across the eight accounts, we saw evidence of the key roles of individuals, particularly in the early setting up phases of a network. However, progress seemed to be strongly associated with a sense of shared leadership, particularly amongst heads and other senior staff. Such an approach seemed to emerge over time, as relationships deepen and trust grows. Being prepared to reveal worries about your own school is potentially threatening within an education service which is so dominated by competition. In a number of the networks, staff visited one another's schools in ways that draw back the veil of secrecy. At the same time, some of the groups began to learn the potential power of sharing data and using external colleagues as critical friends in relation to drawing out implications for further improvement efforts.

All of this points to one of the key challenges: that of finding time. Whilst having access to additional resources is clearly very helpful in this respect, it was evident that, where a group of heads experienced the benefits of collaboration, they were prepared to make strategic decisions to release human resources in order to invest in the strengthening of their partnerships. This reminds us that, as far as schools are concerned, time is the currency used to indicate that something is of importance. In other words, there is no extra time, but if we see something as being a priority, we find the time.

In this sense, attitudes and beliefs are important factors. It is noticeable, for example, that during the early stages the idea of setting up networks was met with a degree of understandable cynicism. In a few of the networks, this was not fully overcome, particularly amongst senior staff.

Progress seemed to be associated with activities around agendas that were determined by schools and that were seen to have the potential to make direct contributions to the core business of teaching and learning. This seemed to create a common sense of purpose and, indeed, a common process for implementation that encouraged the sharing of expertise. The idea of setting up lead teachers to coordinate implementation efforts proved to be particularly effective, and the linking of these staff across schools clearly added considerable value to the process.

Joint staff development events were particularly well received in many of the schools. Then, more specifically, support for schools in difficulty and the mentoring of newly appointed heads proved to be powerful processes. Indeed, it became increasingly apparent that, in the most mature networks, schools were increasingly looking to one another for advice and support. Inevitably, this has implications for the future roles of local authority staff.

Processes of networking remained fluid, as individual schools felt that it was to their benefit to belong to different groupings for different purposes. We also saw how, occasionally, a school may choose to move from one network to another. In this sense, it is better to think of networking as a process rather than as a fixed state. Presumably, then, a feature of an effective local authority would be its capacity to orchestrate networking in order to make good use of all the available expertise to the benefit of all of its children. All of this points to potentially important roles for authority officers in fostering, monitoring, and brokering such processes.

Tensions and uncertainties

Despite the impressive progress that was made in most of the networks, the processes involved continued to be fraught with uncertainties, not least because of an absence of overall policy direction. Consequently, they remained fragile. All of this throws light on the way national policies, as they are interpreted at the local authority level, impact on the actions of schools.

Throughout the 2 years, we noted examples of how these uncertainties played out on the ground, leading to a lack of overall coherence, as those in schools sensed they were receiving competing and, sometimes, contradictory messages as to where they should place their priorities. This was most striking in terms of the continuing tensions between strategies for raising standards, as measured in terms of test and examination scores, and measures taken in relation to notions of social justice and inclusion, with the focus on those learners who remain marginalised despite the efforts made to raise standards.

So, for example, we saw how the two networks that were asked to explore multi-agency working were pulled in different directions. Early on, they were encouraged by local authority colleagues to take on an "assessment for learning" initiative. Then, at a later stage, pressure was put on the two networks to attend training days regarding the idea of "extended schools". These and other initiatives are, of course, all in their own way important. However, as I have already noted, the success of the networks appeared to come from the sense of commitment that occurs when they determine their own improvement agendas. This being the case, it was hardly surprising when some networks started to resist what they saw as "high jacking" of the agenda by the local authority.

In fairness, it is important to note that local authority officers act in the context of pressures (and, sometimes, opportunities) that are created by national agencies. On the other hand, a key role for the local authority must be to create a sense of overall coherence and direction, by drawing staff and partners together around a common mission. More specifically, its aim should be to articulate a clear vision of what the education service should look like that can focus improvement efforts, leaving the networks themselves to generate their own specific goals in relationship to this vision. In this way, I suggest, the tensions that occurred as some networks grew in strength would be much less likely and the power of networking mobilised.

Impact

The experience of these eight networks adds to the growing body of evidence which suggests that processes of networking can strengthen the capacity of schools to respond to learner diversity. Whilst the results were uneven and the progress remained fragile, the evidence was that in Tramton, school-to-school collaboration led to:

- improvements in teaching and learning;
- powerful forms of professional development at all levels, not least that of headteachers;
- a greater capacity for managing change and implementing innovations;
- effective induction of newly appointed headteachers;
- the creation of a more cooperative environment within which external support staff, including those from other agencies, can work more effectively.

All of this occurred through the negotiation of new working relationships within schools and between schools, and between groups of schools and external partners. In the most promising examples, this involved the strengthening of "social capital" in ways described by Hargreaves (2003), such that available expertise was being used more effectively to serve a wider population of learners than is possible when human resources are trapped within the walls of individual institutions.

Some implications

The findings of the 10-year programme of development and research in Tramton do not provide a simple formula that can be used by education systems as they try to develop ways of working that will achieve both excellence and equity. Rather, they suggest a series of propositions around which future actions might be planned. In summary, these are as follows:

- **Schools know more than they use.** Thus the main thrust of development has to be with making better use of existing expertise and creativity within all the member organisations in a local area.
- **The expertise of teachers and educational leaders is largely unarticulated.** Therefore, in order to access the reservoir of unused expertise, it is necessary to create a common language of practice that will facilitate mutual reflection and the sharing of ideas.
- **Evidence is the engine for change.** Specifically, it can help to create space for reappraisal and re-thinking by interrupting existing discourses and by focusing attention on overlooked possibilities for moving practice forward.
- **Networking is socially complex.** Successful networking requires new thinking and, indeed, new relationships at the systems level that foster active connections amongst stakeholders.
- **Leadership must foster interdependence.** There is a need for forms of leadership that encourage the trust, mutual understanding, and shared values and behaviours that will bind members of a network together and make cooperative action possible.

These ideas have implications for what needs to happen within networks of schools, across district education systems and at the national level.

At *the network level*, we saw how the networking between schools that took place in Tramton varied from context to context. This seems inevitable, in that such forms of collaboration involve social learning processes, shaped by particular circumstances, related to history and geography, challenges, and opportunities. Here we note echoes of other research into factors influencing the transfer of practice between teachers (Bragg et al., 2004). This suggests that teacher learning is a social process that is sustained by relationships and trust, that it is a personal and interpersonal process that has to engage with teacher and institutional identity, that this requires conditions that provide support for learner engagement and a willingness to try something out, and, lastly, that the work of transfer has to be sustained over time.

It follows that there can be no one recipe for fostering effective networking. On the other hand, certain ingredients seem to be important. These are to do with:

- **Ownership.** In the contexts where collaboration appeared to pay off, it was evident that those in the partner schools – particularly the headteachers – felt that they had reasonable control over the agendas that were to be the focus of the activities.
- **Levels of involvement.** Whilst the commitment of heads and other senior staff is essential, best practice seemed to involve forms of collaboration that existed at many levels within schools.
- **Practical focus.** Focusing on real world issues, particularly those to do with the core business of teaching and learning, seemed to provide the best type of vehicle for learning how to work together effectively.
- **Making time.** Since successful collaboration demands an investment of people's time and energy, it is hardly surprising that good practice was

associated with flexible management arrangements that provided staff with opportunities to learn from one another.

- **Commitment to values.** In those networks that seem to be maturing into forms of collaboration that looked to be potentially more sustainable, the focus moved from attention to specific projects towards a deeper level of partnership around common beliefs and values.
- **Shared responsibility.** Successful networking leads to changes in organisational cultures and, therefore, demands the sharing of responsibility through new forms of collaborative leadership.

Alongside our experiences of school-to-school collaboration in other settings, the developments in Tramton led us to formulate a model for analysing forms of networking within particular contexts in order to move thinking and practice forward (Chapman & Ainscow, 2007). It takes the form of a *framework for networking* consisting of four interlinked elements, each with its own set of issues for consideration, as shown in Figure 13.1.

The framework pinpoints guiding questions that can be used by those involved in initiating and strengthening networks to develop a greater understanding of their own contexts and their associated processes and practices. Its use requires the development of leadership that will encourage action and shared responsibility at all levels of the system. And, with regard to children's learning experiences, the classroom level is seen as being crucial, since, as became clear in Tramton, teachers *are* decision-makers and, therefore, policy-makers.

Changing policy and practice at the classroom level is particularly difficult, however, in that it most often requires changes in thinking and beliefs. As we have seen, in more mature networks, engaging with evidence of various kinds can be a powerful means of encouraging professional dialogue that can stimulate the sharing of expertise amongst practitioners. Specifically, it can help to create space for reappraisal and rethinking, by interrupting existing discourses and by focusing attention on overlooked possibilities for moving practice forward.

Moving to *implications at that district level,* the changes that occurred in Tramton began to redesign what is meant by the local authority. This involved a move away from the traditional "them and us" relationship between central office staff and schools, to one of shared responsibility. It involved

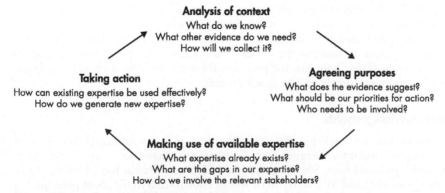

Figure 13.1 A framework for networking.

working together to make use of the pressure for change stemming from national policies, whilst mobilising available human resources at the local level around a common sense of purpose. This is most likely to be achieved when local leadership makes connections between national policies and local priorities. It also means that there is a need to create locally the organisational conditions and climate within which stakeholders will feel encouraged to work together creatively to invent new and more effective responses to old problems – especially those of learners who are not making satisfactory progress.

The emphasis on school-level leadership, within a change model grounded in the notion that a combination of robust national policies and strong school management is the surest way to bring about improvements in teaching and learning, has very significant implications for the roles of local authority staff. It means that they have to adjust their priorities and ways of working in response to the development of collaborative arrangements that are led from within schools. And, as we have seen, at a time when they too are under increasing pressure to deliver improvements in results across their stocks of schools, this can sometimes lead to misunderstandings and tensions between senior staff in schools and their local authority partners.

Despite such difficulties, I cannot conceive of a way for collaboration to continue as a central element of effective school improvement strategies without some form of local co-ordination. As I have indicated, the contributions of local authority staff were significant in the development of collaborative arrangements in Tramton. Specifically, local authority staff had a key role in supporting and challenging schools in relation to the agreed goals of collaborative activities, whilst headteachers shared responsibility for the overall management of improvement efforts within their schools.

This distinction sharpens understanding of the sorts of roles that local authority staffs need to take on: *not* managing and leading change but rather working in partnership with senior people in schools to strengthen collaborative ways of working. In such contexts, they can ensure that specific challenges which derive from their knowledge of the bigger picture across the authority are addressed and also contribute to the clarity of purpose and practical working arrangements, as well as playing an important role in the monitoring and evaluation of progress. At the same time, they can help to broker the sharing of resources and expertise. However, the changes in attitude and practice that this implies are likely to be challenging to the existing thinking of many experienced local authority staff.

Finally, this analysis has *implications for national policy-makers*. If they see school networking as a means of achieving both excellence and equity, they will need to foster greater flexibility at the local level in order that practitioners have the space to analyse their local circumstances and determine priorities accordingly. If that happens, the potential for developments such as those going on in Tramton to grow will be much greater.

Acknowledgements

I must also acknowledge the contributions of local authority partners in "Tramton" and my colleagues Tony Booth, Chris Chapman, Alan Dyson, Anne Francis, Jo Frankham, Sue Goldrick, Andy Howes, Kirstin Kerr, Daniel Muijs, Dave Tweddle, and Mel West, all of whom contributed to the ideas presented in this paper.

Notes

1 I monitored the first phase of development with my colleague Andy Howes as an evaluation commissioned by the local authority. It involved the shadowing of staff, observations of meetings, and a programme of individual interviews with stakeholders (see Ainscow & Howes, 2001).

2 Phase 2 was carried out in partnership with my colleagues Peter Farrell, Andy Howes, and Jo Frankham as part of a larger study funded by the Teaching and Learning Research Programme of the Economic and Social Research Council (Award L139 25 1001).

3 The third phase was an authority commissioned evaluation I carried out with Anne Francis.

References

Ainscow, M. (1999). *Understanding the development of inclusive schools.* London, UK: Falmer.

Ainscow, M., Booth, T., & Dyson, A. (2004). Understanding and developing inclusive practices in schools: A collaborative action research network. *International Journal of Inclusive Education, 8,* 125–140.

Ainscow, M., Booth, T., & Dyson, A. (2006). Inclusion and the standards agenda: Negotiating policy pressures in England. *International Journal of Inclusive Education, 10,* 295–308.

Ainscow, M., Booth, T., Dyson, A., Farrell, P., Frankham, J., Gallannaugh, F., . . . Smith, R. (2006). *Improving schools, developing inclusion.* London, UK: Routledge.

Ainscow, M., Dyson, A., Goldrick, S., & Kerr, K. (2009). Using research to foster inclusion and equity within the context of New Labour education reforms. In C. Chapman & H. Gunter (Eds.), *Radical reform: Perspectives on an era of educational change* (pp. 116–129). London, UK: Routledge.

Ainscow, M., & Howes, A. (2001, September). *LEAs and school improvement: What is it that makes the difference?* Paper presented at the British Education Research Association Conference, Leeds, UK.

Ainscow, M., & Howes, A. (2007). Working together to improve urban secondary schools: A study of practice in one city. *School Leadership and Management, 27,* 285–300.

Ainscow, M., Howes, A.J., Farrell, P., & Frankham, J. (2003). Making sense of the development of inclusive practices. *European Journal of Special Needs Education, 18,* 227–242.

Ainscow, M., Howes, A., & Tweddle, D. (2006). Making sense of the impact of recent education policies: A study of practice. In M. Ainscow & M. West (Eds.), *Improving urban schools: Leadership and collaboration* (pp. 70–80). Maidenhead, UK: Open University Press.

Ainscow, M., & Kaplan, I. (2006). Using evidence to encourage inclusive school development: Possibilities and challenges. *Australasian Journal of Special Education, 29,* 106–116.

Ainscow, M., Muijs, D., & West, M. (2006). Collaboration as a strategy for improving schools in challenging circumstances. *Improving Schools, 9,* 192–202.

Ainscow, M. & West, M. (Eds.). (2006). *Improving urban schools: Leadership and collaboration.* Maidenhead, UK: Open University Press.

Blair, T. (1997). *"Bringing Britain together".* Speech by the Prime Minister, the Rt Hon Tony Blair MP, Stockwell Park School, South London, Monday 8 December 1997. London, UK: Social Exclusion Unit.

Blunkett, D. (1999). *Excellence for the many, not just the few: Raising standards and extending opportunities in our schools.* The CBI President's Reception Address by the Rt. Hon. David Blunkett MP, 19 July 1999, London, UKDfEE.

Bragg, S., Craig, J., Cunningham, I., Eraut, M., Fielding, M., Gillinson, S., . . . Thorp, J. (2004). *Factors influencing the transfer of good practice* (Report on DfES Project JC154/2001/1.). Brighton, UK: University of Sussex.

Brehony, K.J., & Deem, R. (2003). Education policy. In N. Ellison & C. Pierson (Eds.), *Developments in British social policy 2* (pp. 177–193). Basingstoke, UK: Palgrave Macmillan.

Brown, J.S., & Duguid, P. (2000). *Social life of information*. Boston, MA: Harvard Business School Press.

Chapman, C., & Ainscow, M. (2007). *Networking for transformation: Making it happen*. Unpublished pamphlet, University of Manchester, UK.

Department for Education and Employment. (2001). *The code of practice on Local Education Authority–school relations*. London, UK: DfES.

Finkelstein, N.D., & Grubb, W.N. (2000). Making sense of education and training markets: Lessons from England. *American Educational Research Journal, 37*, 601–631.

Giroux, H.A., & Schmidt, M. (2004). Closing the achievement gap: A metaphor for children left behind. *Journal of Educational Change, 5*, 213–228.

Hargreaves, D.H. (2003). *Education epidemic: Transforming secondary schools through innovation networks*. London, UK: DEMOS.

Howes, A., & Ainscow, M. (2006). Collaboration with a city-wide purpose: Making paths for sustainable educational improvement. In M. Ainscow & M. West (Eds.), *Improving urban school: Leadership and collaboration* (pp. 104–116). Maidenhead, UK: Open University Press.

Lave, J., & Wenger, E. (1991). *Situated learning: Legitimate peripheral participation*. Cambridge, UK: Cambridge University Press.

Lipman, P. (2004). *High stakes education*. London, UK: RoutledgeFalmer.

Messiou, K. (2006). Understanding marginalisation in education: The voice of children. *European Journal of Psychology of Education, 21*, 305–318.

Miles, S., & Kaplan, I. (2005). Using images to promote reflection: An action research study in Zambia and Tanzania. *Journal of Research in Special Educational Needs, 5*(2), 77–83.

Mitra, D.L. (2008). Balancing power in communities of practice: An examination of increasing student voice through school-based youth-adult partnerships. *Journal of Educational Change, 9*, 221–242.

O'Neill, O. (2002). *Called to account*. (Lecture 3, Reith Lectures 2002, London, BBC). Retrieved from http://www.bbc.co.uk/radio4/reith2002/lecture3.shtml

Phillips, R., & Harper-Jones, G. (2003). Whatever next? Education policy and New Labour: The first four years, 1997–2001. *British Educational Research Journal, 29*, 125–132.

Schein, E.H. (2001). Clinical inquiry/research. In P. Reason & H. Bradbury (Eds.), *Handbook of action research* (pp. 151–170). London, UK: Sage.

Social Exclusion Unit. (2001). *Preventing social exclusion*. London, UK: Author.

Wenger, E. (1998). *Communities of practice: Learning, meaning and identity*. Cambridge, UK: Cambridge University Press.

Wolf, A. (2002). *Does education matter? Myths about education and economic growth*. London, UK: Penguin Books.

CHAPTER 14

USING EVIDENCE TO PROMOTE EQUITY IN SCHOOLS

Ainscow, M., Dyson, A., Goldrick, S. and West, M. (2012) Making schools effective for all: rethinking the task. *School Leadership and Management* 32(3), 1–17

Introduction

The argument developed in this paper summarises the findings of a five-year study that involved processes of collaborative inquiry among secondary schools in one local authority. The rationale and methodology for this project was informed by the findings of the earlier research described in previous chapters of this book. The paper challenges those leading school improvement to return to their historical purpose, that of ensuring a sound education for every child. We argue that in order to achieve this it is necessary to complement within-school developments with efforts that link schools with one another and with their wider communities. This means that school improvement processes have to be nested within locally led efforts to make school systems more equitable and link the work of schools with area strategies for tackling wider inequities and, ultimately, with national policies aimed at creating a fairer society.

At its point of origin, the school effectiveness movement was rooted in rebellion against conventional explanations of educational failure, particularly those put forward to explain low educational performance in areas characterised by poverty and deprivation (Edmonds 1979). Central to the development of this tradition was the conviction that schools can and should make a difference, regardless of social context.

The argument developed in this article starts from the assumption that school effectiveness and improvement thinking has become domesticated within a political discourse that stifles discussion and equates achievement with measurable outcomes from standardised tests (Slee, Weiner, and Tomlinson 1998; Thrupp 1999). As a result, in national contexts such as our own, where reform policies have been based on a rather narrow view of effectiveness, strategies seeking to bring about school improvement have, in practice, acted as a barrier to the development of educational practices that can serve all students, particularly those in more unfavourable socio-economic contexts.

This article uses evidence from our programme of research carried out with schools and school systems over many years in order to offer an alternative way forward. The approach we describe is built on the principle of equity and uses processes of inquiry to stimulate 'school improvement with attitude'

(Ainscow, Booth, and Dyson 2006). At its best, this approach provides space and opportunities for developing new understandings and generating new practices. However, we argue that such possibilities can only be utilised if potential barriers in the wider context are overcome.

Equitable school improvement

Our research is guided by the principle of equity, which we take to involve notions of inclusion and fairness. As we have worked with schools over many years, we have become aware of the complexities this involves. One way to think about the processes at work is to see them as linked within an 'ecology of equity' (Ainscow et al. 2012). By this, we mean that the extent to which students' experiences and outcomes are equitable is not dependent only on the educational practices of their teachers, or even their schools. Instead, it depends on a whole range of interacting processes that reach into the school from outside. These include the demographics of the areas served by schools, the histories and cultures of the populations who send (or fail to send) their children to the school and the economic realities faced by those populations. Beyond this, they involve the underlying socio-economic processes that make some areas poor and others affluent, and that draw migrant groups into some places rather than others. They are also influenced by the wider politics of the teaching profession, of decision-making at the district level, and of national policy-making and the impacts of schools on one another over issues such as exclusion and parental choice. In addition, they reflect new models of school governance, the ways in which local school hierarchies are established and maintained, and the ways in which school actions are constrained and enabled by their positions in those hierarchies.

It is important to recognise the complexities of interactions between the different elements in this ecology and their implications for achieving more equitable school systems. As we work on improvement projects with schools, we find it helpful to think of three interlinked areas within which equity issues arise. These are:

- *Within schools.* These are issues that arise from school and teacher practices. They include: the ways in which students are taught and engaged with learning; the ways in which teaching groups are organised and the different kinds of opportunities that result from this organisation; the kinds of social relations and personal support that are characteristic of the school; the ways in which the school responds to diversity in terms of attainment, gender, ethnicity and social background; and the kinds of relationships the school builds with families and local communities.
- *Between schools.* These are issues that arise from the characteristics of the local school system. They include: the ways in which different types of school emerge locally; the ways in which these schools acquire different statuses so that hierarchies emerge in terms of performance and preference; the ways in which schools compete or collaborate; the processes of integration and segregation which concentrate students with similar backgrounds in different schools; the distribution of educational opportunities across schools; and the extent to which students in every school can access similar opportunities.
- *Beyond schools.* This far-reaching arena includes: the wider policy context within which schools operate; the family processes and resources which

shape how children learn and develop; the interests and understandings of the professionals working in schools; and the demographics, economics, cultures and histories of the areas served by schools. Beyond this, it includes the underlying social and economic processes at national and – in many respects – at global levels out of which local conditions arise.

Looked at in this way, it is clear that there is much that individual schools can do to tackle issues within their organisations, and that such actions are likely to have a profound impact on student experiences, and perhaps have some influence on inequities arising elsewhere. However, it is equally clear that these strategies do not lead to schools tackling between- and beyond-school issues directly. No school strategy can, for example, make a poor area more affluent, or increase the resources available to students' families, any more than it could create a stable student population, or tackle the global processes underlying migration patterns. But perhaps there are issues of access, or of the allocation of students to schools, that might be tackled if schools work together on a common agenda.

Bearing these arguments in mind, in what follows we explore possibilities for linking within-school, between-schools and beyond-schools strategies in order to develop more equitable improvement approaches.

Improving schools

Over the past 20 years or so we have been privileged to be part of a wider group of colleagues who have carried out research in order to determine effective strategies for improving schools. A feature of this programme of research is that it has involved collaboration with practitioners. In order to develop our argument we will reflect on three of these initiatives.

Improving the Quality of Education for All (IQEA)

This programme of collaborative research began towards the end of the 1980s at the University of Cambridge. Over many years IQEA grew as a result of projects carried out with schools, both in the United Kingdom and overseas (see Ainscow 1999; Clarke, Ainscow, and West 2005; Hopkins 2007; Hopkins, Ainscow, and West 1994; West and Ainscow 2010 for more detailed accounts of some of these projects). These involved teams of researchers working in partnership with colleagues from schools to identify ways in which the learning of all members of the school community – students, parents and staff – could be enhanced.

Working with schools in the IQEA projects was based on a *contract* that attempted to define the parameters for our involvement, and the obligations those involved owed to one another. In particular, the contract emphasised that all staff were consulted; that an in-school team of coordinators were appointed to carry the work forward; that a critical mass of staff were to be actively involved; and that sufficient time would be made available for necessary classroom and staff development activities. Meanwhile, we committed ourselves to supporting the school's developments, usually in the first place for one year. Often the arrangement continued, however, and in some instances we were involved for periods as long as seven years. We provided training for the school coordinators, made regular school visits and contributed to school-based staff development activities. In addition, we attempted to work with the schools in recording and analysing their experiences in a way that also provided data relevant to our own on-going research agendas. These data also contributed to our analysis of these developments.

As a result of such engagements with schools involved in the IQEA project, we evolved a style of collaboration that we referred to as 'working with, rather than working on'. This phrase attempted to sum up an approach that deliberately allows each project school considerable autonomy to determine its own priorities for development and, indeed, its methods for achieving these priorities. In attempting to work in this way, we found ourselves confronted with staggering complexity, and by a bewildering array of policy and strategy options. It was our belief, however, that only through a regular engagement with these complexities could a greater understanding of school improvement be achieved.

Our monitoring of developments in the schools involved in IQEA led us to conclude that such inquiry-based analyses can be a powerful means of stimulating schools' deliberations as they design their own improvement strategies. We also found that they were useful in identifying strategies appropriate to each school's own stage of development. In the case of schools that are relatively low-performing, the initial emphasis was usually placed on gathering evidence that could be used to strengthen system procedures, through the tightening of management and leadership arrangements (West, Ainscow, and Stanford 2005). For schools that were performing more effectively, the focus was likely to be on continuing improvement, not least by looking at within-school variation. We also found that there is always scope for the strengthening of teachers' classroom practices, as no school works equally well for all of its students. These findings from IQEA about the potential of inquiry-based approaches influenced the development of another project focused on schools.

Understanding and developing inclusive practices in schools

This initiative began in 2000 when members of our group won a grant from the Economic and Social Research Council (ESRC) Teaching and Learning Research Programme that enabled us to push forward our ideas about inquiry-based approaches to the development of schools. The initiative, which took the form of a three-year collaborative action research project, involved 25 urban schools, their associated local education authorities and three universities (i.e. Canterbury Christ Church, Manchester and Newcastle). Together we explored ways of developing more inclusive practices in the schools.

We saw inclusion as a value and set of practices about which something was already known. Moreover, as established authors and researchers in the field, we had played our part in generating this prior knowledge (e.g. Ainscow 1999, 2006; Clark et al. 1999; Dyson and Millward 2000). We also knew – from our own work and from others in this field – that acceptance of the value and practices of inclusion was frequently resisted by practitioners who saw themselves as having other priorities and as working within constraints that made inclusive practice impossible. This was particularly the case in the then English policy context where a 'relentless focus on standards' was being imposed on schools by central government (Blair 2005).

We therefore needed a means of releasing practitioners from the constraints of national policy and enabling them to change their value positions and assumptions. We saw the use of research evidence as offering this means.

We made the assumption that, when practitioners were confronted by evidence about their own practices, they would – with appropriate encouragement from their critical friends – begin to recognise the non-inclusive elements of those practices and find ways of making them more inclusive. Fortunately, this is what did most often happen.

What we noted as these developments occurred was neither the crushing of the schools' efforts to become more inclusive by the government's policies for raising standards, nor the rejection of the standards agenda in favour of a radical, inclusive alternative (Ainscow, Booth, and Dyson 2006). In most of the schools, the two agendas remained intertwined. Indeed, the focus on attainment appeared to prompt some teachers to examine issues in relation to the achievements and participation of hitherto marginalised groups that they had previously overlooked. Likewise, the concern with inclusion tended to shape the way the school responded to the imperative to raise standards.

Our analysis revealed how social learning processes within schools influenced people's action and, indeed, the thinking that informed their actions (Ainscow, Nicolaidou, and West 2003). Often this was stimulated by various forms of evidence that created a sense of interruption to existing ways of thinking and working. Particularly powerful techniques in this respect involved the use of mutual observation, sometimes through video recordings, and evidence collected from students about teaching and learning arrangements within a school. Under certain conditions such approaches provided *interruptions* that stimulated self-questioning, creativity and action. In so doing, they sometimes led to a reframing of perceived problems that, in turn, drew attention to overlooked possibilities for addressing barriers to participation and learning.

We concluded, however, that none of this provided a straightforward mechanism for the development of more inclusive practices. We found that any space for reflection that was created as a result of engaging with evidence may sometimes be filled according to conflicting agendas. Indeed, we documented detailed examples of how deeply held beliefs within schools prevented the experimentation that is necessary in order to foster the development of more inclusive ways of working (Ainscow and Kaplan 2006; Howes and Ainscow 2006).

The outcomes of the inclusion project have been widely reported in the scholarly literature (Ainscow et al. 2004; Ainscow, Booth, and Dyson 2006; Ainscow et al. 2006; Dyson, Gallannaugh, and Millward 2003; Howes et al. 2004, 2005). In terms of the development of a methodology for enabling research to contribute to more equitable policy and practice, the main lesson we drew was that it is possible to infuse a critical dimension into a collaborative action-research project, so that issues of social justice (in this case, a focus on inclusion) are considered as practitioners shape their action. We also concluded that the critical friendship of 'outsiders' (in this case, ourselves as researchers) is a way of keeping these issues on the agenda.

An equity research network

The two projects we have described so far clearly have much in common, not least in the way they: sought to stimulate a process of change in practice (i.e. they had an action strand); formulated action with reference to overarching principles; had a research strand that invited practitioners to inquire into their own practice and assumed that such inquiry would impact on the values on which practitioners act; and positioned university researchers as critical friends of and technical supporters for practitioners.

Between 2006 and 2011 we had a chance to explore these ideas in more detail through our involvement in yet another group of schools (see Ainscow et al. 2012 for a detailed account of this project). The initiative was located in an area characterised by socio-economic disadvantage, and social and ethnic segregation. The district's secondary school system comprised a hierarchy of 16 schools, some selective on the basis of attainment or religious faith, with others being non-selective and described as comprehensive schools.

The network grew out of an existing partnership of 4 secondary schools, with 10 other schools joining in at various stages over the five-year period. Whilst the head teachers involved had developed very good working relationships, and this had led to some collaborative activities, they felt that the impact had been limited. Consequently, they decided that there was a need to develop ways of working that would challenge the practices, assumptions and beliefs of staff, and which would help to create a stimulus for further sustainable improvement. With this in mind, they approached us to support and facilitate the use of research to strengthen their network. The schools agreed to fund our involvement.

Through discussions involving the head teachers, it was agreed that equity was a central issue facing each of the partner schools. It soon became evident, however, that what this meant was different in each context, not least in respect to the groups of learners who seemed to be missing out within existing arrangements. As a result, it was agreed that the work of the network should take account of these differences by adopting a broad set of research questions to focus its activities, within which each school would determine its own particular focus. These questions were as follows:

• Which of our learners are most vulnerable to underachievement, marginalisation or exclusion?
• What changes in policy and practice need to be made in order to reach out to these students?
• How can these changes be introduced effectively and evaluated in respect to student outcomes?

In taking the strategic decision to focus attention on groups of learners thought to be missing out within existing arrangements, we were anxious that this might lead to narrowly focused efforts to 'fix' students seen as being in some sense inadequate. However, collecting evidence about these groups usually led to a re-focusing of attention around contextual factors that were acting as barriers to their participation and learning. In this way, most of the projects carried out gradually became mainstream school improvement efforts that had the potential to benefit many students.

As with our earlier projects, staff inquiry groups were set up in each school, usually consisting of five or six members representing different perspectives within their school communities. These groups took part in introductory workshops at which we discussed with them an initial analysis we had made of the area, based on a consideration of various documents, statistics and interviews with a selection of stakeholders, including head teachers, local authority staff, community group representatives and politicians.

Following this process of contextual analysis, we took the staff teams through a process of planning the investigations they intended to carry out. In so doing, we helped them to develop a clearer focus and plan the procedures they would follow. Subsequently, each school team set out to gather evidence about students identified as losing out in some way, the aim being to develop better insights regarding their experiences in the schools. The groups also shared their findings with their colleagues in the partner schools. In these ways, the intention was to deepen understandings of practices, beliefs, assumptions and organisational processes, both within and across the schools in the network.

Taking place as it did over a period of five years of intense government activity to improve educational outcomes – or at least raise the annually reported attainment levels – this was a time of multiple policy initiatives and interventions to drive up standards. Consequently, it is not easy to disentangle particular effects and attribute them to the work of the project teams, rather than the pressures imposed generally on schools over this period of time. Nonetheless, the evidence we collected showed that teachers in the schools themselves felt able to identify changes and to trace these to their involvement in the project. It can be also asserted that these schools contributed fully to the overall increase in examination results recorded in the particular local authority during this period. In fact, the percentage of students gaining five or more A* to C grades at GCSE (General Certificate of Secondary Education) went up from 54.6% in 2005 to 76.5% in 2010, a rise of 22% (during the same period the national average went from 56.3% to 75.3%, or a rise of 19%). Looking at a more inclusive measure of student performance, during the same period the percentage of students gaining five or more A* to G grades went up at almost twice the national average, from 90% to 96.1% (compared to 89% to 92.7% nationally).

Our consideration of what this particular network achieved points to a series of factors that seem to be particularly important for the development of more equitable schools. At their most fundamental, the factors we are concerned with are located in classrooms, where, first and foremost, equity is about attitudes. Put simply, the attitudes of teachers – and of fellow students – can either promote or inhibit a fair, welcoming and inclusive working climate. In a school that is committed to fairness, all students should expect to be welcome in their classrooms – not only in explicit ways, which embrace cultural, social and intellectual differences – but also in implicit ways, so they will not feel marginalised because of feedback (or lack of it) on their behaviour and performance. Because all students are welcome, they can expect positive interactions as a normal part of their classroom experience. As a result, they will feel included, valued and acknowledged.

Then there is the issue of practice. If teachers favour one style it will tend to suit most of those students who are comfortable with that style. In effect, strong teaching orthodoxies can disenfranchise students who are less confident with or less engaged by that approach. Equity, therefore, requires practitioners who understand the importance of teaching the same thing in different ways to different students, and of teaching different things in different ways to the same students.

The network schools could point to examples of good practice in all of these areas before they joined the project. But the issue they were addressing through their involvement was whether they were sure that *all* students could feel they were embraced within these ways of working. In most of the schools there was evidence, too, of changes in classrooms so that specific groups who were felt to be missing out were now more actively engaged in learning, and that this had been achieved through deliberate attention to the attitudes displayed, language used and interactions engineered in lessons, all of which were reflected in the range of teaching approaches used.

Of course, these are the less difficult aspects of equity to deliver. That is not to deny their value, but simply to accept that while adjustments in classroom practices can have significant impact on the experiences of particular students, they may not do much to alter the factors that led to these students 'missing out' in the first place. Often such factors are more intransigent, and therefore more difficult to influence as a single school.

School-to-school collaboration

The approach we have outlined so far is based on the idea of those within schools collecting and engaging with various forms of data in order to stimulate moves to create more equitable arrangements. The accounts we have summarised provide a convincing case for the power of this approach. These accounts have also thrown light on the difficulties in putting such an approach into practice within current policy contexts. This led us to analyse the limitations of within-school strategies, leading us, in turn, to argue that these should be complemented with between-school activities.

In recent years, we have carried out a series of studies that have generated considerable evidence that school-to-school collaboration can strengthen improvement processes by adding to the range of expertise made available (see: Ainscow 2010; Ainscow and Howes 2007; Ainscow, Muijs, and West 2006; Ainscow, Nicolaidou, and West 2003; Ainscow and West 2006; Ainscow, West, and Nicolaidou 2005; Chapman et al. 2010; Muijs, West, and Ainscow 2010; Muijs et al. 2011). Together, these studies indicate that school-to-school collaboration has an enormous potential for fostering system-wide improvement, particularly in challenging urban contexts. More specifically, they show: how collaboration between schools can provide an effective means of solving immediate problems, such as staffing shortages; how it can have a positive impact in periods of crisis, such as during the closure of a school; and, how, in the longer run, schools working together can contribute to the raising of expectations and attainment in schools that have had a record of low achievement. There is also evidence here that collaboration can help to reduce the polarisation of schools according to their position in 'league tables', to the particular benefit of those students who seem marginalised at the edges of the system and whose performance and attitudes cause increasing concern.

For the most part, these studies have focused on situations where schools have been given short-term financial incentives linked to the demonstration of collaborative planning and activity. Nevertheless, they convince us that this approach can be a powerful catalyst for change, although it does not represent an easy option, particularly in policy contexts within which competition and choice continue to be the main policy drivers.

The most convincing evidence about the power of schools working together comes from our recent involvement in the Greater Manchester Challenge. This three-year project, which involved over 1100 schools in 10 local authorities, had a government investment of around £50 million (see Ainscow 2012, for a detailed account of this initiative). The decision to invest such a large budget reflected a concern regarding educational standards in the city region, particularly amongst children and young people from disadvantaged backgrounds. The approach adopted was influenced by an earlier initiative in London (Brighouse 2007).

Reflecting much of the thinking developed in this article, the overall approach of the Challenge emerged from a detailed analysis of the local context, using both statistical data and local intelligence provided by stakeholders. This drew attention to areas of concern and also helped to pinpoint a range of human resources that could be mobilised in order to support improvement efforts. Recognising the potential of these resources, it was decided that networking and collaboration should be the key strategies for strengthening the overall improvement capacity of the system. More specifically, this involved a series of inter-connected activities for 'moving knowledge around' (Ainscow 2012).

So, for example, in an attempt to engage all schools in processes of networking and collaboration, *Families of Schools* were set up, using a data system that groups between 12 and 20 schools on the basis of the prior attainment of their students and their socio-economic home backgrounds. The strength of this approach is that it partners schools that serve similar populations whilst, at the same time, encouraging partnerships amongst schools that are not in direct competition with one another because they do not serve the same neighbourhoods. Led by head teachers, the Families of Schools proved to be successful in strengthening collaborative processes within the city region, although the impact was varied.

In terms of schools working in highly disadvantaged contexts, evidence from the Challenge suggests that school-to-school partnerships are the most powerful means of fostering improvements. Most notably, the *Keys to Success* programme led to striking improvements in the performance of some 160 schools facing the most challenging circumstances. There is also evidence that the progress that these schools made helped to trigger improvement across the system. A common feature of almost all of these interventions was that progress was achieved through carefully matched pairings (or, sometimes, trios) of schools that cut across social 'boundaries' of various kinds, including those that separate schools that are in different local authorities. In this way, expertise that was previously trapped in particular contexts was made more widely available.

Another effective strategy to facilitate the movement of expertise was provided through the creation of various types of *hub schools*. So, for example, some of the hubs provided support for other schools regarding ways of supporting students with English as an additional language. Similarly, so-called 'teaching schools' providing professional development programmes focused on bringing about improvements in classroom practice. Other hub schools offered support in relation to particular subject areas, and in responding to groups of potentially vulnerable students, such as those categorised as having special educational needs. In this latter context, a further significant strategy involved new roles for special schools in supporting developments in the mainstream.

Significantly, we found that such collaborative arrangements can have a positive impact on the learning of students in all of the participating schools. This is an important finding in that it draws attention to a way of strengthening relatively low-performing schools that can, at the same time, help to foster wider improvements in the system. It also offers a convincing argument as to why relatively strong schools should support other schools. Put simply, the evidence is that by helping others you help yourself.

Whilst increased collaboration of this sort is vital as a strategy for developing more effective ways of working, the experience of Greater Manchester showed that it is not enough. The essential additional ingredient is an engagement with data that can bring an element of mutual challenge to such collaborative processes. We found that data were particularly essential when partnering schools, since collaboration is at its most powerful where partner schools are carefully matched and know what they are trying to achieve. Data also matter in order that schools go beyond cosy relationships that have no impact on outcomes. Consequently, schools need to base their relationships on evidence about each other's strengths and weaknesses, so that they can challenge each other to improve.

In order to facilitate this kind of contextual analysis, strategies and frameworks were devised to help schools to support one another in carrying out reviews. In the primary sector, this involved colleagues from another school acting as critical friends to internally-driven review processes; whilst in secondary schools, subject departments took part in 'deep dives', where skilled specialists from another school visited in order to observe and analyse practice, and promote focused improvement activities. The power of these approaches is in the way they provide teachers with opportunities to have strategic conversations with colleagues from another school.

The powerful impact of the collaborative strategies developed in the Greater Manchester Challenge points to ways in which the processes used within individual schools can be deepened and, therefore, strengthened. This requires an emphasis on mutual critique, within schools and between schools, based on an engagement with shared data. This, in turn, requires strong collective commitment from senior school staff and a willingness to share responsibility for system reform. Our study of new patterns of school leadership that are emerging in response to the structural changes occurring in the English education system offers some promise in this respect (Chapman et al. 2008).

Beyond the school gate

An OECD report (2007) argues that educational equity has two dimensions. First, it is a matter of *fairness*, which implies ensuring that personal and social circumstances – for example gender, socio-economic status or ethnic origin – should not be an obstacle to achieving educational potential. Second, it is to do with *inclusion*, which is about ensuring a basic minimum standard of education for all. The report notes that the two dimensions are closely intertwined since, 'tackling school failure helps to overcome the effects of social deprivation which often causes school failure' (11).

The report goes on to argue that a fair and inclusive education is desirable because of the human rights imperative for people to be able to develop their capacities and participate fully in society. It also reminds us of the long-term social and financial costs of educational failure, since those without the skills to participate socially and economically generate higher costs for health, income support, child welfare and security. In addition, increased migration poses new challenges for social cohesion in more and more countries.

Despite the efforts made in response to such arguments, in many parts of the world there remains a worrying gap between the achievements of students from rich and poor families (Kerr and West 2010; UNESCO 2010; Wilkinson and Pickett 2000). The extent of this gap varies significantly between countries. For example, Mourshed, Chijioke, and Barber (2010) argue:

In a world-class system like Finland's, socioeconomic standing is far less predictive of student achievement. All things being equal, a low-income student in the United States is far less likely to do well in school than a low-income student in Finland. Given the enormous economic impact of educational achievement, this is one of the best indicators of equal opportunity in a society . . . . (8–9)

On a more optimistic note, the most recent international comparisons in relation to literacy indicate that the best-performing school systems manage to provide high-quality education for all of their students. For example:

Canada, Finland, Japan, Korea and the partner economies Hong Kong-China and Shanghai-China all perform well above the OECD mean performance and students tend to perform well regardless of their own background or the school they attend. They not only have large proportions of students performing at the highest levels of reading proficiency, but also relatively few students at the lower proficiency levels. (OECD 2010, 15)

The implication is that it is possible for countries to develop education systems that are both excellent and equitable. The question is: what needs to be done to move policy and practice forward?

Within the international research community, there is evidence of a division of opinion regarding how to respond to this question. On the one hand, there are those who argue that what is required is a school-focused approach, with better implementation of the knowledge base that has been created through many years of school effectiveness and improvement research (e.g. Hopkins, Reynolds, and Gray 2005; Sammons 2007). Such researchers point to examples of where this approach has had an impact on the performance of schools serving disadvantaged communities (e.g. Chenoweth 2007; Stringfield 1995). On the other hand, there are those who argue that such school-focused approaches can never address fundamental inequalities in societies that make it difficult for some young people to break with the restrictions imposed on them by their home circumstances (Dyson and Raffo 2007).

Such arguments point to the danger of separating the challenge of school improvement from a consideration of the impact of wider social and political factors. This danger is referred to by those who recommend more holistic reforms that connect schools, communities and external political and economic institutions (e.g. Anyon 1997; Crowther et al. 2003; Levin 2005; Lipman 2004). These authors conclude that it is insufficient to focus solely on the improvement of individual schools. Rather, such efforts must be part of a larger overarching plan for system-wide reform that must include all stakeholders, at the national, district, institutional and community levels.

An obvious possibility is to combine the two perspectives by adopting strategies that seek to link attempts to change the internal conditions of schools with efforts to improve local areas. This approach is a feature of the highly acclaimed Harlem Children's Zone (Whitehurst and Croft 2010), a neighbourhood-based system of education and social services for the children of low-income families in New York. The programme combines education components (e.g. early childhood programmes with parenting classes; public charter schools), health components (including nutrition programmes), and neighbourhood services (one-on-one counselling for families; community centres;

and a centre that teaches job-related skills to teenagers and adults). Dobbie and Fryer (2009) describe the Children's Zone as 'arguably the most ambitious social experiment to alleviate poverty of our time' (1). Having carried out an in-depth analysis of statistical data regarding the impact of the initiative, they conclude:

> ... high-quality schools or high-quality schools coupled with community investments generate the achievement gains. Community investments alone cannot explain the results. (25)

Our recommendations are based on this combined approach, although we are well aware that pressures created by national policies can lead to strategic dilemmas in so doing, particularly when schools feel obliged to demonstrate rapid increases in test and examination scores.

The analysis we have made of the ways in which external factors limit the possibilities for developing equitable schools offers vivid illustrations of the complexities involved (see Ainscow et al. 2012). In so doing, it makes a convincing case for carrying out an analysis of the wider context within which schools work. We have had considerable experiences of conducting such analyses in school districts. This has convinced us that transforming educational provision in relation to local neighbourhoods and services depends on identifying local priorities and ways of developing sustainable responses to these. To do this, it is necessary to engage in forms of contextual analysis that probe beneath the surface of headline performance indicators in order to understand how local dynamics shape particular outcomes; and to identify the key underlying factors at work and determine which of these factors can be acted upon and by whom.

This marks a shift in thinking about local transformation from a surface-level, quick-fix response – concerned with manipulating headline figures – to a deeper response, which by addressing issues in context aims to achieve sustainable and long-term improvements. In this way, the purpose is to produce a rich and actionable understanding of local issues. To help achieve this, the analysis may be bounded in one of three ways – none of which are mutually exclusive:

- *By the unit of action* – for example, a contextual analysis might focus on issues in an administratively defined area, such as a district or local authority, where there are already structures in place that can be used to drive action.
- *By geographical and social boundaries* – the analysis might focus on issues in an area that has clear physical boundaries, for example, main roads or imagined boundaries, such as a housing estate that residents strongly identify with – or some combination of the two.
- *By issues* – the analysis might focus on understanding a particular issue, such as poor school attendance or teenage gang membership. In these instances, while retaining a local focus, the analysis might extend beyond a particular neighbourhood or administrative area.

We have found that sometimes a contextual analysis may highlight issues that shape local circumstances but which local actors are not in a position to change – for example, global recession leading to the decline of local industry. However, the analysis should be able to identify how local processes and dynamics are being shaped by this; what is locally actionable; and what unit(s) of action can be utilised to develop an appropriate response.

In order to understand the complex dynamics at work in an area, as well as exploring outcome data, it is necessary to enable people who live and work there to talk about their understandings of local issues. We have found that a loose research framework can help to provide the freedom needed for this, while also ensuring that the data generated can be usefully compared, and used to create shared understandings and strategies (Ainscow et al. 2012).

Rethinking relationships

In thinking about how the strategies we have outlined in this article might be used more widely, it is essential to recognise that they do not offer a set of techniques that can simply be lifted and transferred to other contexts. Rather, they offer an overall approach to improvement that is driven by a set of values and uses processes of contextual analysis in order to create strategies that fit particular circumstances. What is also distinctive in the approach is that it is mainly led from within schools in order to make more effective use of existing expertise and creativity.

We argue that closing the gap in outcomes between those from more- and less-advantaged backgrounds will only happen when what happens to children *outside* as well as *inside* schools changes. This means changing how families and communities work, and enriching what they offer to children. In this respect, we have seen encouraging experiences of what can happen when what schools do is aligned in a coherent strategy with the efforts of other local players – employers, community groups, universities and public services (Ainscow 2012; Cummings, Dyson, and Todd 2011). This does not necessarily mean schools doing more, but it does imply partnerships beyond the school, where partners multiply the impacts of each other's efforts.

All of this has implications for the various key stakeholders within education systems. In particular, teachers, especially those in senior positions, have to see themselves as having a wider responsibility for all children and young people, not just those that attend their own schools. They also have to develop patterns of internal organisation that enable them to have the flexibility to cooperate with other schools and with stakeholders beyond the school gate (Chapman et al. 2008). It means, too, that those who administer area school systems have to adjust their priorities and ways of working in response to improvement efforts that are led from within schools.

There is a key role for governments in all of this. The evidence from the English experience over the past 20 years suggests that attempts to command and control from the centre stifle as many local developments as they stimulate (Ainscow and West 2006; Gray 2010; Whitty 2010). Consequently, central government needs to act as an enabler, encouraging developments, disseminating good practice and holding local leaders to account for outcomes. All of this depends on the currency of knowledge exchange and, therefore, requires cultural change. This requires a new approach to national policy – one that can respond to local factors, while also providing a unifying understanding of equity that can help to create coherence and foster collaboration across reform efforts (Ainscow 2005).

Conclusion

The arguments we have developed in this article are intended to challenge those leading school improvement to return to their historical purpose, that of ensuring a sound education for every child. We have suggested that in order to achieve this it is necessary to complement within-school developments with efforts that link schools with one another and with their wider communities. For this to happen, we propose five organisational conditions that need to be in place:

Condition 1: Schools have to collaborate in ways that create a whole-system approach. If, as we have argued, equity issues can arise between schools, then an approach to promoting equity is needed which crosses school boundaries. Put simply, all schools in an area need to assume some level of accountability for all of the children who live in that area. This means that the prioritisation of institutional advantage that is so characteristic of the current school system needs to be replaced by an approach that acknowledges the *mutuality* of schools.

Condition 2: Equity-focused local leadership is needed in order to coordinate collaborative action. Whether local authorities are any longer the appropriate vehicles for local coordination and policy-making is a moot point, but it is clear that some source of local leadership is needed, and that such leadership has to be concerned with equity issues across the area, rather than with the advantage of this or that institution. In this respect, we have seen a number of contexts in which senior staff from a group of schools have worked together in providing such a lead.

Condition 3: Development in schools must be linked to wider community efforts to tackle inequities experienced by children. Local coordination is not simply about managing schools into some sort of productive relationship with each other. It is also about linking the work of schools with that of other agencies, organisations and community groups that are concerned with the social and economic well-being of the area. Working individually, schools are helpless to tackle the deprivation and associated disadvantages that some of their students experience. Yet, there is no reason in principle why they cannot look beyond their gates and develop more holistic approaches to local problems in collaboration with other stakeholders.

Condition 4: National policy has to be formulated in ways that enable and encourage local actions. None of the developments we are suggesting will be possible without a national policy framework that encourages schools to orientate themselves towards wider equity issues. In our own country the perverse consequences of successive governments' education policies are all too evident – the narrow focus on measured attainment; the conflation of crude benchmarks of school performance with students' real achievements; the encouragement of schools to view themselves as self-interested institutions competing against each other rather than working in the interests of all children; the weakening of local leadership from local authorities; and the repeated attempts to solve deep-seated social and educational problems by improving, reforming and, ultimately, closing down the schools where those problems became manifest. Yet this is not the whole story of education policy over the past two decades. The nascent forms of school collaboration we have described owed much to a policy emphasis on schools working together, and an unheralded yet crucial shift away from the 'lone school' model for providing education.

Condition 5: Moves to foster equity in education must be mirrored by efforts to develop a fairer society. Needless to say, even the most powerful area-based approaches to promoting equity are likely to have little more than palliative effects in the context of the powerful socio-economic forces that engender inequality and lead to marginalisation. There is, therefore, an important sense in which, in the absence of more fundamental social reforms, efforts to develop greater equity and service integration are inevitably doomed to failure. Yet, powerful as the forces that produce inequality and marginalisation might be, they are not entirely overwhelming. Policy in our country and elsewhere can and does make a difference to levels of poverty, to social segregation and integration, and to the gaps between rich and poor. Even without radical political change, different governments, as a matter of record, have made different decisions that exacerbate or ameliorate the impact of both underlying socio-economic processes and global influences.

Our conclusion is, therefore, that just as there is a complicated ecology of equity in and around schools, so there need to be multi-dimensional strategies to tackle equity issues. Specifically, school improvement processes need to be nested within locally led efforts to make school systems more equitable and to link the work of schools with area strategies for tackling wider inequities and, ultimately, with national policies aimed at creating a fairer society.

References

Ainscow, M. 1999. *Understanding the development of inclusive schools*. London: Routledge.

Ainscow, M. 2005. Developing inclusive education systems: What are the levers for change? *Journal of Educational Change* 6, no. 2: 109–24.

Ainscow, M. 2006. From special education to effective schools for all: A review of progress so far. In *The handbook of special education*, ed. L. Florian, 146–59. London: Sage.

Ainscow, M. 2010. Achieving excellence and equity: Reflections on the development of practices in one local district over 10 years. *School Effectiveness and School Improvement* 21, no. 1: 75–91.

Ainscow, M. 2012. Moving knowledge around: Strategies for fostering equity within educational systems. *Journal of Educational Change* (in press).

Ainscow, M., T. Booth, and A. Dyson. 2004. Understanding and developing inclusive practices in schools: A collaborative action research network. *International Journal of Inclusive Education* 8, no. 2: 125–39.

Ainscow, M., T. Booth, and A. Dyson. 2006. Inclusion and the standards agenda: Negotiating policy pressures in England. *International Journal of Inclusive Education* 10, nos. 4–5: 295–308.

Ainscow, M., T. Booth, A. Dyson, P. Farrell, J. Frankham, F. Gallannaugh, A. Howes, and R. Smith. 2006. *Improving schools, developing inclusion*. London: Routledge.

Ainscow, M., A. Dyson, S. Goldrick, and M. West. 2012. *Developing equitable education systems*. London: Routledge.

Ainscow, M., and A. Howes. 2007. Working together to improve urban secondary schools: A study of practice in one city. *School Leadership & Management* 27, no. 3: 285–300.

Ainscow, M., and I. Kaplan. 2006. Using evidence to encourage inclusive school development: Possibilities and challenges. *Australasian Journal of Special Education* 29, no. 2: 12–21.

Ainscow, M., D. Muijs, and M. West. 2006. Collaboration as a strategy for improving schools in challenging circumstances. *Improving Schools* 9, no. 3: 192–202.

Ainscow, M., M. Nicolaidou, and M. West. 2003. Supporting schools in difficulties: The role of school-to-school cooperation. *NFER Topic* 30: 1–4.

Ainscow, M., and M. West, eds. 2006. *Improving urban schools: Leadership and collaboration*. Maidenhead: Open University Press.

Ainscow, M., M. West, and M. Nicolaidou. 2005. Putting our heads together: A study of headteacher collaboration as a strategy for school improvement. In *Improving schools in difficult circumstances*, ed. C. Clarke, 117–36. London: Continuum.

Anyon, J. 1997. *Ghetto schooling: A political economy of urban educational reform.* New York: Teachers College Press.

Blair, T. 2005. Higher standards: Better schools. Speech on education at 10 Downing Street. http://www.pm.gov.uk/output/Page8363.asp (accessed October 24, 2005).

Brighouse, T. 2007. The London challenge: A personal view. In *Education in a global city*, ed. T. Brighouse and L. Fullick, 71–94. London: Institute of Education, Bedford Way Papers.

Chapman, C., M. Ainscow, J. Bragg, F. Gallannaugh, D. Mongon, D. Muijs, and M. West. 2008. *New models of leadership: Reflections on ECM policy, leadership and practice.* Nottingham: NCSL.

Chenoweth, K. 2007. *It's being done: Academic success in unexpected schools.* Cambridge, MA: Harvard Education Press.

Clark, C., A. Dyson, A. Millward, and S. Robson. 1999. Theories of inclusion, theories of schools: Deconstructing and reconstructing the 'inclusive school'. *British Educational Research Journal* 25, no. 2: 157–77.

Clarke, P., M. Ainscow, and M. West. 2005. Learning from difference: Some reflections on school improvement projects in three countries. In *International developments in school improvement*, ed. A. Harris, 77–89. London: Continuum.

Crowther, D., C. Cummings, A. Dyson, and A. Millward. 2003. *Schools and area regeneration.* Bristol: The Policy Press.

Cummings, C., A. Dyson, and L. Todd. 2011. *Beyond the school gate: Can full service and extended schools overcome disadvantage?* London: Routledge.

Dobbie, W., and R.G. Fryer. 2009. *Are high-quality schools enough to close the achievement gap? Evidence from a bold social experiment in Harlem.* Cambridge, MA: Harvard University Press.

Dyson, A., F. Gallannaugh, and A. Millward. 2003. Making space in the standards agenda: Developing inclusive practices in schools. *European Educational Research Journal* 2, no. 2: 228–44.

Dyson, A., and A. Millward. 2000. *Schools and special needs: Issues of innovation and inclusion.* London: Paul Chapman.

Dyson, A., and C. Raffo. 2007. Education and disadvantage: The role of community-orientated schools. *Oxford Review of Education* 33, no. 3: 297–314.

Edmonds, R. 1979. Effective schools for the urban poor. *Educational Leadership* 37, no. 1: 15–34.

Gray, J. 2010. Probing the limits of systemic reform: The English case. In *Second international handbook of educational change*, ed. A. Hargreaves, A. Lieberman, M. Fullan, and D. Hopkins, 293–308. Dordrecht: Springer.

Hopkins, D. 2007. *Every school a great school: Realizing the potential of system leadership.* Maidenhead: Open University Press.

Hopkins, D., M. Ainscow, and M. West. 1994. *School improvement in an era of change.* London: Cassell.

Hopkins, D., D. Reynolds, and J. Gray. 2005. *School improvement lessons from research.* London: DfES.

Howes, A., and M. Ainscow. 2006. Collaboration with a city-wide purpose: Making paths for sustainable educational improvement. In *Improving urban schools: Leadership and collaboration*, ed. M. Ainscow and M. West, 104–16. Maidenhead: Open University Press.

Howes, A., T. Booth, A. Dyson, and J. Frankham. 2005. Teacher learning and the development of inclusive practices and policies: Framing and context. *Research Papers in Education* 20, no. 2: 131–46.

Howes, A., J. Frankham, M. Ainscow, and P. Farrell. 2004. The action in action research: Mediating and developing inclusive intentions. *Educational Action Research* 12, no. 2: 239–57.

Kerr, K., and M. West, eds. 2010. *Insight 2: Social inequality: Can schools narrow the gap?* Macclesfield: British Education Research Association.

Levin, B. 2005. Thinking about improvements in schools in challenging circumstances. Paper presented at the American Educational Research Association, April, in Montreal, Canada.

Lipman, P. 2004. *High stakes education: Inequality, globalisation and urban school reform.* New York: Routledge.

Mourshed, M., C. Chijioke, and M. Barber. 2010. *How the world's most improved school systems keep getting better.* London: McKinsey & Company.

Muijs, D., M. Ainscow, C. Chapman, and M. West. 2011. *Collaboration and networking in education.* London: Springer.

Muijs, D., M. West, and M. Ainscow. 2010. Why network? Theoretical perspectives on networking. *School Effectiveness and School Improvement* 21, no. 1: 5–26.

OECD (Organisation for Economic Co-operation and Development). 2007. *No more failures: Ten steps to equity in education.* Paris: OECD.

OECD (Organisation for Economic Co-operation and Development). 2010. *PISA 2009 results: Overcoming social background – equity in learning opportunities and outcomes.* Vol. II. Paris: OECD.

Sammons, P. 2007. *School effectiveness and equity: Making connections.* Reading, MA: CfBT.

Slee, R., G. Weiner, and S. Tomlinson. 1998. *School effectiveness for whom?: Challenges to the school effectiveness and school improvement movements.* London: Falmer.

Stringfield, S. 1995. Attempting to improve students' learning through innovative programs – the case for schools evolving into high reliability organizations. *School Effectiveness and School Improvement* 6, no. 1: 67–96.

Thrupp, M. 1999. *Schools making a difference: Let's be realistic!* Buckingham: Open University Press.

UNESCO (United Nations Educational, Scientific and Cultural Organisation). 2010. *EFA global monitoring report: Reaching the marginalized.* Paris: UNESCO/Oxford University Press.

West, M., and M. Ainscow. 2010. Improving schools in Hong Kong: A description of the improvement model and some reflections on its impact on schools, teachers and school principals. In *School leadership – international perspectives*, ed. S. Huber, 1–18. London: Springer.

West, M., M. Ainscow, and J. Stanford. 2005. Sustaining improvement in schools in challenging circumstances: A study of successful practice. *School Leadership & Management* 25, no. 1: 77–93.

Whitehurst, G.J., and M. Croft. 2010. *The Harlem Children's Zone, promise neighborhoods, and the broader, bolder approach to education.* Washington, DC: The Brookings Institution.

Whitty, G. 2010. Marketization and post-marketization in education. In *Second international handbook of educational change*, ed. A. Hargreaves, A. Lieberman, M. Fullan, and D. Hopkins, 405–14. Dordrecht: Springer.

Wilkinson, R., and K. Pickett. 2000. *The spirit level.* London: Allen Lane.

CHAPTER 15

TOWARDS SELF-IMPROVING SCHOOL SYSTEMS

Ainscow, M. (2013) Developing more equitable education systems: reflections on a three-year improvement initiative. In V. Farnsworth and Y. Solomon (eds.), *Reframing educational research: Resisting the 'what works' agenda.* London: Routledge[1]

Introduction

The chapter describes and analyses the work of a large-scale improvement project in England in order to find more effective ways of fostering equity within education systems. The project provided me with a remarkable opportunity to test out ideas from my earlier research. Building on these ideas, the initiative involved an approach based on an analysis of local context, and used processes of networking and collaboration in order to make better use of available expertise. Reflecting on the impact and difficulties involved in using such an approach on such a large scale, the chapter draws out lessons that may be relevant to other contexts. Consideration is also given to the implications for policy makers, practitioners and community stakeholders. The argument presented in this chapter is more fully developed in my book *Towards self-improving school systems: lessons from a city challenge* (Routledge, 2015).

As countries make efforts to improve their national education systems, equity continues to be a major challenge. Put simply, how can schools ensure that every child is treated fairly, particularly those from less advantaged backgrounds? England is a useful context to consider when thinking about this issue, as noted in a 2007 OECD study which reported that the impact of socio-economic circumstances on young people's attainment was more marked in the UK than in any other of the 52 countries considered.

Recent years have seen intensive efforts by successive British governments to address such concerns. These efforts have been part of an intensification of political interest in education, especially regarding standards and the management of the state system (Whitty, 2010). Competition between schools is seen to be the key to 'driving up standards', while also further reducing the control of the local authority over provision. All of this is intended to 'liberate' schools from the bureaucracy of local government and establish a form of marketplace. In this way, it is intended that families will have greater choice as to which school their youngsters will attend. At the same time, there has been a huge number of specific policy initiatives aimed at addressing the equity agenda (Ainscow, Dyson, Goldrick and West, 2012).

Predictably, government statements point to improvements in test and examination scores, arguing that the impact of the various interventions has been significant. Within the research community, however, there are a variety of views, including some who argue that there has been very little impact, particularly among learners from disadvantaged backgrounds, and that the apparent improvements in measured performance are not supported by detailed analysis of national data (Meadows, Herrick and Feiler, 2007; Sammons, 2008; Tymms, 2004). Concern has also been expressed that improvements in test and examination scores may have been achieved by the use of particular tactics – some of which are, to say the least, dubious – such as orchestrated changes in school populations, the exclusion of some students and the careful selection of the courses students follow. All of this casts doubt on both the authenticity of improvement claims and the sustainability of whatever progress is made (Gray, 2010). There is also a worry that the various national strategies, whatever their benefits, have tended to reduce the flexibility with which schools can respond to the diverse characteristics of their students (Ainscow, Mujis and West, 2006).

Meanwhile, it has been argued that the development of the educational marketplace, coupled with the recent emphasis on policies fostering greater diversity of schools, has created a quasi-selective system in which the poorest children, by and large, attend the lowest-performing schools (Ainscow, 2012). Consequently, the low achieving and, many would argue, the least advantaged schools, fall progressively further and further behind their high-performing counterparts. In terms of these effects, through selective advantaging and disadvantaging of schools, those policies that have generally led to increased standards have also increased rather than decreased disparities in education quality and opportunity between advantaged and less privileged groups. The policy priority, therefore, is to find ways of continuing to improve the education system but in a way that fosters equity.

A city challenge

Between 2007 and 2011, I led a large-scale initiative that set out to address this important policy agenda across ten local authorities[2] in England (Ainscow, 2012). Known as the Greater Manchester Challenge, the project involved a partnership between national government, local authorities, schools and other stakeholders, and had a government investment of around £50 million. The decision to invest such a large budget reflected a concern regarding educational standards in the region, particularly among children and young people from disadvantaged backgrounds. The approach adopted was influenced by an earlier initiative in London (Brighouse, 2007).

The Greater Manchester city region is home to a population of 2.5 million people, and has over 600,000 children and young people. Across the region, there are approximately 1,150 schools and colleges. The area is diverse in a number of ways, with very high levels of poverty. Children and young people come from a range of ethnic and cultural backgrounds, with a high proportion whose families have Asian heritage. Nearly 16 per cent have a first language other than English.

A detailed study of patterns of school attendance in Greater Manchester confirms the concerns noted earlier about the impact of national policies on the educational experiences of young people from disadvantaged backgrounds (Robson, Deas and Lymperopoulou, 2009). In particular, it shows that deprived students who attend low-performing schools do worse than deprived students who attend higher-performing schools. And, since such students go disproportionately to poor-performing schools, this exacerbates the gulf between the results of deprived and non-deprived students, thereby acting as a significant driver of social polarisation.

The overall aims of the Challenge project were related to these concerns. They were to raise the educational achievement of all children and young people, and to narrow the gap in educational achievement between learners from disadvantaged backgrounds and their peers. A vision document, developed through extensive consultation between the national and local partners, led to a worrying proliferation of what were described as 'pledges', as the various stakeholders – nationally and locally – attempted to promote their own areas of interest.

In an attempt to create a sense of common purpose within this over ambitious agenda, it was eventually agreed that the focus of Challenge activities would be on 'three As'. These were that all children and young people: should have high *Aspirations* for their own learning and life chances; are ensured *Access* to high-quality educational experiences; and *Achieve* the highest possible standards in learning. It was immediately obvious that these goals would necessitate reforms at all levels of the education service. This being the case, the aim was to encourage experimentation and innovation, rather than simply doing more of the same. Significantly, there was government approval for taking this approach, including the active involvement of a minister.

The Challenge also set out to take advantage of new opportunities provided as a result of adopting an approach that drew on the strengths that existed in different parts of the city region. These included possibilities for: tackling educational issues that cut across local authority boundaries (such as declining school performance at the secondary school stage, the development of personalised learning pathways for older students); linking educational issues to broader social and economic agendas (such as population mobility, employment, transport, housing, community safety, health); and the freer exchange of expertise, resources, and lessons from innovations.

After three years the impact was significant in respect to overall improvements in test and examination results and, indeed, the way the education system carries out its business. So, for example, Greater Manchester primary schools now outperform national averages on the tests taken by all children in England. And, in the public examinations taken by all young people at 16, in 2011 secondary schools in Greater Manchester improved faster than schools nationally, with the schools serving the most disadvantaged communities making three times more improvement than schools across the country. During the same period, the number of schools below the Government's floor standard[3] decreased more than it did in other areas of the country. In addition, the proportion of 'good' and 'outstanding' schools, as determined by the national inspection system, increased, despite the introduction of a more challenging framework (see Hutchings, Hollingworth, Mansaray, Rose and Greenwood, 2012 for a detailed independent evaluation of the impact of City Challenge).

Within such a large-scale and socially complex project it is, of course, difficult to make causal claims in respect to the factors that led to these improvements, particularly within an initiative that incorporated such a wide range of strategies. It is also the case that I walk a delicate line here in using these measures to describe the success of the intervention, given that I have already expressed concerns about their reliability and impact. And, of course, my ambiguous role – both the leader of the project and a researcher trying to make sense of what was going on – has to be borne in mind when considering the conclusions I present.

Keeping these caveats in mind, in what follows I reflect on statistical data compiled as part of the formal monitoring of the impact of the project and qualitative evidence collected through numerous informal observations and conversations, plus more occasional formal interviews with stakeholders, in order to draw out some lessons. This leads me to indicate some of the social and political complexities involved.

A framework for analysis

The approach used by the Challenge emerged from a detailed analysis of the local context, using both statistical data and local intelligence provided by stakeholders. This drew attention to areas of concern and also helped to pinpoint a range of human resources that could be mobilised in order to support improvement efforts. Recognising the potential of these resources, it was decided that networking and collaboration should be the key strategies for strengthening the overall improvement capacity of the system.

In trying to make sense of the complex processes involved I have found it useful to see them in relation to what my colleagues and I have recently described as an *ecology of equity* (Ainscow, 2012). By this we mean that the extent to which students' experiences and outcomes are equitable is not dependent only on the educational practices of their teachers, or even their schools. Instead, it depends on a whole range of interacting processes that reach into the school from outside. These include the demographics of the areas served by schools, the histories and cultures of the populations who send (or fail to send) their children to the school and the economic realities faced by those populations. Beyond this, they involve the underlying socio-economic processes that make some areas poor and others affluent, and that draw migrant groups into some places rather than others. They are also influenced by the wider politics of the teaching profession, of local authority decision-making and of national policy making, and the impacts of schools on one another over issues such as exclusion and parental 'choice'. In addition, they reflect new models of school governance, the ways in which local school hierarchies are established and maintained, and the ways in which school actions are constrained and enabled by their positions in those hierarchies.

It is helpful, therefore, to think of three interlinked arenas within which equity issues arise. These relate to: *within school* factors that arise from existing policies and practices; *between school* factors that arise from the characteristics of local school systems; and *beyond school* factors, including the wider policy context, family processes and resources, and the demographics, economics, cultures and histories of local areas. In what follows I examine the work of the Greater Manchester Challenge in relation to each of these sets of factors, remembering that, in practice, they interact.

Within school factors

Our earlier research had thrown light on the sorts of strategies needed in order to foster improvements in schools facing challenging circumstances (Ainscow and West, 2006; West, Ainscow and Stanford, 2005). Inevitably such research attempts to identify common elements, as it seeks to determine the ingredients that combine into success. However, useful as it is to know what these ingredients are, it is equally important to recognise that they do not readily come together into any one 'recipe' that will transform a school. Therefore, a note of caution is necessary. Yes, there do seem to be common ingredients, but these need to be mixed in different proportions and added in a different order according to the school's circumstances. This suggests that possibly the most important attribute of leaders in a school facing challenging circumstances is the ability to analyse the context as quickly as possible, as suggested by Harris and Chapman (2002).

So, for example, it is clear that focusing on teaching and focusing on learning are both important, and that once a school is into a cycle of improvement, both are kept under regular evaluation and review. However, whether to start from teaching and progress to its impact on learning, or to begin by looking at learning and then explore the implications for teaching, needs to be considered in context. A school with a static and exhausted teaching force is unlikely to respond to having current practices placed under the microscope, but may be engaged by looking at the learning needs and problems of the pupils. Conversely, in a school with relatively inexperienced teachers but poor subject leadership, staff may respond very positively to measures that focus on teaching approaches that reduce the number of classroom problems they are encountering.

Our earlier research had shown how the use of evidence to study teaching can help to foster the development of more inclusive practices (Ainscow *et al.*, 2006). Specifically, it can help to create space for reappraisal and rethinking by interrupting existing discourses, and by focusing attention on overlooked possibilities for moving practice forward. Particularly powerful techniques in this respect involve the use of mutual observation, sometimes through video recordings (Ainscow, 1999, 2003), and evidence collected from students about teaching and learning arrangements within a school (Ainscow and Kaplan, 2006; Messiou, 2006; Miles and Kaplan, 2005). Under certain conditions such approaches provide 'interruptions' that help to make the familiar unfamiliar in ways that stimulate self-questioning, creativity and action. In so doing they can sometimes lead to a reframing of perceived problems that, in turn, draws the teacher's attention to overlooked possibilities for addressing barriers to participation and learning.

However, such enquiry-based approaches to the development of practice are far from straightforward. An interruption to thinking that is created as a group of teachers engage with evidence may not necessarily lead to a consideration of new ways of working. Indeed, we had documented examples of how deeply held beliefs within a school may prevent the experimentation that is necessary in order to foster the development of more inclusive ways of working (Ainscow and Kaplan, 2006; Howes and Ainscow, 2006). This reminds us that it is easy for educational difficulties to be pathologised as difficulties inherent within students. This is true not only of students with disabilities and those defined as having special educational needs, but also of those whose socio-economic status, race, language and gender renders them problematic to particular teachers in particular schools. Consequently, it is necessary to explore ways of developing the capacity of those within schools to reveal and challenge deeply entrenched, deficit views of 'difference', which define certain types of students as 'lacking something' (Trent, Artiles and Englert, 1998). This involves being vigilant in scrutinising how deficit assumptions may be influencing perceptions of certain students.

Bearing these ideas in mind, the Challenge placed particular emphasis on supporting within-school efforts to improve practice. Most notably, what we referred to as the 'Keys to Success' programme led to striking improvements in the performance of some 200 schools serving the most disadvantaged communities. There was also evidence that the progress that these schools made helped to trigger improvements across the system.

The approach used in each of the Keys to Success schools was particular, based on a detailed analysis of the local context and the development of an improvement strategy that fitted the circumstances. A team of expert advisers had a central role here, working alongside senior school staff in carrying out the initial analysis and, where necessary, mobilising external support. A common feature of almost all of these interventions, however, was that progress was achieved through carefully matched pairings of schools that cut across social 'boundaries' of various kinds, including those that separate schools in different local authorities. In this way, expertise that was previously trapped in particular contexts was made more widely available.

Crossing boundaries sometimes involved what seemed like unlikely partnerships. For example, a highly successful school that caters for children from Jewish Orthodox families worked with an inner city primary school – the largest primary school in the city region – to develop more effective use of assessment data and boost the quality of teaching and learning. This school had a high percentage of Muslim children, many of whom learn English as an additional language. Over a period of 18 months, the partnership contributed to significant improvements in test results, and throughout the school the majority of students reached nationally determined expectations for their ethnic groups. It also led to a series of activities around wider school issues, such as the creative arts and the use of student voice, where the two schools shared their expertise.

Another partnership involved a primary school that had developed considerable expertise in teaching children to read, supporting a secondary school in another local authority where low levels of literacy have acted as a barrier to student progress. And in another example, involving an outstanding grammar school[4] partnering with a low-performing inner city comprehensive school in another local authority, the impact on attendance, behaviour and examination results was remarkable.

Through such examples we saw how boundaries to do with cultures, religion, age group of students and selection could be crossed in order to facilitate the exchange of expertise. Significantly, these examples also indicated that such arrangements can have a positive impact on the learning of students in both of the partner schools. This is an important finding in that it draws attention to a way of strengthening relatively low-performing schools that can, at the same time, help to foster wider improvements in the system. It also offers a convincing argument as to why a relatively strong school should support other schools. Put simply, the evidence is that by helping others you help yourself.

While increased collaboration of this sort is vital as a strategy for developing more effective ways of working, the experience of Greater Manchester shows that it is not enough. The essential additional ingredient is an engagement with evidence that can bring an element of mutual challenge to such collaborative processes. We found that this is particularly essential in the partnering of schools, since collaboration is at its most powerful when partner schools are carefully matched and know what they are trying to achieve. Evidence also matters in order that schools go beyond cosy relationships that have no impact on outcomes. Consequently, schools need to base their relationships on evidence about each other's strengths and weaknesses, so that they can challenge each other to improve.

In order to facilitate this kind of contextual analysis, various strategies and frameworks were devised to help schools to support one another in carrying out reviews. In the primary sector, this involved colleagues from another school acting as critical friends to internally driven review processes; while in secondary schools, subject departments were involved in 'deep dives', where skilled subject specialists from another school visit to observe and analyse practice in order to promote focused improvement activities. The power of these approaches is in the way they provide teachers with opportunities to have strategic conversations with colleagues from another school.

Between school factors

Our earlier research had suggested that collaboration between differently performing schools can reduce polarisation within education systems, to the particular benefit of learners who are performing relatively poorly (Ainscow, 2010; Ainscow and Howes, 2007; Ainscow, Muijs and West, 2006; Ainscow and West, 2006). It does this by both transferring existing knowledge and, more importantly, generating context-specific new knowledge.

With this in mind, an attempt to engage all schools in the city region in processes of networking and collaboration was made through the creation of socalled 'Families of Schools'. This involved the use of a data system that grouped schools on the basis of the prior attainment of their students and their socioeconomic home backgrounds. There were 58 primary Families and 11 secondary, each of which had between 12 and 20 schools from different local authorities. The strength of this approach is that it groups together schools that serve similar populations while, at the same time, encouraging partnerships among schools that are not in direct competition with one another because they do not serve the same neighbourhoods.

Varied performance among Family members offered possibilities for using differences as a resource to stimulate the sharing of expertise and joint efforts to innovate in order to: improve the performance of every school; increase the numbers of outstanding schools; reduce the gap between high- and low-performing groups of learners; and improve outcomes for particular vulnerable groups of students. We found, however, that for this to happen schools had to dig more deeply into the comparative data in order to expose areas of strength that could be used to influence performance across their Family, while also identifying areas for improvement in every school.

With this in mind, the average performance for each Family – both in terms of overall attainment and recent improvement trends – provided a benchmark against which overall goals for each of the partner schools could be set. At the same time, the analysis of data with regard to sub-groups of students (e.g. boys and girls; those eligible for free school meals; minority groups) and different subject areas also enabled a Family to work on the issue of within-school variations. The collective goal, then, was to move all of the Family members forward in respect to an agreed improvement agenda.

In thinking about how to make this happen, we found that it is important to be sensitive to the limitations of statistical information. What brings such data to life is when 'insiders' start to scrutinise and ask questions as to their significance, bringing their detailed experiences and knowledge to bear on the process of interpretation. The occasional involvement of colleagues from partner schools can deepen such processes, not least because of the ways in which they may notice things or ask questions that those within a school may be overlooking.

Even then there remain other limitations that have to be kept in mind. Statistics provide patterns of what exists: they tell us what things are like but give little understanding as to why things are as they are, or how they came to be like that. This is why qualitative evidence is needed to supplement statistical data. As I have indicated, mutual observation among colleagues and listening to the views of learners can be a powerful means of challenging thinking and provoking experimentation. Again, here, there is potential for schools to support one another in collecting and engaging with such evidence in a way that has the potential to make the familiar unfamiliar. Of course, all of this necessitates a commitment of time in order to take advantage of such opportunities, a factor that, unfortunately, some head teachers found difficult to accept.

Led by head teachers, the Families of Schools proved to be successful in strengthening collaborative processes within the city region. So, for example, primary schools in one Family worked together to strengthen leadership in each school. This included head teachers visiting one another to carry out 'learning walks', during which colleagues had opportunities to reflect upon and debate noticeable differences in practices. Eight schools in another primary Family identified a shared desire to build stronger relationships with the children's homes – for example, parents of children with English as an additional language where there were communication issues, or groups of students with lower attendance. And in the secondary sector, schools within one of the Families used a web-based system where students could showcase their work via podcasts, videos and blogs, allowing teachers, parents and students from their own and other schools to view and comment on their efforts.

However, involvement of schools in the Families remained patchy and there were concerns that too often those that might most benefit chose not to do so. Our monitoring of what went on suggests certain conditions that led to higher involvement and a greater impact on student achievement. These included a collective commitment to: improve the learning of every student, in every school in the group; analyse statistical data, using professional insights in order to identify areas that need addressing; and pinpoint expertise within the schools that could be used to address these concerns. It also required collaborative activities involving people at different levels, including, in some instances, children and young people; and a small number of head teachers taking on the role of leading these collaborative activities.

In moving collaboration forward in a way that supports development within a Family of Schools, we found that shared leadership was a central driver. This requires the development of leadership practices that involve many stakeholders in collectively sharing responsibility. Often this necessitates significant changes in beliefs and attitude, and new relationships, as well as improvements in practice. The goal is to ensure that collaboration is between school communities, and not restricted to head teachers, since arrangements that rely on one person are unlikely to survive the departure of those individuals who brokered them.

Beyond school factors

In developing the strategy for the Challenge, I was conscious of the danger of separating strategies for school improvement from a consideration of the impact of wider context factors. This danger is referred to by those writers who recommend more holistic reforms that connect schools, communities, and external political and economic institutions (e.g. Anyon, 1997; Crowther, Cummings, Dyson and Millward, 2003; Levin, 2005; Lipman, 2004). These authors conclude that it is insufficient to focus solely on the improvement of schools. Rather, such efforts must be part of a larger overarching plan for system-wide reform that must include all stakeholders, at the national, district, institutional and community levels.

In pursuing the goals of the Challenge we introduced a series of strategies in order to inject further innovation and pace into the system. Each of these initiatives was led by one of the local authority partners and focused on educational issues facing all local authorities, linking improvement efforts to broader social and economic agendas. Importantly, this led to the involvement of local businesses, professional sports clubs, universities, and arts and media organisations. For example, the four universities in Greater Manchester worked together on an initiative known as 'Higher Futures for You', the aim of which was to raise self-belief and aspirations among primary school children from disadvantaged backgrounds. Through carefully orchestrated visits to local places of employment, 10- and 11-year-old students were helped to understand the career opportunities that could be available to them. During a final workshop, the children shared their knowledge with their parents. This initiative, which worked with some 200 primary schools, was originally developed by the head teacher of one school. Through the Challenge, this creative project reached many more children and families.

Another initiative set out to explore the use of learner voice as a strategy for rethinking what schools offer to their students. In carrying out this work a partnership was developed with an independent charity that promotes democratic citizenship and life skills. This led to an additional focus on the experience of young people outside of school. As a result, schools across Greater Manchester collaborated in addressing the question: *In developing children as participative citizens in designing the way things are in school, can we achieve greater civic participation beyond school?* The schools involved were enthused by the opportunity provided, and in some instances became committed to widen and deepen the involvement of students (and parents).

In another experimental initiative – known as 'Better Futures' – 16 students from disadvantaged backgrounds shared jobs in three major companies. Each student attended their internship one day per week throughout the year and caught up with missed schoolwork during the rest of the week. The evidence suggests that parents were very positive once they saw the impact on children's social skills in their home environment. Meanwhile, within school, aspirations changed, so did attitudes to catch up on missed school work, as the students made links between a good career and attaining targets at school. There was evidence, too, of shifts in aspirations – for example, from mechanic to engineer, childcare to business, and 'don't knows' to IT and law. The approach was subsequently developed in many more schools, involving other business organisations.

Reflections

Central to the strategies I have described were attempts to develop new, more fruitful working relationships: within and between schools; between schools and their wider communities; and between local and national government. A helpful theoretical interpretation that can be made of these strategies is that, together, they help to strengthen *social capital*. In other words, they create pathways through which expertise and lessons from innovations can spread.

In recent years, the work of Robert Putnam (2000) has been influential in making the idea of social capital a focus for research and policy discussion. Interestingly, he notes that the term was first used in 1916 by a supervisor of schools in West Virginia. Writing about the more recent situation in the United States, Putnam states that 'what many high-achieving school districts have in abundance is social capital, which is educationally more important than financial capital' (2000, p. 306). He also suggests that this can help to mitigate the insidious effects of socio-economic disadvantage.

Reflecting on his work with schools serving disadvantaged communities – also in the United States – Payne comes to a similar conclusion. Thinking specifically about school contexts that are characterised by low levels of social capital, he argues:

> Weak social infrastructure means that conservatives are right when they say that financial resources are likely to mean little in such environments. It means that expertise inside the building is likely to be underutilized, and expertise coming from outside is likely to be rejected on its face. It means that well-thought-out programs can be undermined by the factionalized character of teacher life or by strong norms that militate against teacher collaboration.
>
> (2008, p. 39)

Mulford (2007) suggests that by treating social relationships as a form of capital, they can be seen as a resource, which can then be drawn on to achieve organisational goals. There are, he explains, three types of social capital, each of which throws further light on the processes that could be developed within an education system. The first of these is 'bonding social capital' – this relates to what can happen among work colleagues within a school. 'Bridging social capital' is what can occur between schools through various forms of networking and collaboration. And finally, 'linking social capital' relates to stronger relationships between a school and wider community resources.

As I have explained, the work of the Greater Manchester Challenge involved a series of interconnected strategies that appeared to foster stronger social capital of all three types. These strategies helped to break down social barriers within schools, between schools, and between schools and other stakeholders, in order to facilitate the sorts of mutual benefit that I have described. However, it is important to recognise that, within the context of changing and, at times, contradictory national policies, the gains made through such approaches were hard won, and remained fragile and easily lost. Here, continuing tensions regarding priorities and preferred ways of working between national and local policy makers, and, indeed, between schools and local authorities, were factors that continued to create barriers to progress. So, for example, those near to central government remained pre-occupied with achieving short-term gains in test and examination scores in ways that can create barriers to efforts for promoting sustainable improvements. Coupled with this was a mistrust of local authorities – the staff of which were sometimes seen as part of the problem, rather than part of the solution – and doubts about the need to have separate strategies that fit particular contexts.

Certainly, the creation of education systems where improvement is driven by schools themselves, and that involves cooperation between schools, and between schools and other community organisations, begs questions regarding the roles of local authorities. Indeed, it raises the possibility that the involvement of a middle-level administrative structure may not even be necessary. The authors of an influential McKinsey report, having analysed 'how the world's most improved school systems keep getting better', express their surprise at the critical role that what they call the 'mediating layer' plays between school delivery and central government (Mourshed, Chijioke and Barber, 2010). This leads them to conclude that sustaining improvements in the longer term requires 'integration and intermediation' across each level of the system, 'from the classroom to the superintendent or minister's office'.

The authors of the report go on to suggest that the specific functions the mediating layer plays are: providing targeted support to schools; acting as a buffer between central government and the schools, while interpreting and communicating the improvement objectives in order to manage any resistance to change; and enhancing the collaborative exchange between schools, by facilitating the sharing of best practices, helping them to support each other, share learning and standardise practices.

Our experience in Greater Manchester suggests that local authority staff can have an important role to play, not least in acting as the conscience of the system – making sure that all children and young people are getting a fair deal within an increasingly diverse system of education. In order to do this, they need to know the big picture about what is happening in their communities, identifying priorities for action and brokering collaboration. This requires significant structural and cultural change, with local authorities moving away from a command and control perspective, towards one of enabling and facilitating collaborative action. I experienced many situations where local authority colleagues found these changes challenging, particularly during a time of reducing budgets. Nevertheless, I remain committed to the view that local coordination – the presence of an effective 'mediating layer' – is vital.

Concluding thoughts

The argument I have developed in this chapter does not take the form of a simple 'what works' formula. Rather it offers a way of thinking about system level improvement that involves an analysis of particular contexts in order to develop strategies that make better use of available energy and expertise. My suggestion is that this 'way of thinking' offers more promise than suggestions that seek to impose externally generated, one-size-fits-all improvement mechanisms.

There are, however, some rather obvious questions that can be asked about my analysis, not least in relation to my status within the Challenge initiative. As a researcher, I was provided with a remarkable opportunity to put into practice ideas that had emerged from years of investigating ways of developing more effective, equitable schools and education systems. At the same time it placed me in a position of having privileged access to information regarding the way decisions are made within an education system, from the levels of government ministers and senior civil servants, through to that of teachers in the classroom. All of this provided frequent reminders of the social complexity involved when trying to bring about changes in the way that a system does its business.

On the other hand, as the person charged with the task of championing the Challenge, how far can my interpretations be trusted, not least because my efforts to collect data about the processes involved were largely carried out in an incidental way? My response to this concern is that, while readers must take it into account in determining the weight of my argument, they should recognise that my 'insider' stance enabled me to experience things in ways that researchers rarely do. It is also worth adding that, throughout the three years, a small group of my academic colleagues acted as critical friends, reading the frequent discussion papers I prepared in order to stimulate debate with stakeholders within the project and offering their more detached views.[5] In particular, I invited them to challenge the interpretations I was making and to draw my attention to any evidence that I was falling into the trap of becoming an agent of central government.

Another obvious question relates to the large amount of funding involved. Put simply, how far were the successes of the Challenge the result of the investment of additional money into the system? And, therefore, how viable are the approaches I am recommending without extra resources? This remains an area of debate within my mind. Certainly, the project involved a lot of additional finance. On the other hand, over the previous decade or so, far more money had been invested in the system through a plethora of national improvement strategies that had led to very little improvement in the performance of schools across the city region.

Notes

1   The work described in this chapter is the product of the efforts and creativity of many colleagues in the schools, local authorities and communities of Greater Manchester. Particular thanks must go to the splendid team of advisers and civil servants who worked with me on the project. Their efforts were in themselves a demonstration of the power of collaboration.

2   There are 152 English local authorities. They are democratically accountable for providing a range of services for their local communities, including education. The ten local authorities in Greater Manchester are: Bolton, Bury, Oldham, Manchester, Rochdale, Salford, Stockport, Tameside, Trafford and Wigan.

3   This is the minimum standard set by the Government, below which schools are subject to some form of intervention.

4   Grammar schools select students academically at the age of 11. In general they do not tend to cater for young people from economically disadvantaged backgrounds.

5   Chris Chapman, Alan Dyson, Peter Farrell, Denis Mongon and Mel West acted as critical friends throughout the project and, in so doing, contributed many ideas to the analysis presented in this chapter.

References

Ainscow, M. (1999). *Understanding the development of inclusive schools*. London: Routledge.

Ainscow, M. (2003). Using teacher development to foster inclusive classroom practices. In T. Booth, K. Nes and M. Stromstad (eds) *Developing inclusive teacher education*. London: RoutledgeFalmer.

Ainscow, M. (2010). Achieving excellence and equity: reflections on the development of practices in one local district over 10 years. *School Effectiveness and School Improvement*, 21(1), 75–92.

Ainscow, M. (2012). Moving knowledge around: strategies for fostering equity within educational systems. *Journal of Educational Change*, 13(3), 289–310.

Ainscow, M. and Howes, A. (2007). Working together to improve urban secondary schools: a study of practice in one city. *School Leadership and Management*, 27(3), 285–300.

Ainscow, M. and Kaplan, I. (2006). Using evidence to encourage inclusive school development: possibilities and challenges. *Australasian Journal of Special Education*, 29(2), 106–116.

Ainscow, M. and West, M. (eds) (2006). *Improving urban schools: Leadership and collaboration*. London: Open University Press.

Ainscow, M., Booth, T., Dyson, A., with Farrell, P., Frankham, J., Gallannaugh, F., Howes, A. and Smith, R. (2006). *Improving schools, developing inclusion*. London: Routledge.

Ainscow, M., Dyson, A., Goldrick, S. and West, M. (2012). *Developing equitable education systems*. London: Routledge.

Ainscow, M., Muijs, D. and West, M. (2006). Collaboration as a strategy for improving schools in challenging circumstances. *Improving Schools*, 9(3), 192–202.

Anyon, J. (1997). *Ghetto schooling: A political economy of urban educational reform*. New York: Teachers College Press.

Brighouse, T. (2007). The London Challenge: a personal view. In T. Brighouse and L. Fullick (eds) *Education in a global city* (pp. 71–94). London: Institute of Education Bedford Way Papers.

Crowther, D., Cummings, C., Dyson, A. and Millward, A. (2003). *Schools and area regeneration*. Bristol: The Policy Press.

Gray, J. (2010). Probing the limits of systemic reform: the English case. In A. Hargreaves, A. Lieberman, M. Fullan and D. Hopkins (eds) *Second international handbook of educational change* (pp. 293–307). Dordrecht: Springer.

Harris, A. and Chapman, C. (2002). *Leadership in schools in challenging circumstances*. Report to the National College for School Leadership.

Howes, A. and Ainscow, M. (2006). Collaboration with a city-wide purpose: making paths for sustainable educational improvement. In M. Ainscow and M. West (eds) *Improving urban school: Leadership and collaboration* (pp. 104–116). Maidenhead: Open University Press.

Hutchings, M., Hollingworth, S., Mansaray, A., Rose, R. and Greenwood, C. (2012). *Research report DFE-RR215: Evaluation of the city challenge programme*. London: DfE.

Levin, B. (2005, April). *Thinking about improvements in schools in challenging circumstances*. Paper presented at the American Educational Research Association, Montreal.

Lipman, P. (2004). *High stakes education: Inequality, globalisation and urban school reform*. New York: Routledge.

Meadows, S., Herrick, D. and Feiler, A. (2007). Improvements in national test reading scores at Key Stage 1: grade inflation or better achievement? *British Educational Research Journals*, 33(1), 47–59.

Messiou, K. (2006). Understanding marginalisation in education: the voice of children. *European Journal of Psychology of Education*, 21(3), 305–318.

Miles, S. and Kaplan, I. (2005). Using images to promote reflection: an action research study in Zambia and Tanzania. *Journal of Research in Special Educational Needs*, 5(2), 77–83.

Mourshed, M., Chijioke, C. and Barber, M. (2010). *How the world's most improved school systems keep getting better*. London: McKinsey & Company.

Mulford, B. (2007). Building social capital in professional learning communities: importance, challenges and a way forward. In L. Stoll and K. Seashore Louis (eds)

Professional learning communities: Divergence, depth and dilemmas. London: Open University Press.

Putnam, R. D. (2000). *Bowling alone*. New York: Simon & Schuster.

Sammons, P. (2008). Zero tolerance of failure and New Labour approaches to school improvement in England. *Oxford Review of Education*, 34(6), 651–664.

Trent, S. C., Artiles, A. J. and Englert, C. S. (1998). From deficit thinking to social constructivism: a review of theory, research and practice in special education. *Review of Research in Education*, 23, 277–307.

Tymms, P. (2004). Are standards rising in British primary schools? *British Educational Research Journal*, 30(4), 477–494.

West, M., Ainscow, M. and Stanford, J. (2005). Sustaining improvement in schools in challenging circumstances: a study of successful practice. *School Leadership and Management*, 25(1), 77–93.

Whitty, G. (2010). Marketization and post-marketization in education. In A. Hargreaves, A. Lieberman, M. Fullan and D. Hopkins (eds) *Second international of educational change* (pp. 405–413). Dordrecht: Springer.

INDEX